Lecture Notes in Computer Science 2822
Edited by G. Goos, J. Hartmanis, and J. van Leeuwen

Springer
Berlin
Heidelberg
New York
Hong Kong
London
Milan
Paris
Tokyo

Nadia Bianchi-Berthouze (Ed.)

Databases in Networked Information Systems

Third International Workshop, DNIS 2003
Aizu, Japan, September 22-24, 2003
Proceedings

 Springer

Series Editors

Gerhard Goos, Karlsruhe University, Germany
Juris Hartmanis, Cornell University, NY, USA
Jan van Leeuwen, Utrecht University, The Netherlands

Volume Editor

Nadia Bianchi-Berthouze
University of Aizu
Department of Computer Software, Database Systems Lab.
Tsuruga Ikki Machi 965-8580, Aizu Wakamatsu, Japan
E-mail: nadia@u-aizu.ac.jp

Cataloging-in-Publication Data applied for

A catalog record for this book is available from the Library of Congress

Bibliographic information published by Die Deutsche Bibliothek
Die Deutsche Bibliothek lists this publication in the Deutsche Nationalbibliografie;
detailed bibliographic data is available in the Internet at <http://dnb.ddb.de>.

CR Subject Classification (1998): H.2, H.3, H.4, H.5, C.2

ISSN 0302-9743
ISBN 3-540-20111-4 Springer-Verlag Berlin Heidelberg New York

Springer-Verlag Berlin Heidelberg New York
a member of BertelsmannSpringer Science+Business Media GmbH

http://www.springer.de

Typesetting: Camera-ready by author, data conversion by DA-TeX Gerd Blumenstein
Printed on acid-free paper   SPIN 10953600   06/3142   5 4 3 2 1 0

Preface

The understanding of data semantics in Web-based information systems is the object of intensive research efforts. The large volume of data on the Internet originates a need for accessing the semantic content of that information. Furthermore, it requires the personalizing of its search and integration to various types of users. Two approaches have been proposed in the research literature: integration of Web technologies with database technologies and use of meta-languages such as XML. These solutions offer highly structured or semi-structured data that allow users to perform queries at a higher semantic level. These also facilitate the dynamic personalization of Web-based applications. Therefore, it is now important to address the question of how one can efficiently query and search large collections of XML documents. And it is also necessary to find new solutions, both to support dynamic architectures for Web-based applications and to model users' search and result presentation criteria.

The third international workshop on Databases in Networked Information Systems (DNIS 2003) was held on September 22–24, 2003 at the University of Aizu in Japan on the occasion of its 10th anniversary. The workshop program included research contributions, and invited contributions. The session on *Web Intelligence* included invited papers by Professor Jiming Liu and Professor Cyrus Shahabi. The session on *Information Interchange and Management Systems* included invited papers by Professor Tosiyasu L. Kunii, Professor Elisa Bertino, and Professor Marc Sifer. The session on *Information Interchange Among Cyber Communities* had invited papers by Professor Toyoaki Nishida, Professor Masaru Kitsuregawa, and Dr. Umeshwar Dayal. Finally the session on *Knowledge – Annotation and Visualization* included the invited contribution by Professor Daniel Keim.

The sponsoring organizations and the organizing committee deserve praise for the support they provided. I would like to thank the members of the program committee for their support and all the authors who submitted the results of their research to DNIS 2003.

The workshop received invaluable support from the University of Aizu. In this context, I would like to thank Professor Ikegami, President of the University of Aizu, and Professor Mirenkov, Head of the Department of Computer Software, for making the financial support available. I would like to express my gratitude to the members and chairman of the International Affairs Committee, for supporting the workshop proposal, as well as to the faculty members at the university for their cooperation and support.

September 2003   Nadia Bianchi-Berthouze

Organization

The DNIS 2003 international workshop was organized by the Database Systems Laboratory, University of Aizu, Aizu-Wakamatsu City, Fukushima, 965-8580 Japan.

Executive Committee

Honorary Chair: T. L. Kunii, Kanazawa Institute of Technology, Japan
Program Chair: N. Bianchi-Berthouze, University of Aizu, Japan
Executive Chair: S. Bhalla, University of Aizu, Japan

Program Committee

D. Agrawal, University of California, USA
E. Bertino, University of Milan, Italy
S. Bhalla, University of Aizu, Japan
N. Bianchi-Berthouze, University of Aizu, Japan
P.C.P. Bhatt, Indian Institute of Information Technology, India
J. Biskup, University of Dortmund, Germany
P. Bottoni, University "La Sapienza" of Rome, Italy
L.F. Capretz, University of Western Ontario, Canada
M. Capretz, University of Western Ontario, Canada
B. Chidlovskii, Xerox Research Center Europe, France
U. Dayal, Hewlett-Packard Laboratories, USA
S. Grumbach, INRIA, France
J. Herder, Dusseldorf University of Applied Sciences, Germany
S. Jajodia, George Mason University, USA
Q. Jin, Waseda University, Japan
R. Khosla, La Trobe University, Australia
M. Kitsuregawa, University of Tokyo, Japan
A. Kumar, University of Colorado, USA
J. Li, University of Tsukuba, Japan
G. Mansfield, Tohoku University, Japan
K. Myszkowski, Max-Planck-Institut für Informatik, Germany
P.K. Reddy, International Institute of Information Technology, India
O. Zaiane, University of Alberta, USA

Additional Reviewers

F. Andres	I. Paik	M. Simmert	H. Yu
A. Bergholz	O.D. Sahin	L. Sznuk	
V. Kluev	C. Shahabi	T. Tamura	

Sponsoring Institution

International Affairs Committee, University of Aizu
Aizu-Wakamatsu City, Fukushima 965-8580, Japan

VIII   Organization

Table of Contents

Information Interchange among Cyber Communities

Knowledge – Annotation and Visualization

The World Wide Wisdom Web (W4)

Jiming Liu

Web Intelligence Consortium (WIC) & Computer Science Department
Hong Kong Baptist University
Kowloon Tong, Hong Kong
jiming@comp.hkbu.edu.hk
http://robotics.comp.hkbu.edu.hk/~jiming

Abstract. In this talk, I will address the research and development needs for creating the new paradigm shift in Internet computing. In particular, I will present one of the most promising answers to such needs, called *World Wide Wisdom Web* (W4), and identify several challenges and enabling technologies in building the W4.

1   The Emergence of Web Intelligence (WI)

Web Intelligence (WI) was first introduced by Zhong (Japan), Liu (Hong Kong), Yao (Canada), and Ohsuga (Japan) in 2000 [6], as a joint research effort in developing the next generation Web-based intelligent systems, through combining their expertise in Data-Mining, Agents, Information Retrieval, and Logic.

Broadly speaking, WI encompasses the scientific research and development that explores the fundamental roles as well as practical impacts of Artificial Intelligence (AI), such as autonomous agents and multi-agent systems, machine learning, data mining, and soft-computing, as well as advanced Information Technology (IT), such as wireless networks, grid computing, ubiquitous agents, and social networks, on the next generation of Web-empowered products, systems, services, and activities. WI is the key and the most urgent research field of IT today.

2   Web Intelligence (WI) as a Promising Field of Research and Development

As much more detailed blueprints and issues of Web Intelligence (WI) were evolved and specified in recent years [4, 5, 7, 8], numerous WI related research studies and business enterprises have been established around the world. WI companies and research centers or labs have been launched around the globe in USA, Europe, Japan, and India, etc. Each of them focuses on certain specific WI issues or products/services. As a result, today WI has become a well-defined IT research field, publicly recognized and promoted by the IEEE Computer Society.

In the meantime, international forums, such as IEEE International Conference on Web Intelligence (WI01, WI03) and Atlantic Web Intelligence Conference (AWIC03), were also organized with overwhelming interests and positive

N. Bianchi-Berthouze (Ed.): DNIS 2003, LNCS 2822, pp. 1–4, 2003.

responses. Successful experiences in the development of WI technologies have been reported as special issues in leading journals and magazines, and documented in details in the first ever hardcover text on Web Intelligence published by Springer in 2003 [9].

The challenges of Internet computing research and development in the next decade will be Web Intelligence (WI) centric, focusing on how we can intelligently make the best use of the widely available Web connectivity. The new WI technologies to be developed will be precisely determined by *human needs in a post-industrial era*; namely:

1. **information** empowerment;
2. **knowledge** sharing;
3. virtual **social** clustering;
4. **service** enrichment;
5. practical **wisdom** development.

In this talk, I will argue that one of the most promising paradigm shifts in WI will be driven by the notion of *wisdom*. Developing the **World Wide Wisdom Web** (W4) will become a tangible goal for WI researchers and practitioners. The W4 will enable us to *optimally* utilize the global connectivity, as offered by the Web infrastructure, and most importantly, to gain the practical wisdoms of living, working, and playing, in addition to information search and knowledge queries.

3   WIC: A Consortium for the W4 Research and Development

In order to best exchange and coordinate the W4 research and development efforts, and effectively promote and share the WI technologies, Ning Zhong (Maebashi Institute of Technology, Japan) and Jiming Liu (Hong Kong Baptist University), together with Edward A. Feigenbaum (Stanford University, USA), Setsuo Ohsuga (Waseda University, Japan), Benjamin Wah (University of Illinois at Urbana-Champaign, USA), Philip Yu (IBM T. J. Watson Research Center, USA), and L.A. Zadeh (UC Berkeley, USA), formally established the Web Intelligence Consortium (WIC) in 2002.

The WIC is an international non-profit organization dedicated to the promotion of world-wide scientific research and industrial development in the era of Web and agent intelligence, through collaborations among world-wide WI research centers and organizational members, technology showcase at WI conferences and workshops, WIC official book and journal publications, WIC newsletter, and WIC official releases of new industrial solutions and standards.

4   Towards Wisdom Oriented Computing

The paradigm of **wisdom oriented computing** is aimed at providing not only a medium for seamless information exchange and knowledge sharing [2] but also a type of *man-made resources for sustainable knowledge creation, and scientific and social evolution*. The W4 will reply on *grid-like service agencies* that self-organize, learn, and evolve their courses of actions in order to perform service tasks as well as their identities and interrelationships in communities. They will also cooperate and compete among themselves in order to optimize their as well as others resources and utilities.

Self-organizing, learning agents are computational entities that are capable of self-improving their performance in dynamically changing and unpredictable task environments. In [3], Liu has provided a comprehensive overview of several studies in the field of **autonomy oriented computing**, with in-depth discussions on self-organizing and adaptive techniques for developing various embodiments of agent based systems, such as autonomous robots, collective vision and motion, autonomous animation, and search and segmentation agents. The core of those techniques is the notion of synthetic or emergent autonomy based on behavioral self-organization.

5   Turing Test in the 21st Century

In order to effectively develop the new generation WI systems, we need to define *benchmark* applications, *i.e.*, a new *Turing Test*, that will capture and demonstrate the W4 capabilities.

Take the wisdom oriented computing benchmark as an example. We can use a service task of compiling and generating a market report on an existing product or *a potential market report on a new product*. In order to get such service jobs done, an information agent on the W4 will mine and integrate available Web information, which will in turn be passed onto a market analysis agent. Market analysis will involve the quantitative simulations of customer behavior in a marketplace, instantaneously handled by other serviced agencies, involving a large number of grid agents [1]. Since the number of variables concerned may be in the order of hundreds or thousands, it can easily cost a single system years to generate one predication.

References

[1] Berman, F.: From TeraGrid to knowledge grid. Communications of the ACM, 44:27-28, 2001. 3
[2] Berners-Lee, T., Hendler, J., Lassila, O.: The semantic Web. Scientific American, 284:34-43, 2001. 2
[3] Liu, J.: Autonomous Agents and Multiagent Systems, World Scientific Publishing, 2001. 3
[4] Liu, J., Zhong, N., Yao, Y.Y., Ras, Z.W.: The Wisdom Web: New challenges for Web Intelligence (WI). Journal of Intelligent Information Systems, Kluwer Academic Publishers, 20(1):5-9, 2003. 1
[5] Yao, Y.Y., Zhong, N., Liu, J., Ohsuga, S.: Web Intelligence (WI): Research challenges and trends in the new information age. N. Zhong, Y.Y. Yao, J. Liu, and S. Ohsuga (eds.), Web Intelligence: Research and Development, LNAI 2198, pages 1-17, Springer, 2001. 1

[6] Zhong, N., Liu, J., Yao, Y.Y., Ohsuga, S.: Web Intelligence (WI). In Proceedings of the 24th IEEE Computer Society International Computer Software and Applications Conference (COMPSAC 2000), pages 469-470, IEEE Computer Society Press, Taipei, Taiwan, October 25-28, 2000. 1

[7] Zhong, N., Yao, Y.Y., Liu, J., Ohsuga, S. (eds.): Web Intelligence: Research and Development, LNAI 2198, Springer, 2001. 1

[8] Zhong, N., Liu, J., Yao, Y.Y.: In search of the Wisdom Web. IEEE Computer, 35(11):27-31, November 2002. 1

[9] Zhong, N., Liu, J., Yao, Y.Y. (eds.): Web Intelligence, Springer, 2003. 2

Web Information Personalization: Challenges and Approaches*

Cyrus Shahabi[1] and Yi-Shin Chen[2]

[1] Department of Computer Science
University of Southern California
Los Angeles, CA 90089-2561, USA
shahabi@usc.edu
http://infolab.usc.edu/
[2] Integrated Media Systems Center
University of Southern California
Los Angeles, CA 90089-2561, USA
yishinc@imsc.usc.edu

Abstract. As the number of web pages increases dramatically, the problem of the information overload becomes more severe when browsing and searching the WWW. To alleviate this problem, personalization becomes a popular remedy to customize the Web environment towards a user's preference. To date, *recommendation systems* and *personalized web search systems* are the most successful examples of Web personalization. By focusing on these two types of systems, this paper reviews the challenges and the corresponding approaches proposed in the past ten years.

1 Introduction

The World Wide Web (WWW) is emerging as an appropriate environment for business transactions and user-organization interactions, because it is convenient, fast, and cheap to use. The witness to this fact is the enormous popularity of e-Commerce and e-Government applications. However, since the Web is a large collection of semi-structured and structured information sources, Web users often suffer from information overload. To alleviate this problem, personalization becomes a popular remedy to customize the Web environment for users.

Among all personalization tools, recommendation systems are the most employed tools in e-commerce businesses. Recommendation systems are usually used to help the customers to locate the products they would like to purchase. In essence, these systems apply data analysis techniques to progressively generate a list of recommended products for each online customer. The most famous example in e-commerce is the *"Customers who bought"* feature used in Amazon.com™, which is basically applied to every product page on its websites. With the help of this feature, the Amazon.com™'s system recommends

---

* This research has been funded in part by NSF grants EEC-9529152 (IMSC ERC) and IIS-0082826, and unrestricted cash gifts from Microsoft, NCR, and Okawa Foundation.

similar products to the current buyer based on the purchase histories of previous customers who bought the same product.

Contrary to the recommendation systems, the personalized web search systems[1] have received little attention from the e-commerce domain, even though search engines have become the indispensable tools in our daily lives. Generally, most modern search engines, e.g., Google[2], Yahoo![3], and AltaVista[4] do not return personalized results. That is, the result of a search for a given query is identical, independent of the user submitting the query. Hence, by ignoring the user's preferences during the search process, the search engines may return a large amount of irrelevance data. To illustrate, consider the search query for the keywords "web usage". By this query, some users may look for the information regarding the usage of the *spider* web, while other users may be interested in documents related to the statistical data about World Wide Web usage.

In summary, both the recommendation systems and the personalized web search systems face the same obstacle of "ambiguity" in users' needs[5]. Moreover, both types of systems share the same challenge of striking a compromise between the amount of processed data and the efficiency of the retrieval process. We review the challenges and the proposed approaches for both system types in the remainder of this paper. Section 2 reviews the work on the recommendation systems. In Section 3, the work on the search systems is discussed.

2   Recommendation Systems

Various statistical and knowledge discovery techniques have been proposed and applied for recommendation systems. To date, most recommendation systems are designed either based on *content-based filtering* or *collaborative filtering*. Both types of systems have inherent strengths and weaknesses, where content-based approaches directly exploit the product information, and the collaboration filtering approaches utilize specific user rating information.

2.1   Content-Based Filtering

Content-based filtering approaches are derived from the concepts introduced by the Information Retrieval (IR) community. Content-based filtering systems are usually criticized for two weaknesses:

1. **Content Limitation**: IR methods can only be applied to a few kinds of content, such as text and image, and the extracted features can only capture certain aspects of the content.

---

[1] Note that the web search system is a more general term than *search engine* where the search system includes search engines, search agents, and metasearch systems.

[2] http://www.google.com

[3] http://www.yahoo.com

[4] http://www.altavista.com

[5] The ambiguity comes from user perceptions or the disagreements among users' opinions.

2. **Over-Specialization**: Content-based recommendation system provides recommendations merely based on user profiles. Therefore, users have no chance of exploring new items that are not similar to those items included in their profiles.

2.2   Collaborative Filtering

The collaborative filtering (CF) approach remedies for these two problems. Typically, CF-based recommendation systems do not use the actual content of the items for recommendation. Collaborative filtering works based on the assumption that if user x interests are similar to user(s) y interests, the items preferred by y can be recommended to x. Moreover, since other user profiles are also considered, user can explore new items. The nearest-neighbor algorithm is the earliest CF-based technique used in recommendation systems [16, 17]. With this algorithm, the similarity between users is evaluated based on their ratings of products, and the recommendation is generated considering the items visited by nearest neighbors of the user. In its original form, the nearest-neighbor algorithm uses a two-dimensional user-item matrix to represent the user profiles. This original form of CF-based recommendation systems suffers from three problems:

1. **Scalability**: The time complexity of executing the nearest-neighbor algorithm grows linearly with the number of items and the number of users. Thus, the recommendation system cannot support large-scale applications such as Amazon.com™, which provides more than 18 million unique items for over 20 million users.
2. **Sparsity**: Due to large number of items and user reluctance to rate the items, usually the profile matrix is sparse. Therefore, the system cannot provide recommendations for some users, and the generated recommendations are not accurate.
3. **Synonymy**: Since contents of the items are completely ignored, latent association between items is not considered for recommendations. Thus, as long as new items are not rated, they are not recommended; hence, false negatives are introduced.

In order to solve these problems, a variety of different techniques have been proposed. Some of techniques, such as dimensionality reduction [11, 8], clustering [29], and Bayesian Network [10, 9], mainly are remedies for the scalability problem. These techniques extract characteristics (patterns) from the original dataset in an offline process and employ only these patterns to generate the recommendation lists in the online process. Although this approach can reduce the online processing cost, it often reduces the accuracy of the recommending results. Moreover, the online computation complexity keeps increasing with the number of patterns.

Some other techniques, such as association rules [30, 11], content analysis [12, 13, 15], categorization [18, 14], are emphasized on alleviating the sparsity and synonymy problems. Basically, these techniques analyze the Web usage data (from Web server logs) to capture the latent association between items. Subsequently, based on both item association information and user ratings, the recommendation systems can thus generate better recommendation to users. However, the online computation time concurrently increases, as more data are incorporated into the recommendation progress. Additionally, because Web usage data from the server side are not reliable [24], the item association generated from Web server logs might be wrong.

2.3   Yoda

In an earlier work [1], we introduced a hybrid recommendation system - *Yoda*, which simultaneously utilizes the advantages of *clustering, content analysis*, and *collaborate filtering* (CF) approaches. Basically, Yoda is a two-step approach recommendation system. During the offline process, Yoda generates cluster recommendation lists based on the Web usage data from the client-side through clustering and content analysis techniques. This approach not only can address the scalability problem by the preprocessing work, but also can alleviate the sparsity and synonymy problems by discovering latent association between items. Since the Web usage data from the client-side can capture real user navigation behaviors, the item association discovered by the Yoda system would be more accurate. Beside the cluster recommendation lists, Yoda also maintains numerous recommendation lists obtained from different experts, such as human experts of the Website domain, and the cluster representatives of the user ratings. By these additional recommendation lists, Yoda is less impacted by the preprocessing work as compared to other systems.

During the online process, for each user who is using the system, Yoda estimates his/her confidence values to each expert, who provides the recommendation list, based on his/her current navigation behaviors through the PPED distance measure [23] and our GA-based learning mechanism. Subsequently, Yoda generates customized recommendations for the user by aggregating across recommendation lists using the confidence value as the weight. In order to expedite the aggregation step, Yoda employs an optimized fuzzy aggregation function that reduces the time computation complexity of aggregation from $O(N \times E)$ to $O(N)$, where N is the number of recommended items in the final recommendation list to users and E is the number of recommendation lists maintained in the system. Consequently, the online computation complexity of Yoda remains the same even if number of recommendation lists increases.

In sum, the time complexity is reduced through a model-based technique, a clustering approach, and the optimized aggregation method. Additionally, due to the utilization of content analysis techniques, Yoda can detect the latent association between items and therefore provides better recommendations. Moreover, Yoda is able to collect information about user interests from implicit web navigation behaviors while most other recommendation systems [16, 17, 11, 9, 10] do not have this ability and therefore require explicit rating information from users. Consequently, Yoda puts less overhead on the users.

Since content analysis techniques only capture certain characteristics of products, some desired products might not be included in the recommendation lists produced by analyzing the content. For example, picking wines based on brands, years, and descriptors might not be adequate if "smell" and "taste" are more important characteristics. In order to remedy for this problem, in [2] we extended Yoda to incorporate more recommendation lists than just web navigation patterns. These recommendation lists can be obtained from various experts, such as human experts and clusters of user evaluations.

Meanwhile, because PPED is specially designed for measuring the similarity between two web navigation patterns including related data such as browsed items, view time, and sequences information, it can only be used for estimating confidence values to navigation-pattern clusters. Therefore, a learning mechanism is needed for obtaining the complete confidence values of an active user toward all experts. We proposed a learning mechanism that utilizes users' relevance feedback to improve confidence values automatically using genetic algorithms (GA) [5].

To the best of our knowledge, only a few studies [4, 3] incorporate GA for improving the user profiles. In these studies, users are directly involved in the evolution process. Because users have to enter data for each product inquiry, they are often frustrated with this method. On the contrary, in our design, users are not required to offer additional data to improve the confidence values. These confidence values are corrected by the GA-based learning mechanisms using users' future navigation behaviors. Our experimental results indicated a significant increase in the accuracy of recommendation results due to the integration of the proposed learning mechanism.

3   Personalized Web Search Systems

A variety of techniques have been proposed for personalized web search systems. These techniques, which are adopted from IR systems, face a common challenge, i.e., evaluating the accuracy of retrieved documents. The common evaluation method applied in IR systems is *precision and recall*, which usually requires relevance feedback from users. However, obtaining relevance feedback explicitly from users for personalized web search systems is extremely challenging due to the large size of WWW, which consists of billions of documents with a growth rate of 7.3 million pages per day [33]. Therefore, it is very time consuming and almost impossible to collect relevance judgments from each user for every page resulting from a query.

In order to incorporate user preferences into search engines, three major approaches are proposed: *personalized page importance, query refinement*, and *personalized metasearch systems*. Consider each approach in turn.

3.1   Personalized Page Importance

In addition to the traditional text matching techniques, modern web search engines also employ the importance scores of pages for ranking the search results.

The most famous example is the *PageRank* algorithm , which is the basis for all web search tools of Google [34]. By utilizing the linkage structure of the web, PageRank computes the corresponding importance score for each page. These importance scores will affect the final ranking of the search results. Therefore, by modifying the importance equations based on user preference, the PageRank algorithm can create a personalized search engine.

Basically, personalized importance scores are usually computed based on a set of favorite pages defined by users. In *topic-sensitive PageRank* [36], the system first pre-computes web pages based on the categories in *Open Directory*. Next, by using the pre-computation results and the favorite pages, the system can retrieve "topic-sensitive" pages for users. The experimental results [36] illustrated that this system could improve the search engine. However, this technique is not scalable, since the number of favorite pages is limited to 16 [35].

With the aim of constructing a scalable and personalized PageRank search engine, Jeh and Widom [35] proposed a model based on *personalized PageRank vector (PPV)*. PPV represents the distribution of selection in the model. The selection of PPV prefers pages related to input favorite pages. For example, the pages linked by the favorite pages and the pages linked to these favorite pages have higher selected possibilities. Each PPV can be considered as a personalized view of the importance of pages. Therefore, by incorporating PPV during the selection process, the search engine can retrieve pages closer to user preferences.

In general, since these techniques require direct inputs from users, the system increases the usage overhead. As a result, instead of saving time from identifying relevant web pages, users could possibly spend more time to personalize the search.

3.2 Query Refinement

Instead of modifying the algorithms of search engines, researchers [37, 38, 39, 40] proposed assisting users with the query refinement process. Generally, the query refinement process of these systems consists of three steps.

1. **Obtaining User Profiles from User**: The user profiles could be explicitly entered by users or implicitly learned from user behaviors. For example, WebMate [39] automatically learns the users' interested domains through a set of interesting examples; Persona [40] learns the taxonomy of user interests and disinterests from user's navigation history; the system proposed by Liu et al. [38] can learn user's favorite categories from his/her search history. Different from these systems, the client-side web search tool proposed by Chau et al. [37] requires direct inputs about interesting phrases from users.
2. **Query Modification**: The systems first adjust the input query based on the corresponding user profile. Subsequently, the modified query is outsourced to search engines. For instance, the system proposed by Liu et al. [38] maps the input query to a set of interesting categories based on the user profile and confines the search domain to these categories. In Websifter [42], after

a user submits his/her intent, Websifter formulates the query based on user's search taxonomy and then submits the query to multiple search engines[6].

3. **Refinement**: After receiving the query results from the search engine, the systems refine the response. Occasionally, some search systems would further filter the irrelevant pages. For example, in the Persona system [40], the search results are ranked according to authoritativeness with a graph based algorithm. The returned set in Persona only contains the top n documents. Furthermore, Persona would refine the results if the user provides positive or negative feedback on the response.

In general, maintaining efficiency is the major challenge of the query refinement approach. That is, the time complexity of the proposed techniques grows with the size of user profiles, e.g., the number of interested categories, keywords, and domains.

3.3 Personalized Metasearch Systems

It has been reported [41] that the search engine coverage decreases steadily as the estimated web size increases. In 1999, no search engine can index more than 16% of the total web pages. Consequently, searching data by employing only a single search engine could result in a very low retrieval rate. To solve this problem, metasearch systems, such as MetaCrawler[7], Dogpile[8], and McFind[9], are proposed to increase the search coverage by combining several search engines.

Ideally, by merging various ranked results from multiple search engines into one final ranked list, metasearch systems could improve the retrieval rate. However, since metasearch systems expand the search coverage, the information overload problem could possibly be intensified. In order to improve the accuracy of returned results, researchers proposed different techniques for incorporating user preferences into metasearch systems.

The first type of personalized metasearch systems [37, 42, 45] adopt the query refinement approach. Typically, these metasearch systems modify the input query based on the corresponding user profile. Some systems[37, 45] can further select the outsourcing search engines based on user's intent. Since these systems exploit the query refinement approach, they also inherit the scalability problem from the query refinement approach.

The second types of personalized metasearch systems [43, 44] emphasize on the merging procedures. By considering user preferences during the merging process, the systems could retrieve different documents even with the same set of input lists from search engines. For example, in Inquirus 2 [44], users can assign (explicitly or implicitly) weights to different search engines and categories. The final rankings of results in Inquirus 2 are aggregated with a weighted average

---

[6] Note that aggregating the results from different search engines is the problem of *metasearch*, which is described later in Section 3.3.

[7] http://www.metacrawler.com/

[8] http://www.dogpile.com/

[9] http://www.mcfind.com/

process. For another instance, the personalized metasearch engine proposed by Zhu et al. [43] merges the lists based on explicit relevance feedback. In this system, users can assign "good" or "bad" scores to returned pages. With content-based similarity measure, the system could evaluate final scores to all pages. Note that the importance degrees of search engines are not considered in this merging technique.

In general, most metasearch systems emphasize on one-phase merging process, i.e., the system only considers the final score of each page returned from a search engine. However, the final score provided by each search engine is composed of several similarity values, where each value corresponds to a feature. For instance, the similarity values can be derived based on the corresponding titles of the pages, the URLs of the pages, or the summaries generated by the search engine. For another example, assume the query submitted by the user is "SARS WHO", the metasearch system can obtain different scores from the same search engine with similar queries (e.g., "SARS WHO", "SARS and WHO organization", "SARS on Who magazine", and "Severe Acute Respiratory Syndrome and WHO organization") that are generated by a query modification process. Therefore, merging these query scores based on user preferences should also be considered.

In our recent work [46], we introduced a new concept, *two-phase decision fusion*, where scores returned from the search engines are aggregated based upon user perceptions on both search engines and the relevant features. Our experimental results indicate that as compared to a traditional decision fusion approach, the retrieval accuracy of the two-phase decision fusion approach is significantly improved.

References

[1] Shahabi, C., Banaei-Kashani, F., Chen Y.-S., McLeod, D.: Yoda: An Accurate and Scalable Web-based Recommendation System. In Proceedings of Sixth International Conference on Cooperative Information Systems (2001) 8

[2] Shahabi, C., Chen, Y.-S.: An Adaptive Recommendation System without Explicit Acquisition of User Relevance Feedback. Distributed and Parallel Databases, Vol. 14. (2003) 173–192 9

[3] Moukas, A.: Amalthea: Information discovery and filtering using a multiagent evolving ecosystem. In Proceedings of 1st Int. Conf. on The Practical Applications of Intelligent Agents and MultiAgent Technology (1996) 9

[4] Sheth, B., Maes, P.: Evolving Agents for Personalized Information Filtering. *Proceedings of the Ninth IEEE Conference on Artificial Intelligence for Applications* (1993) 9

[5] Holland, J.: *Adaption in Natural and Artificial Systems*. University of Michigan Press, Ann Arbor, Michigan 9

[6] Konstan, J., Miller, B., Maltz, D., Herlocker, J., Gordon, L., Riedl, J.: Applying Collaborative Filtering to Usenet News. Communications of the ACM Vol. 40 (3) (1997)

[7] Shahabi, C., Zarkesh, A. M., Adibi, J., Shah, V.: Knowledge Discovery from Users Web Page Navigation. In *Proceedings of the IEEE RIDE97 Workshop* (1997)

[8] Sarwar, B., Karypis, G., Konstan, J., Riedl, J.: Application of Dimensionality Reduction in Recommender System – A Case Study. In *Proceedings of ACM WebKDD 2000 Web Mining for e-Commerce Workshop* (2000)   7

[9] Kitts, B., Freed D., Vrieze, M.: Cross-sell, a fast promotion-tunable customer-item recommendation method based on conditionally independent probabilities. In*Proceedings of the sixth ACM SIGKDD international conference on Knowledge discovery and data mining* (2000) 437-446   7, 8

[10] Breese, J., Heckerman, D., Kadie, C.: Empirical Analysis of Predictive Algorithms for Collaborative Filtering. In *Proceedings of the Fourteenth Conference on Uncertainty in Artificial Intelligence* (1998) 43–52   7, 8

[11] Sarwar, B., Karypis, G., Konstan, J., Riedl, J.: Analysis of Recommendation Algorithms for e-Commerce. In *Proceedings of ACM e-Commerce 2000 Conference* (2000)   7, 8

[12] Balabanovi, M., Shoham, Y.: Fab, content-based, collaborative recommendation. Communications of the ACM, Vol 40(3) (1997) 66–72   7

[13] Balabanovi, M.: An Adaptive Web page Recommendation Service. In *Proceedings of Autonomous Agents* (1997) 378-385   7

[14] Kohrs, A., Merialdo, B.: Using category-based collaborative filtering in the Active WebMuseum. In *Proceedings of IEEE International Conference on Multimedia and Expo*, Vol 1 (2000) 351–354   7

[15] Lieberman, H., Dyke, N., Vivacqua, A.: Let's Browse, A Collaborative Browsing Agent. Knowledge-Based Systems, Vol 12 (1999) 427–431   7

[16] Shardanand, U., Maes, P.: Social Information Filtering, Algorithm for automating "Word of Mouth". In *Proceedings on Human factors in computing systems*(1995) 210–217   7, 8

[17] Resnick, P., Iacovou, N., Suchak, M., Bergstrom, P., Riedl, J.: GroupLens, An Open Architecture for Collaborative Filtering of Netnews. In *Proceedings of ACM conference on Cumputer-Supported Cooperative Work* (1994) 175–186   7, 8

[18] Good, N., Schafer, J., Konstan, J., Borchers, J., Sarwar, B., Herlocker, J., Riedl, J.: Combining Collaborative Filtering with Personal Agents for Better Recommendations. In *Proceedings of the 1999 Conference of the American Association of Artifical Intelligence* (1999) 439–446   7

[19] Pazzani, M., Billsus, D.: Learning and Revising User profiles: The Indentification of Interesting Web Sites. Machine Learning, Vol 27 (1997) 313–331

[20] Tan, A., Teo, C., Learning User Profiles for Personalized Information Dissemination. In *Proceedings of Int'l Joint Conf. on Neural Network* (1998) 183–188

[21] Lam, W., Mukhopadhyay, S., Mostafa J., Palakal, M.: Detection of Shifts in User Interests for Personalized Information Filtering. In *Proceedings of the 19th Int'l ACM-SIGIR Conf on Research and Development in Information Retrieval* (1996) 317–325

[22] Goldberg, D. E.: Genetic Algorithms in Search, Optimisation, and Machine Learning. Addison-Wesley, Wokingham, England (1989)

[23] Shahabi, C., Banaei-Kashani, F., Faruque, J., Faisal, A.: Feature Matrices: A Model for Efficient and Anonymous Web Usage Mining. In *Proceedings of EC-Web* (2001)   8

[24] Shahabi, C., Banaei-Kashani, F., Faruque, J.: A Reliable, Efficient, and Scalable System for Web Usage Data Acquisition. In *WebKDD'01 Workshop in conjunction with the ACM-SIGKDD* (2001)   8

[25] Fagin, R.: Combining Fuzzy Information from Multiple Systems. In *Proceedings of Fifteenth ACM Symposyum on Principles of Database Systems* (1996)

[26] Hunter, A.: Sugal Programming manual. http://www.trajan-software.demon.co.uk/sugal.htm (1995)

[27] Wu, L., Faloutsos, C., Sycara, K., Payne, T.: FALCON: Feedback Adaptive Loop for Content-Based Retrieval. In *Proceedings of Int'l. Conf. on Very Large Data Bases* (2000)

[28] Knorr, E., Ng, R., Tucakov, V.: Distance-Based Outliers: Algorithms and Applications. *The VLDB Journal*, Vol 8(3) (2000) 237–253

[29] Mobasher, B., Cooley, R., Srivastava, J.: Automatic personalization based on Web usage mining. *Communications of the ACM*, Vol 43(8) (2000) 142–151 7

[30] Mobasher, B., Dai, H., Luo, T., Nakagawa, M.: Web Data Mining: Effective personalization based on association rule discovery from web usage data. In *Proceeding of the Third International Workshop on Web Information and Data Management* (2001) 7

[31] Rui, Y., Huang, T., Ortega, M., Mehrotra, S.: Relevance feedback: a power tool for interactive content-based image retrieval. *IEEE Transactions on Circuits and Systems for Video Technology*, Vol 8(5) (1998) 644–655

[32] Knuth, D. Seminumerical Algorithm. *The Art of Computer Programming Volume 2*, 1997

[33] Lyman, P., Varian, H. R.: How Much Information . *Retrieved from* http://www.sims.berkeley.edu/research/projects/how-much-info/internet.html (2000) 9

[34] Google: Google Technology. *Retrieved from http://www.google.com/technology/* (2003) 10

[35] Jeh, G., Widom, J.: Scaling Personalized Web Search. *Proceedings of the 12th International World Wide Web Conference* (2003) 10

[36] Haveliwala, T. H.: Topic-sensitive PageRank. *Proceedings of the 11th International World Wide Web Conference* (2002) 10

[37] Chau, M., Zeng, D., Chen, H.: Personalized Spiders for Web Search and Analysis. *Proceedings of ACM/IEEE Joint Conference on Digital Libraries* (2001) 10, 11

[38] Liu, F., Yu, C. T., Meng, W.: Personalized web search by mapping user queries to categories. *Proceedings of CIKM* (2002) 10

[39] Chen, L., Sycara, K.: WebMate : A Personal Agent for Browsing and Searching. *Proceedings of the 2nd International Conference on Autonomous Agents* (1998) 10

[40] Tanudjaja, F., Mui, L.: Persona: a contextualized and personalized web search. *35th Annual Hawaii International Conference on System Sciences* (2002) 10, 11

[41] Lawrence, S., Giles, C. L.:   Accessibility of Information on the Web . *Nature*, Vol 400 (1999) 107–109 11

[42] Scime, A., Kerschberg, L.: WebSifter: An Ontology-Based Personalizable Search Agent for the Web . *Proceedings of International Conference on Digital Libraries: Research and Practice* (2000) 10, 11

[43] Zhu, S., Deng, X., Chen, K., Zheng, W.: Using Online Relevance Feedback to Build Effective Personalized Metasearch Engine. *Proceedings of Second International Conference on Web Information Systems Engineering* (2001) 11, 12

[44] Glover, E., Lawrence, S., Birmingham, W. P., Giles, C. L.:   Architecture of a Metasearch Engine that Supports User Information Needs. *Proceedings of Eighth International Conference on Information and Knowledge Management* (1999) 11

[45] Glover, E., Flake, G.W., Lawrence, S., Birmingham, W.P., Kruger, A., Giles, C.L., Pennock, D.M.: Improving Category Specific Web Search by Learning Query Modifications. *Proceedings of Symposium on Applications and the Internet* (2001) 11

[46] Chen, Y.-S., Shahabi, C., Burns, G.: Two-Phase Decision Fusion Based On User Preferences. *submitted for reviewing* (2003) 12

An Adaptive E-commerce Personalization Framework with Application in E-banking

Qiubang Li and Rajiv Khosla

School of Business
La Trobe University, Melbourne,
Victoria, Australia
{L.Qiubang,R.Khosla}@latrobe.edu.au

Abstract. Internet Personalized services are irresistible developing trend for e-commerce. More and more researchers are committed to personalization field. Many personalization approaches are static and lack of means to improve the personalized tasks. This paper proposes an adaptive e-commerce personalization framework using traditional data mining techniques and agent technology as well as user feedback optimisation mechanism to improve the personalized services to the e-commerce customer. The behaviours of all the agents in the framework are carefully considered and the framework has been applied to an online banking system.

1   Introduction

Today's World Wide Web market is becoming more competitive, so it's more important than ever to provide customers with an interactive, personal Web experience. Personalization (sometimes called information customization) means to provide such personalized services to customer. It is like, in a sense, bank staff and customer with one-one relationships to discuss the special needs of the customer. The objective of web personalization systems in e-commerce is to identify customers online, understand and predict their buying patterns, identify what they want or need without requiring them to ask for it explicitly, and deliver appropriate offers in personalized formats directly to them[2].

Currently, four basic techniques of, rule-based filtering, content-based filtering, collaborative filtering and learning-agent technology, are used for web personalization.

- Rules-based filtering poses users a series of questions (or asks them to meet a set of criteria), and then delivers content appropriate to their responses. The criteria can be anything from making sure a user lives in a state served by the company sponsoring the site, making sure the site offers products that meet specific needs. Examples of rules-based filtering questions include: What is your zip code? Are you male or female? Do you use a Mac or a PC? Is your camping trip scheduled for winter or summer? This approach differs from basic personalization by providing users with specific content based on their responses. Users are led

N. Bianchi-Berthouze (Ed.): DNIS 2003, LNCS 2822, pp. 16-26, 2003.

down a path by answering a set of yes/no or multiple-choice questions of increasing specificity and relevance.

- Content-based techniques from the information-filtering and Web database management communities use keywords, string matching, link patterns, and manually compiled identifiers to provide simple "Web query languages" for personalization. Examples include WebSQL, WebOQL, and Florid. For an excellent survey of these and other content-based techniques with a database flavor, see [3].

- Collaborative filtering (also called *group filtering*), meanwhile, is designed to serve relevant material to users by combining their own personal preferences with the preferences of like-minded others. The book selling in Amazon.com, is perhaps the best-known example of this approach. The site asks users to rate books on a scale. At the most basic level, it works like this: If one user loves *Harry Potter* and *The King of Torts*, and another loves *Harry Potter* and *Harry Potter Schoolbooks Box Set*, then Amazon.com suggests that the first user check out *Harry Potter Schoolbooks Box Set*. In this way, users collaborate (albeit without truly interacting) to make recommendations to each other.

- Learning agent technology or nonintrusive personalization, instead of asking users explicitly rating products, tracks users' movements around the e-business web site and alters what is presented based on their click trails. Using implicit rating is mainly motivated by its removing the cost to the evaluator of examining and rating the item and remaining a computational cost in storing and processing the implicit rating data that is hidden from the user[4].

Among these, no single personalization technology or model works best: It depends on what you are trying to accomplish. Collaborative filtering and rules-based filtering are not mutually exclusive. In fact, it's often desirable to offer users the opportunity to input information, while at the same time leading them where you want them to go. Most collaborative filtering technologies let Web builders weigh certain criteria more highly than others, adding some rules-based rigidity to help control where users actually go. This is the advantage of hybrid system, which will be adopted in this paper. Further details will be discussed in the next section.

This paper is organized as follows: In the next section, the adaptive e-commerce personalization framework is proposed. Section 3 illustrates some agent definitions of the framework. Section 4 provides some experiment results. Section 5 is related work in the field. Finally, the last section concludes the paper.

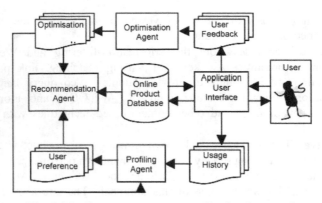

Fig. 1. Adaptive e-commerce personalization framework

2   Framework of E-commerce Personalization

The architecture of personalization is a multi-agent, distributed, and complex system. From fine-grained to coarse-grained, there are three layers, which is sufficient to the domain[5], technology-oriented agent layer, optimisation agent layer, and task-oriented (problem solving) agent layer[6,7]. Technology-oriented agent layer focused on solving any specific problem. It is a reactive layer of personalization implementation hierarchy, which needs to accept external sensor input and response immediately. The optimisation agent layer is in the middle layer of the personalization implementation hierarchy answering customers or users in a knowledge-level view of the agent environment. The task-oriented agent layer (also called problem-solving agent layer in [6]), which is the uppermost implantation hierarchy of personalization system, interacts with users or customers directly. It seems to the users or customers who possess all the resources of the personalization system. The task-oriented agent layer coordinates various tasks and finally produces the global behaviours of the personalization system.   This paper only deals with technology agent layer and problem solving (task-oriented) agent layer.

The adaptive framework is shown in Fig. 1. It is a hybrid system using personalization techniques fusing rule-based filtering, content-based filtering and learning agent technology. The function of recommendation agent is to extracting of rules from user preference, searching similar product results, and recommending based on online product database.

When users express any interests to an online product in the online shopping mall, recommendation agent try to recommend similar products to the customer simultaneously. The construction work of recommendation system agent can be found at [8] by Li and Khosla. Its architecture is shown in Fig. 2. The problem solving agents of data mining algorithm agents, and parallel processing agents shown in Fig. 2 work sequentially to get the recommendation results based on the interests of customer. The recommendation results, together with retrieving product result for customer's enquiry, are re-organized to corresponding web-page format and feedback to the active online customer. The data mining algorithm agents consist of transaction frequency agent, association rule agent, and collaborative filtering agent. They mutually coordinate together and acquire the necessary information based on the tremendous purchase history of customers. One of most significant problem for recommendation is cold-start[9]. It can be solved by offering a search result list to the customers, which is enlightened from [10] by Chen and Sycara 1997.

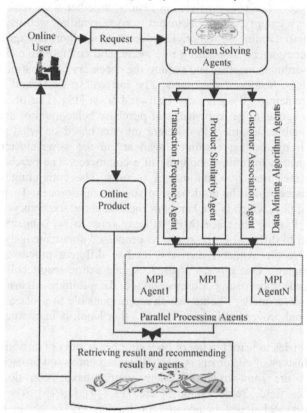

Fig. 2. The architecture of recommendation agent

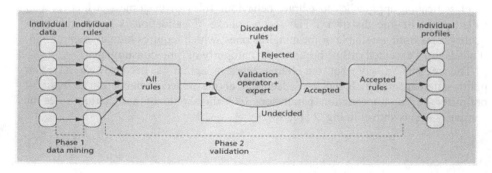

Fig. 3. A profile-build process using data mining techniques from [1]

Fig. 2 is the architecture of multi-agent automatic recommendation system. An online user who stays at the computer makes an enquiry about a product. The front-end web-based database management system will retrieve what the customer wants for the customer. The data mining algorithm agents, and parallel processing agents shown in Fig. 2 work together to get the recommendation results based on the interests of customer. The recommendation results, together with retrieving product result for customer's enquiry, are re-organized to corresponding web-page format and feedback to the active online customer. The data mining algorithm agents consist of transaction frequency agent, association rule agent, and collaborative filtering agent. They mutually coordinate together and acquire the necessary information based on the tremendous purchase history of customers. The internal structure and algorithms in detail of the aforementioned agents can be found from [11]. The principle of data mining algorithm agents to get knowledge of purchase behaviours of customers here is to classify available customers to different clusters based on what products they already bought. It means that customers who are in the same cluster share most similar purchase habits for online shopping in e-commerce. The purchase history of customers sometimes runs into millions of records. The computing time of data mining algorithms becomes the bottleneck in such circumstances. To accelerate the process of data mining, which is the kernel of the automatic recommendation system, we use Message Passing Interface (MPI) (Please refer to [12]) agents to feed our available raw data to different processes to be processed simultaneously. It uses MPI command to divide the available data and feed to different processes in a multi-processor environment. One process is used as calculation result collector and the others as data processors using aforementioned data mining algorithms. This is similar to client/server mode. Clients, which are responsible to process raw data, are comparable to serial process and server, on the other hand, is in charge of collecting process result.

Profiling agent tries to learn buying or browsing behaviours of customers. The data source of usage history of customers is web pages users browsed or user click-stream logs whose data are semi-structured. Many works have been done by active researchers in this field. Some examples are [13, 14] [1, 15]. The data mining profiling customer techniques is adopted in this paper, which is suggested by Adomavicius et al. [1] and Li et al.[14]. Two phases of data mining and validation are applied in this approach. The objective of data mining phase is to use association or classification approaches to extract behaviour rules of customers, which is also called phase of rule discovery. The second phase of validation is to identify high quality rules from unreliable or meaningless ones, which requires human intervention. It needs to be executed offline because of its property of time-consuming.

The reason we say that our frame work adaptive is because we have an optimisation agent, which gets user's feedback about the recommendation as input, to optimise the recommendation parameters like thresholds of association rules or similarity agents shown in Fig. 2 [11, 16].

Table 1. Behaviour definition of recommendation agent

Name :	Recommendation Agent
Goals:	Make recommendation to customers
Some Tasks:	Association rule, similarity, and frequency computing
Task Constraints:	Homogeneous clusters Response time less than 30 seconds
Precondition:	Preprocessed online structured data for further processing
Postcondition:	Cross-validated recommendation quality.
Communicates with:	Profiling agent and optimisation agent
Communication Constructs:	Customer association agent, product similarity agent, transaction frequency agent, parallel processing agent
Linguistic/non-linguistic features:	User preference, cluster data, optimisation result
Internal Tools	Nearest neighbor algorithm, association algorithm, and frequency algorithm
External Tools:	Domain: Bank data model and database
Actions:	Change learning parameters Invoke optimisation agent Send recommendation results to customer

3   Agent Definition of the Framework

In this section we outline the agent design of the recommendation agent and profiling agent. An overview of the agent based design architecture is shown in Fig. 1.

The agent definitions of agents describe the agent behaviors like input, output, internal structure etc. Tables 1 and 2 are agent definition of recommendation agent and profiling agent respectively. The role of recommendation agent is to offer recommendations to customers effectively and efficiently. Effective means the quality of recommendation should be high and efficient means the response time of recommendation should very rapid (usually less than 30 seconds). The recommendation agent integrate data mining agents of nearest neighbor, association rule, and frequency computing with parallel processing agent to warrant the response requirement set by online users or customers whose patience to a link clicked is normally less than 30 seconds [16]. The improvement of recommendation quality solely relies on the cooperation of profiling agent and optimization agent. The profiling agent can study user behavior and present the relevant information (user preference in this case) to the user via recommendation agent. Its role is to produce rules according to the purchase trails left in the online e-commerce website. The agents are capable of autonomous behaviour both in the reactive as well as in the proactive task execution modes[17], as in our profiling agent both classification of pre-defined clusters and agent technology embedding data mining techniques are used, which can cluster customers automatically. The profiling process is executed offline and usually updates its user preferences in an off-peak usage of the e-commerce services.

Table 2. Behaviour definition of profiling agent

Name :	Profiling Agent
Goals:	Collecting customer-behaviours
Some Tasks:	Collecting customer data, customer profiling
Task Constraints:	Homogeneous clusters
Precondition:	Preprocessed semi-structured data for further processing
Postcondition:	Cross-validated profiling quality.
Communicates with:	Recommendation agent
Communication Constructs:	Similarity-based rule grouping, template-based filtering, redundant-rule elimination
Linguistic/non-linguistic features:	Rules, cluster data, web pages
Internal Tools	Rule-generating algorithm
External Tools:	Domain: online semi-structured web pages and server logs
Actions:	Data validation Rule extraction Rule validation

4 Experiment to the Architecture

The ability of the financial institutions like banks to collect data far outstrips their ability to explore, analyze and understand it. For that reason, in the past five years banks have moved aggressively towards applying data mining techniques especially in the personalization area. Given the cost savings with Internet banking, the banks seem now keen to apply data mining techniques to study online transaction behaviour of their clients and offer personalized services to customers. Fig. 4 shows a highly simplified data model of a bank with both Internet and branch (face-to-face) banking facilities, which is used as a testbed in this paper. From Fig. 4, we can see that are 11 tables connected together in the testbed. In this paper, data in saving (1056320 records), loan (682 records), and credit card (892 records) are mainly used for bank personalization service.

4.1 Product Similarity

The similarity agent is used to determine clusters of customers with similar transactional behaviour. The loan account and credit account transaction records shown in Table 3 have been used to cluster similarities in two-product transaction behaviour. The fields "Loan_Dur" and "Loan-Stat" stand for Loan duration and Loan status respectively. Fig. 5 is a diagram shown how many groups of people who share similar behaviours in the saving account. We can observe that most largest cluster is about 550 customers and the scale of some customers is less than two, which means these customers have no people with similar interests.

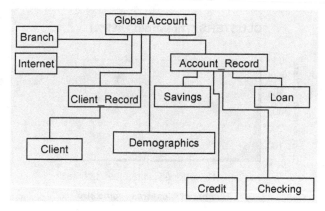

Fig. 4. Simplified data model of a bank

4.2   Profiling Rules of Banking Products

By implementing profiling agent and applying it to banking products, we get following rules for our experiment.

- More transactions are done from the district where there are more inhabitants.
- More transactions are did by those clients whose average salary is also high.
- There are 10 clients who have both minus account balance and bad loans.
- We have 39 customers who have minus account balance out of them above 11 customers either have bad loans or credit card so that the reason they have negative account balance but we couldn't find the reason that why 39-11=28 customers have minus account balance.
- Account_id 3948 used his credit card to pay his payment the most of 212 times for all credit card holders.
- Most of the customers used credit card for household payments.
- In general it would be advisable to set business goal to promote credit card usage.

Table 3. Loan Account and Credit Card Transactions

Account_id	Card_Type	Av_Trans	Balance	Loan_Amt	Loan_Dur	Loan_Stat
790	1	7559	28826	208128	48	2
1843	1	4922	31652	105804	36	1
2167	1	8557	34109	170256	24	1
2824	2	5213	38281	50460	60	3
3050	1	7280	51572	82896	12	1
3166	1	5657	23730	177744	48	4
4337	1	11133	46132	51408	24	1
4448	1	6946	36681	192744	36	1
4894	1	9070	43671	117024	24	1

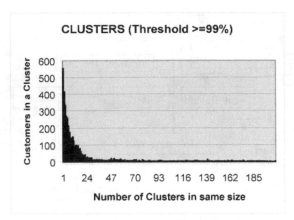

Fig. 5. Similarity visualization of computing result

5   Related Work

Currently, many web-based companies use collaborative filtering techniques which is heavily based on getting human intervention for personalization purpose. NetPerceptions tries to obtain or learns user preferences and discover Web information sources that correspond to their preferences, and possibly those of other individuals with similar interests using explicit rating from users [18]. The information inferences are mainly based on previous personal history and data accumulated from customers with similar attribute. Similar cases can be found at GroupLens [19,20] and Firefly [21]. Some other examples using same approach includes WebWatcher [22] and Syskill & Webert [23]. Syskill & Webert is a system that utilizes user profile and learns to rate Web pages of interest using Bayesian classifier and can suggest web pages based on their relevance to the user interest.

Another personalization approach of Webmate [10] adopting a keyword vector to represent categories of user interest learns a user profile incrementally and facilitates user browsing and searching in the Web by using their profiles. Cooley et al. [24], and Buchner and Mulvenna [25] have applied data mining techniques to extract usage patterns from Web logs, for the purpose of deriving marketing intelligence. Shahabi et al. [26], Yan et al. [27], and Nasraoui et al. [28] have proposed clustering of user sessions to predict future user behaviour. As users regularly use multiple channels (e.g. web, email, mobile devices), personalization even can apply to this cross-channel. Pazzani [29]suggests a solution for the mobile web in his paper of "Personalization for the Mobile Web: A Position Paper".

6   Conclusion

Information explosion on the internet is compelling researchers to develop, better and better services for e-business and e-commerce Especially customer personalization service in e-commerce to attract potential customer is of paramount importance.

However the huge data available nowadays is a barrier to extract useful information. This paper, firstly, develops an e-commerce personalization framework for online customisation and applies it in the e-banking domain. Secondly, The agent behaviours of agents in the framework are defined. Finally, the framework is tested by actual banking data.

References

[1]   Adomavicius, G. and A. Tuzhilin, *Using Data Mining Methods to Build Customer Profiles.* IEEE Computer, 2001. **34**(2): p 74-82.

[2]   Ha, S.H., *Helping online customers decide through Web personalization.* Intelligent Systems, IEEE, 2002. **17**(6): p. 34 -43.

[3]   Lawrence, S. and C.L. Giles, *Searching the World Wide Web.* Science, 1998. **280**(5,360): p. 98-100.

[4]   Nichols, D. Implicit Rating & Filtering. in FIFTH DELOS WORKSHOP on Filtering and Collaborative Filtering. 1997. Budapest, Hungary: ERCIM.

[5]   Sycara, K., *Multiagent Systems.* AI Magazine, 1998. **19**(2): p. 79-92.

[6]   Khosla, R. and T. Dillon, *Engineering Intelligent Hybrid Multi-Agent Systems.* 1997: Kluwer Academic Publishers, MA, USA. 425.

[7]   Khosla, R., I. Sethi, and E. Damiani, *Intelligent Multimedia Multi-Agent Systems: A Human-Centerd Approach.* 2000: Kluwer Academic Publishers, MA, USA. 333.

[8]   Li, Q. and R. Khosla. Multi-agent Architecture for Automatic Recommendation System in E-commerce. in 5th International Conference on Enterprise Information Systems. 2003. Angers, France.

[9]   Schein, A., A. Popescul, and L. Ungar. Methods and Metrics for ColdStart Recommendations. in the 25th annual International ACM SIGIR Conference on Research and Development in Information Retrieval. 2002.

[10] Chen, L. and K. Sycara. WebMate: A Personal Agent for Browsing and Searching. in the 2nd International Conference on Autonomous Agents and Multi Agent Systems, AGENTS '98. 1998: ACM.

[11] Li, Q. and R. Khosla. Intelligent Agent-Based Framework for Mining Customer Buying Habit in E-Commerce. in Fourth International Conference on Enterprise Information Systems. 2002.

[12] Gropp, W., E. Lusk, and A. Skjellum, *Using MPI Portable Parallel Programming with Message-Passing Interface.* second ed. 2000, Cambridge Massachusetts London England: The MIT press.

[13] Schechter, S., M. Krishnan, and M.D. Smith. Using path profiles to predict HTTP requests. in 7th International World Wide Web Conference. 1998. Brisbane, Australia.

[14] Li, Q., *Profiling Customer Buying Habit Project.* 2002, La Trobe University.

[15] Dai, H. and B. Mobasher. Using Ontologies to Discover Domain-Level Web Usage Profiles. in the Second Workshop on Semantic Web Mining and the 6th European Conference on Principles and Practice of Knowledge Discovery in Databases (PKDD'02). 2002. Helsinki, Finland.

[16]   Li, Q. and R. Khosla. Adopting High Performance Computing to Implement E-commerce Intelligent Agent. in 6th International Conference/Exhibition on High Performance Computing in Asia Pacific Region (HPC Asia 2002). 2002. Bangalore, India.

[17]   Bohte, S., W.B. Langdon, and H.L. Poutre, *On current technology for information filtering and user profiling in agent-based systems.* 2000, CWI, Center for Mathematicas and Computer Science: Amsterdam, the Netherland.

[18]   Sarwar, B., et al. Item-based collaborative filtering recommendation algorithms. in The tenth international World Wide Web conference on World Wide Web. 2001.

[19]   Konstan, J., et al., *GroupLens: applying collaborative filtering to Usenet news.* Communications of the ACM, 1997. **40**(3): p. 77-87.

[20]   Herlocker, J., et al. An algorithmic framework for performing collaborative filtering. in 1999 Conference on Research and Development in Information retrieval. 1999.

[21]   Shardanand, U. and P. Maes. *Social information filtering: algorithms for automating "word of mouth".* in *Conference on Human Factors and Computing Systems.* 1995. Denver, Colorado, United States: ACM Press/Addison-Wesley Publishing Co. New York, NY, USA.

[22]   Armstrong, R.C., T. Joachims, and T. Mitchell Webwatcher: A learning apprentice for the world wide web. in AAAI Spring Symposium on Information Gathering from Heterogeneous, Distributed Environments. 1995.

[23]   Pazzani, M., J. Muramatsu, and D. Billsus. *Syskill & Webert: Identifying interesting web sites.* in *AAAI Spring Symposium.* 1996. Stanford, CA.

[24]   Cooley, R., B. Mobasher, and J. Srivastava, *Data Preparation for Mining World Wide Web Browsing Patterns.* Journal of Knowledge and Information Systems, 1999. **1**(1).

[25]   Buchner, A. and M.D. Mulvenna, Discovering internet marketing intelligence through online analytical web usage mining. SIGMOD Record, 1998. **27**(4): p. 54-61.

[26]   Shahabi, C., et al. Knowledge discovery from users Web-pages navigation. in Workshop on Research Issues in Data Engineering. 1997. Birmingham, England.

[27]   Yan, T., et al. From user access patterns to dynamic hypertext linking. in 5th International World Wide Web Conference. 1996. Paris, France.

[28]   Nasraoui, O., et al. Mining Web access logs using relational competitive fuzzy clustering. in Eight International Fuzzy Systems Association World Congress. 1999.

[29]   Pazzani, M.J., Personalization for the Mobile Web: A Position Paper. 2003.

Accessing Hidden Web Documents by Metasearching a Directory of Specialty Search Engines

Jacky K. H. Shiu, Stephen C. F. Chan, and Korris F. L. Chung

Department of Computing
The Hong Kong Polytechnic University
Hung Hom, Kowloon, Hong Kong.
{cskhshiu,csschan,cskchung}@comp.polyu.edu.hk

Abstract. Many valuable Web documents have not been indexed by general search engines and are only accessible through specific search interfaces. Metasearching groups of specialty search engines is one possible way to gain access to large amount of such hidden Web resources. One of the key issues for returning quality metasearch results is how to select the most relevant specialty search engines for a given query. We introduce a method for categorizing specialty search engines automatically into a hierarchical directory for metasearching. By utilizing the directory, specialty search engines that have a high possibility of having relevant information and resources can be easily selected by a metasearch engine. We evaluate our algorithm by comparing the directory built by the proposed algorithm with another one that was built by human-judgments. In addition, we present a metasearch engine prototype, which demonstrates that such a specialty search engine directory can be beneficial in locating essential but hidden Web resources.

1   Introduction

As the size of the World Wide Web increase dramatically, general Internet search engines cannot completely satisfy the information needs of all Internet users. A study shows that major search engines only indexed small fractions of the total Web pages [14]. To increase the coverage of the Internet, *metasearch engines* have been developed and widely investigated. Though metasearch engines combine the coverage of different general search engines, the coverage of the Internet still limited because many of the resources indexed are overlapped in different general search engines. In addition, as metasearch engines combine search results from a number of search engines, the difficulty in finding target information in the search results increased because of the increased size of the combined result list.

One of the obstacles to increasing the coverage of general search engines is that many documents available on the Internet are not "*crawlable*" to their software robots. Robots cannot index documents that are encapsulated by a search interface and generated dynamically by Web servers. In this paper, we use the term *specialty search engines* [6] to represent such kinds of specific search interfaces on the Web. As the technologies for dynamically serving Web documents improve continuously, the number of Web site managing documents in such a way increases considerably,

N. Bianchi-Berthouze (Ed.): DNIS 2003, LNCS 2822, pp. 27–41, 2003.

making it increasing difficulties for general search engine to increase their coverage significantly. A study shows that resources that are not indexed by general search engines are hundreds of times greater than those were indexed [3].

As a result, the exploration of the valuable resources covered by specialty search engines poses a standing challenge. One solution is again metasearching. By using a directory to organize a variety of specialty search engines, we believe that it is possible to efficiently select specialty search engines which contain the target relevant information and resources for a given query. Therefore, the excessive cost of querying unsuitable search engines can be reduced. Metasearch engines can benefit from the proposed directory and more hidden but valuable data on the Web can be made accessible without degrading the quality of search results.

The rest of the paper is organized as follows. Section 2 gives the necessary background to the problem. Section 3 describes the algorithm designed to categorize specialty search engines automatically into a hierarchical category structure. Section 4 explains the experiments done to validate the categorization algorithm. Section 5 presents a metasearch engine prototype as a case study to show how metasearch engines can benefit from such a specialty search engine directory. Finally, Section 6 presents our conclusion on the study.

2   Background

The major standing challenge for the metasearching environment is how to select suitable search engines for metasearching when a particular query is given. Many approaches for collection, database and server selection have been proposed in the past. Representative systems that are similar in the basis of their methodology are grouped together and summarized in this section.

2.1   Based on Theoretical Model

Callan et al. [4] introduced the CORI algorithm for providing collection selection based on the inference network model of information retrieval. The algorithm was widely evaluated in different studies, and the performance is outstanding. Meng et al. [Meng99] also proposed methods for estimating the usefulness of text databases based on the probabilistic model. Additionally, Fuhr [7] presented a decision-theoretic model for selecting data sources based on the retrieval cost and some typical information retrieval parameters.

2.2   Based on Past Performance

As metasearching in the Web environment and metasearching distributed text collections have different characteristics, using only theoretic-based algorithms may not be sufficient. Focusing on metasearch engines, some selection methods are developed based on past performances of the search engines. SavvySearch [6] categorizes search engines into a hierarchical directory for searching. While searching, users need to specify the category to search, and search engines will be selected based on what category has been chosen. MetaSEEK [2] is another metasearch index that considers past performance. It utilizes the historical information of queries searched to handle new query, and select the highest performance search engine to do metasearching. Conversely, the Inquirus2 [9] metasearch engine considers individual user's past feedback. Search engines are grouped into different categories. When submitting queries, users need to specify their information needs by selecting a category in which to search. In addition, to guarantee the search quality at a certain level when utilizing the past performances of the search engines, the system needs to be executed for some period of time in order to collect enough historical information for the prediction. As a result, there are selection methods developed based on a pre-built centralized index approach.

2.3   Based on Meta-index or Content Summary

Most of the traditional selection algorithms use statistical data to characterize the contents of each data source. Statistical data of each data source are combined as a large centralized index that can be referred to as *meta-index* or *content summaries*. It usually includes the document frequencies of words which appear in the data source with other simple statistics. Relevant data sources are selected by evaluating the degree of similarity between the given query and the meta-index. ProFusion [8] uses meta-index in terms of a set of hand-built knowledge base. Each search engine has one tailor-made knowledge base. Selection is made by mapping the given query to the knowledge bases for the most relevant search engine to search. Yuwono et al. [16] ranked distributed text server by developing a centralized broker which maintains a document frequencies table for each server. Another method that also requires the cooperation of databases is GlOSS [11]. The meta-index is constructed by combining the indices of the databases, which are document frequencies of words. When a query is accepted, databases are ranked according to their appropriateness to the given query. This is done by estimating the number of documents in each database for which query similarity was greater than a predefined threshold. A score will be created for each database through summing up the similarities values, and databases will be chosen according to the scores. Instead of using the statistical information of words contained to characterize a collection, Xu et al. [15] proposed to use the phase information accompanied by query expansion. It was believed that carrying out a collection selection within such kind of distributed retrieval systems will be effectively poorer comparing to a single centralized retrieval system. Because most of the databases do not release the required information to the public, it is sometime difficult to build the meta-index in the Web environment although meta-index is widely investigated and is one of the promising selection algorithms.

2.4   Based On Probe Query

As developing methods for building a meta-index that requires large cooperation of databases is believed to be impractical and not scalable, researchers have developed methods based on *probe queries* to create a meta-index without the cooperation of databases. The idea of probe queries draws on the nature of search engine (or searchable database) in that it returns a set of results for any given query. By sending a set of sample queries to a search engine and then, downloading and analyzing the documents from the search results, statistical information can be extracted. This kind of information will be considered as a representative of all the documents inside that search engine. Callan et al. [5] introduced query-based sampling approach to sampling text database contents via the normal process of running queries and retrieving documents. Using this kind of probe queries, indexing or categorizing a database needs no cooperative work, which is important when applying search engine selection in the Web environment. Another probe query method introduced by Hawking et al. [12] is called Lightweight Probes (LWP). A small amount of probe queries will be submitted to each of the databases at querying time. The probe results are non-random, which can greatly improve the efficiency of the probing process. The advantage of using probe queries to select search engines is that a metasearch engine can address a new search engine without cooperation. On the other hand, since the set of probe queries is usually static, the results returned from a search engine are non-random. Whether a search engine can be characterized correctly highly depends on the quality of the probe queries selected.

3   Search Engine Categorization

In this section, we further explain the search engine categorization algorithm that was highlighted in [13]. To categorize specialty search engines into a hierarchical directory, we collect sample documents from them. Search engines are then characterized based on the contents of the sampled documents. Document sampling techniques will be used to collect sets of documents contained in different search engines being categorized. After analyzing the statistical data extracted from the documents, each search engine will be ranked for each category in the hierarchy according to how relevant they are to those categories. And finally, by keeping only the most relevant search engines in each category, a directory of specialty search engines can be built. Compared to other human-edited Web directories like Yahoo! [18], the categorization process we proposed here is more efficient as it can be done in an automatic manner.

3.1   Document Sampling

The sampling method we used here is *probe queries*. The idea of probe queries exploit the nature of search engine being that it always returns a set of results considered relevant to a given query. The sample queries we used were generated using words from a predefined hierarchical category.

Instead of constructing a hierarchy from scratch, we decided to utilize a well-known category hierarchy: the DMOZ Open Directory Project (ODP) [17], for categorizing search engines. Currently, the ODP is the largest and most comprehensive human-edited directory for the Web. Tens of thousands volunteer editors are employed to maintain the directory and this makes the directory more updated compared to other human-edited directories. As shown in later section, a simplified branch of the ODP is selected for our implementation.

The rationale behind the sampling method is that search engines belonging to a category should be able to return search results that are relevant to that category. As a result, search engines can be categorized by measuring the relevancies of documents returned. For example, a query "*C programming*" should retrieve a number of relevant documents from a computer-related search engine, while a query "*Chicago Bulls*" is likely to retrieve few or no document from the same search engine. Compared to other methods like [Callen99] that generates probe queries by randomly choosing words from a general dictionary, and [8] that constructs probe queries manually, our method raises the effectiveness by binding probes to words relevant to the categories.

3.2   Relevancy Calculation

Our final search engine directory groups different specialty search engines for metasearching. Each sub-category contains a number of engines, ranked according to their relevancies to the category. To estimate the relevancy of a search engine to a category, a corresponding *relevancy score* will be computed. Our approach first calculates the frequencies of terms in each document, and then the values will be adjusted by the weights according to the ranking position of the documents. Finally, the values will be used to compute the relevancy scores by including the hierarchical information.

We believe that the hierarchical structure of the category tree can be exploited as extra information to augment the precision of the categorization process in the computation of the final relevancy score. In other words, the relevancy score of a search engine with respect to a category will be influenced by the search engine's term frequency values in different but related categories. In short, the relevancy score $R_{S,C}$ of the search engine S for the category C which has nc number of immediate child is given by:

$$R_{S,C} = TF_{S,C} + \sum_{i=1}^{nc} \beta \left(\frac{link_i}{L} \times R_{S,i} \right) \quad (1)$$

where $TF_{S,C}$ is term frequency values calculated for the sample documents returned by S, $R_{S,i}$ is the relevancy score of the i-th child category, $link_i$ is the number of links indexed in ODP for the child category i and L is the total number of links indexed for all the immediate child of C. β is a constant to control how much the hierarchical information should affect the final relevancy score.

The ODP link information is used to give different weights to different categories. We believe that for a parent category, its child categories should not be treated as equally important. We assign weights to categories by using the number of links indexed in the ODP as the factor to identify the importance of a category. That is, for a category, the larger the number of links contained, the higher the weight.

The final step of the categorization process is to eliminate irrelevant search engines from the categories. After performing the procedures described in the previous sections, each category in the hierarchy contains the same number of search engines.

Table 1. Specialty search engines selected for the experiments

Search Engine	URL	Description
Apple	www.apple.com	computer company
CBS Sportsline	cbs.sportsline.com/u/cbs/sports/	TV channel
IBM	www.ibm.com	computer company
Java Sun	java.sun.com	Java official site
Sun Microsystems	www.sun.com	computer company
Tucows	www.tucows.com	software downloads
NASA Spacelink	spacklink.nasa.gov	US NASA web site
Macromedia	www.macromedia.com	software company
Borland	www.borland.com	software company
Internet.com	www.internet.com	Internet news
Redhat	www.redhat.com	Linux and software company
Science News Online	www.sciencenews.org	science news
Discovery Channel	dsc.discovery.com	TV channel
U.S. Nation Library of Medicine	www.nlm.nih.gov	Library
RFC Editor Webpage	www.rfc-editor.org	RFC collections
Prevline	www.health.org	health organization
Manufacturing.net	www.manufacturing.net	manufacturing news and articles
The Whitaker Foundation	www.whitaker.org/news	biomedical engineering news
The Internet Bookshop	www.bookshop.co.uk	online bookshop
ebay	www.ebay.com	online bid company

One method that can be used to eliminate irrelevant search engines is to make every category keep an equally n number of search engines. This method is simple, but it is hard to define n. Also, a number of high score search engines may be eliminated. Alternatively, we can eliminate search engines within categories based on the standard deviation of the relevancy scores.

After performing all the categorization procedures, a hierarchical directory of specialty search engine category is produced. The produced directory contains numbers of sub-categories in a hierarchical structure. Each sub-category contains numbers of relevant search engines that are ranked according their relevancy scores. The next section explains the experiments done to evaluate the described categorization algorithm.

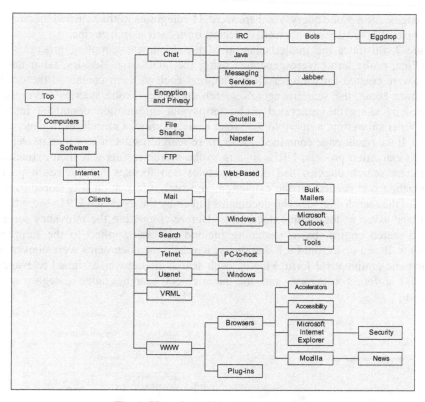

Fig. 1. The selected hierarchical structure

4   Validation for the Categorization Algorithm

In this section, we will first describe how the proposed categorization algorithm is implemented. Second, we describe how we evaluate the performance of the proposed categorization algorithm by comparing the rankings of the search engines produced by the algorithm to those constructed by human judgments.

4.1   Experiment Setup

As mentioned in the previous section, only a subset of the ODP hierarchy will be needed. The sub-category "*Top / Computers / Software / Internet / Client*" is selected with some child categories we believe are not significant are excluded. Table 1 shows the 20 specialty search engines selected for the experiments. Most of them are computer-related and only a few of them focused on other domains. On the other hand, Figure 1 shows the hierarchical structure.

The first step of the categorization algorithm was the document sampling process. Probe queries were generated using the selected hierarchy and were sent to all selected search engines. In order to reduce the time required to parse the search results and download the documents, only the top 50 documents were downloaded for each search engine for a probe query. As there were 34 categories in the selected hierarchy, a maximum of 1,700 documents were collected from each search engine.

Figure 2 illustrates the implementation of the document sampling processes in detail. First, probe terms were generated using the ODP data. Besides, tailor-made profiles were created for each search engine, and each of them contained the detail information about the search engine's search interface. Probe queries were then generated by using the generated probe terms and information contained in the profile. After submitting a query to the target search engine, a search result page was returned. If the result page contained one or more search results, it was then passed to the result extraction process. URLs linking to the search results was then extracted. As different search engines had different styles and formats for the result page, customization was needed for the extraction, and such information was stored in the profiles of the search engines. The documents linked by the extracted URLs were then fetched and saved as the sample documents. Before computing the relevancy scores for each search engine, basic stemming method [1] was applied to the sampled documents. Based on a hand-built dictionary, words in the documents were converted to their basic grammatical form. Finally, each search engine was assigned relevancy scores for different category, and the hierarchical search engine category was produced.

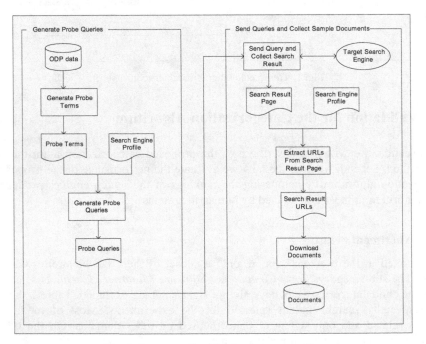

Fig. 2. Processes flow for document sampling

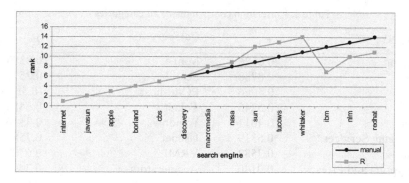

Fig. 3. Category bulk mailers

4.2   Experimental Results

Another set of rankings of those search engines is obtained by human judgments. The evaluation of the categorization algorithm was made by comparing the rankings produced by the algorithm to those produced manually. The experiment indicates that the rankings using these methods were similar. Manual ranking of Search engines were obtained by the following method. First, 20 computer proficient were invited as testers to perform the experiments. Approximately 340 rounds of experiments were conducted. In each round, the testers were given a subject term (*e.g. "mail tools"*) and a set of Web pages fetched from different specialty search engines. They were required to evaluate the relevance between the subject and the set of pages by assigning a relevancy score to each subject-page pair. The scores ranged from 1 (totally irrelevant) to 6 (highly relevant). In fact, each round of the experiment was used to collect the judgments of the proficient for a particular category. The subject given is actually the probe query used for that category, and the pages presented were the sample documents fetched from different specialty search engines. As the proficient had no idea which page corresponded to which search engine, he unknowingly assigned scores for the search results of different search engines. By averaging the relevancy scores from different testers, manual-judged rankings of the search engines were obtained.

For each sub-category listed in Figure 1, both human-judged rankings and the rankings derived from the proposed algorithm were collected and compared. We chose the rankings for the category *"Top / Computers / Software / Clients / Mail / Windows / Bulk Mailers"* as an example and the comparison results are shown in Figure 3. As shown in the figure, the rankings derived by the algorithm (R) stayed very close to those judged by humans (*manual*). R ranked the top 6 search engines, exactly the same as *manual*; and the 7th and 8th rankings given by R only had 1 rank different from those given by *manual*. Although R was not able to rank all search engines exactly the same as *manual*, it produced highly similar rankings.

Table 2. Correlation coefficients of all categories

Category	r_s	Category	r_s
Eggdrop	0.8626	Mail	0.8393
Bots	0.8788	Search	0.2571
IRC	0.4066	PC-to-host	-0.5636
Java	0.5245	Telnet	0.6484
Jabber	0.4011	Windows	0.3516
Messaging Services	0.6319	Usenet	0.7582
Chat	0.7582	VRML	0.6703
Encryption and Privacy	0.0140	Accelerators	0.3497
Gnutella	0.6364	Accessibility	0.6835
Napster	0.7902	Security	0.8462
File Sharing	0.5209	Microsoft Internet Explorer	0.6967
FTP	0.6044	News	0.4560
Web-Based	0.0462	Mozilla	0.4670
Bulk Mailers	0.8418	Browsers	0.5560
Microsoft Outlook	0.8059	Plug-ins	0.4901
Tools	0.6544	WWW	0.3714
Windows	0.5172	Clients	0.5588
Average r_s			0.5392
Percentage of categories having a positive r_s			97%
Percentage of categories having a r_s greater then 0.5			65%

In order to gain insight into the performance of the proposed categorization algorithm, we used the *Spearman's rank correlation coefficient* to measure the correlation between the rankings and used the results to explain the comparison. For each category, we computed the correlation coefficient (r_s) between the human-judged rankings and the rankings given by the categorization algorithm. The computed coefficient of the example "*Bulk Mailers*" category is 0.8418, indicating that the rankings given by our algorithm was highly similar to those produced by human judgment. Besides, Table 2 listed the computation results for the remaining categories:

As shown in the above figure, many of the categories had a high coefficient score. The average coefficient of all the categories was 0.5392, which indicated a positive correlation. In addition, there was a positive coefficient in 97% of the categories, with 65% of these greater than 0.5. The above results indicated that the proposed categorization algorithm could categorize search engine with a high accuracy, and the quality of the produced search engine category was promising.

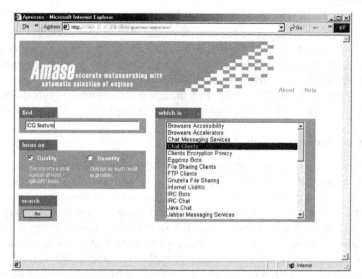

Fig. 4. User interface of Amase

5   The Experimental Metasearch Engine

In this section, we present *"Amase – Accurate Metasearching with Automatic Selection of Engines"*, an experimental metasearch engine prototype developed to demonstrate the effectiveness of the specialty search engine directory produced by the proposed categorization algorithm. Since the selected hierarchical structure and specialty search engines are limited in terms of size and domain as described in previous section, Amase only capable for metasearching resources inside the *Internet Clients* domain. Search results of Amase show that hidden valuable resources can be made accessible and only relevant specialty search engine will be selected from the directory for metasearching.

5.1   User Interface

Figure 4 presents the user interface of Amase. As shown in the figure, there are four components: *"find"*, *"which is"*, *"focus-on"* and *"search"*. To submit a query to Amase, the user first needs to input some search keywords into the *"find"* section, which is the same as querying traditional search engines. Next, the user has to select a descriptive term in the list box inside the *"which is"* section. The selected term call "describe-term" will serve as context to help the user explain the former inputted keywords. For example, if a user wants to discover the function of an Internet chat client named "ICQ", his query may be *"find*: ICQ feature, *which is*: Chat Clients".

After entering the search keywords and selected suitable description, the user can choose one of the search options inside the *"focus-on"* section. The *"Quality"* option indicates that the user wants only the most relevant documents. When this option is set, Amase will select only the top results from different specialty search engines for the users. This option can provide users a small set of highly accurate results in a very short process time. On the other hand, the "*Quantity*" option indicates that the user may want to collect a large set of the search results. When this option is set, Amase will return all the search results collected from different specialty search engines to the users. This option can provide support to users when they want to do some broad review on a specific topic. After selecting suitable options, the user can start the metasearch by pressing the "*Go*" button in the "*Search*" section. Figure 5 shows the search result listing the user received for the above example.

5.2   Evaluation of the Search Results

The performance of Amase was studied by making a series of sample searches using Amase, and comparing the results with that of a general search engine. The general search engine we used was Google [10], which is one of the most successful general search engines on the Internet. Google was chosen not only because of its reputation, but also because of its ability to restrict search to only the sub-categories of the Open Directory. Amase requires the user to submit query with one set of search terms and one set of describe-terms, which is used to implicitly specify the search domains. Using the same set of search terms to query another general search engine may lead to incomparable results since the search results returned by the general search engine belong to all kinds of domains. Therefore, Google was selected in experiments.

We present here the preliminary results of a comprehensive set of tests which is under going. Ten equivalent queries were sent to both Amase and Google. When querying Google, the search was restricted to the category selected by Amase in order to have an equal searching domain. For example, if the describe-term selected when querying Amase is "*Mail Clients*" and the category associated with the term is "*Top / Computers / Software / Internet / Clients / Mail*", the query sending to Google would also be restricted to the same category. Table 3 listed the queries issued and the number of search results returned.

Fig. 5. Returned search results

Table 3. Search results returned by Amase and Google

Describe term	Search term	Results by Amase	Results by Google	Equal page
Mail Clients	check mail	150	230	0
Mail Clients	junk mail	150	29	0
Mail Clients	anti spam	150	71	0
Mail Clients	virus	150	42	0
Mail Clients	mail broadcast	150	6	0
Chat Clients	multimedia chat	100	2	0
Chat Clients	voice messages	100	6	0
Chat Clients	web-based	100	13	0
Chat Clients	random chat	100	15	0
Chat Clients	instant messaging	100	45	0

As shown in the figure, Amase was able to return more number of search results than Google. In particular, we tried to compare the search results by finding the occurrences of the search results returned by Amase to those returned by Google. The results listed in the "*Equal Page*" column indicated that none of the search results returned by Amase was returned by Google, which indicated the ability of Amase in accessing hidden valuable resources on the Internet. The search results returned from Amase also show that while restricted the searches within specific domains or topics, Amase was able to locate more resources. Therefore, by applying metasearching to search specialty search engines, the coverage on the Internet would be increased and users could obtain more significant search results. Moreover, the search engine selection problem of metasearch engine could be alleviated by the directory automatically built by the proposed algorithm, and resulting in more accurate and effective metasearching.

6   Conclusions

In this paper, we presented a categorization algorithm which can automatically categorize specialty search engines into a hierarchical structure. We found that our algorithm is able to categorize specialty search engines, and construct a sensible specialty search engine directory similar to that built by humans. We also presented the experimental metasearch engine *Amase*, which exploits the proposed directory. Experimental results show that general search engines seems to concentrated on general resources and may missed some of the resources available in specialty search engines, and the proposed directory of specialty search engine is valuable in selecting relevant specialty search engines for metasearching.

Acknowledgement

The research reported in this paper was partially supported by The Hong Kong Polytechnic University Research Grants G-W059 and A-PE35.

References

[1]   R. Baeza-Yates, B. Ribeiro-Neto "Modern Information Retrieval". *ACM Press / Addison-Wesley Longman* (1999)

[2]   A. B. Benitez, M. Beigi, and S. F. Chang "Using Relevance Feedback in Content-Based Image Metasearch". *IEEE Internet Computing*, Vol.2, No.4, pp.59-69 (1998)

[3]   Michael K. Bergman "The Deep Web: Surfacing Hidden Value". *The Journal of Electronic Publishing*, Vol.7, Issue 1 (2001)

[4]   James P. Callan, Z. Lu and W. Bruce Croft "Searching distributed collections with inference networks". *Proceedings of the 18th ACM-SIGIR International Conference*, Seattle, Washington, USA, July 1995, pp.12-20 (1995)

[5]   J. Callan, M. Connell, and A. Du "Automatic Discovery of Language Models for Text Databases". *Proceedings of ACM-SIGMOD International Conference on Management of Data*, Philadelphia, Pennsylvania, USA, 1-3 June 1999, pp.479-490 (1999)

[6]   D. Dreilinger, Adele E. Howe "Experiences with Selecting Search Engines Using Metasearch". *ACM Transactions on Information Systems*, Vol.15, No.3, pp.195-222 (1997)

[7]   N. Fuhr "A decision-theoretic approach to database selection in networked IR". *ACM Transactions on Information Systems*, Vol.17, No.3, pp.229-249 (1999)

[8]   S. Gauch, G. Wang, and M. Gomez "Profusion: Intelligent fusion from multiple, distributed search engines". *Journal of Universal Computer Science*, Vol.2, No.9, pp.637-649 (1996)

[9]   E. Glover, S. Lawrence, W. Birmingham, C. Lee Giles "Architecture of a Metasearch Engine that Supports User Information Needs". *Proceedings of the 8th International Conference on Information Knowledge Management*, Kansas City, MO, November 1999, pp.210-216 (1999)

[10]   http://www.google.com, 2003

[11]   L. Gravano, H. Garcia-Molina, A. Tomasic "GlOSS: Text-source discovery over the Internet". *ACM Transactions on Database Systems*, Vol.24, No.2, pp.229-264 (1999)

[12]   D. Hawking, P. Thistlewaite "Methods for information server selection". *ACM Transactions on Information Systems*, Vol.17, No.1, pp.40-76 (1999)

[13]   Jacky K. H. Shiu, Stephen C F Chan and Korris F L Chung "Developing a Directory of Search Engines for Meta-Searching" To appear in *Proceedings of the 4th International Conference on Intelligent Data Engineering and Automated Learning*, Hong Kong, 21-23 March 2003 (2003)

[14]   S. Lawrence, C. Lee Giles "Accessibility of information on the Web". *Nature*, Vol.400 pp.107-109 (1999)

[15]   J. Xu and J. Callan   "Effective   retrieval   with   distributed   collections". *Proceedings of the 21st International ACM-SIGIR Conference*, Melbourne, Australia, 24-28 August 1998, pp.112-120 (1998)

[16]   B. Yuwono and D. L. Lee "Server ranking for distributed text retrieval systems on the Internet". *Proceedings of the 5th Annual International Conference on Database Systems for Advanced Applications*, Melbourne, Australia, April 1997, pp.41-49 (1997)

[17] http://dmoz.org, 2003
[18] http://www.yahoo.com, 2003

Hidden Schema Extraction in Web Documents

Vincenza Carchiolo, Alessandro Longheu, and Michele Malgeri

Dipartimento di Ingegneria Informatica e delle Telecomunicazioni
Facoltà di Ingegneria – V.le A. Doria 6 – I95125 – Catania
Tel. +39-095-738-2359 – Fax +39-095-738-2397
{car,alongheu,mm}@diit.unict.it

Abstract. One of the main limitation when accessing the web is the lack of explicit schema about the logical organization of web pages/sites, whose presence may help in understanding data semantics. Here, an approach to extract a logical schema from web pages based on HTML source code analysis is presented. We define a set of primary tags actually used to give a structural/logical backbone to the page. Primary tags are used to divide the page into collections, which represent distinct *structural* page sections; these are finally mapped into *logical* sections according to their semantics, providing a logical page schema. The structuring methodology is applied to some real web pages to test the approach.

1   Introduction

The World Wide Web can be seen as the largest (almost chaotic) data warehouse, from which possibly any information can be accessed. Though, the absence of an explicit schema about the logical organization of web pages/sites represents a significant limitation when accessing and retrieving information from the web; indeed, an explicit logical schema would help in understanding data semantics, making it easier and time-saving for users to locate desired information, whereas current data comprehension is mainly based on intuition [1].

Web data belong to semi-structured data class, i.e. data with self-contained schema [2], [3], [4], hence the need of extracting schema to improve data management arises [5], [6]. Schema for web data can be constructed at different levels: giving a schema for a set of logically related sites viewing them as a whole, or examining a single site [7], or finally structuring single pages.

Our work aims at structuring web pages in order to provide them with a logical schema, i.e. to divide page contents into semantically distinct parts. Such a schema is actually implicitly embedded into the page, hence the term *hidden* schema. This division comes from the fact that information placed inside a web page generally do not form a monolithic block, rather it is possible to divide the page into a set of *logical sections* which aim to reflect the logical structure given by the author. Logical sections we introduce come from considering typical web pages, and are:

N. Bianchi-Berthouze (Ed.): DNIS 2003, LNCS 2822, pp. 42-52, 2003.
© Springer-Verlag Berlin Heidelberg 2003

- *document information* section, containing metadata about the page (e.g. DTD, author);
- *logical heading* section, used to present the page/site, e.g. title or logo of the site;
- *logical footer* section, containing information as link to webmasters, copyright notices, etc.;
- *logical link* section, a set of HTML tags representing a physical link (e.g. clickable images);
- *index* section, a group of logical links having similar properties (e.g. navigation menus) [9];
- *logical data* section, data where the semantic of the page is mainly placed.
- *interactive* section, i.e. forms for users interaction, as search bar in search engines.

To extract logical sections, our approach tends to combine both structural and semantic information about the page [8]; in particular, we first model the page as a tree according to the hierarchy of HTML tags, then we locate some specific tags having a primary role when giving a structure to the page. We use such *primary* nodes to create *collections*, where each collection is a subtree (rooted at one of these nodes) collecting a set of consecutive HTML tags presenting similar structures; in other words, collections are introduced to divide the page into distinct *structural* sections. Collections are finally mapped into logical sections exploiting their semantics; this paper however does not deal with this last issue (more details can be found in [8]).

Here we first introduce primary tags and their properties, then we define collections together with the algorithm used for their extraction, finally applying it to some sample pages to test the approach.

2   Structuring Methodology

2.1   Primary Tags

The idea of primary tags comes from the fact that some tags in web pages are actually used to give a structural/logical backbone to the page; more specifically, we consider tags with the following features: tags used to arrange page elements (text, images) in a tabular or similar representation, e.g. *<table>*, *<frame>*; tags used to separate page elements, as *<hr>*; tags used to manage forms to allow user interactions. Based on these considerations, primary tags are: *table, hr, frame, form* (this set is small in order to limit the number of collections). We associate to a primary node a set of properties:

- the list of primary tag *attributes*, so e.g. *<table>* and *<table* BORDER=1 WIDTH="75%" CELLPADDING=6 ALIGN="RIGHT">* will be considered different (probably even semantically);
- the *relative depth*, i.e. the number of *primary* nodes from root (*<html>*) to the current node;
- the *absolute depth*, i.e. the number of nodes from root to current node (the ordinary depth);

```
<table>
<tr><td>
<a href...>...</a><br>
<a href...>...</a><br>
</td><td>
<a href...><img src..>...</a><br>

<a href...>...</a><br>      <br>
<a href...><font...>...</font></a><p>
</td></tr></table>
```

Fig. 1. An example of collection

- the *number of levels*, i.e. the average absolute depth from current node to its leaves (average is required when several subtrees depart from the current node);
- the *number of leaves*, considered just if the primary node *directly* contains leaves (i.e. no other nodes, primary or not, must be present between the primary node and its leaves).

2.2   Collections

We define the *collection* as *a set of consecutive HTML tags containing repeated similar structures*. For instance, Fig.1 represents a collection made of hyperlinks (the similarity here derives from the fact that some links embed tags, others do not). Collections extraction aims at giving a structural backbone to the page, in order to further discover logical sections, each made by one or more collections semantically related.

To extract collections, we first find each deepest primary node and evaluate its properties; in particular, relative and absolute depth are used to quantify the position of each primary with respect to others in the tree, while the number of leaves and the number of levels represent the horizontal (respectively, vertical) dimension of the Html tags subtree rooted at a given primary node.

Then, we compare *brothers* subtrees (i.e. whose roots have the same primary node as ancestor) through a *distance* function expressed as a weighted sum of the properties associated to each subtree's root (i.e. to each primary node) [8]:

$$D(t_1,t_2) = P_{MAX}^A \frac{N_{DA}}{N_A} + P_{MED}^A \frac{N_{EADV}}{N_A} + P_{POS}\left(\frac{\Delta_{AD}}{Max_{AD}} + \frac{\Delta_{NL}}{Max_{NL}}\right) + P_L \frac{\Delta_L}{Max_L} \tag{1}$$

Distance is evaluated for each brother subtrees pair to establish whether they are similar, using a proper threshold. If brother subtrees are similar (distance less than threshold), they belong to the same collection, and the collection grows until other similar brother subtrees are found. When there are no more similar subtrees, the current collection stops and a new collection is created, while when brother subtrees are all examined, the algorithm continues from the upper level of the tree. This method tends to emulate the schema that intuition suggests.

Table 1. Explanation of distance formula parameters

Name	Meaning
N_{DA}	Number of attributes present in just one root
N_A	Total number of attributes (used to normalize N_{DA}, N_{EADV}) present in both roots
$P^A{}_{MAX}$	Weight for attributes present in just one root
N_{EADV}	Number of attributes present in both roots but with different values
$P^A{}_{MED}$	Weight for attributes present in both roots but with different values
Δ_{AD}	Difference between subtrees absolute depths
Max_{AD}	the maximum absolute depth between the two subtrees
Δ_{NL}	Difference between subtrees number of levels
Max_{NL}	the maximum number of levels between the two subtrees
P_{POS}	Weight used for position parameters (i.e. absolute depth and number of levels)
Δ_L	Difference between number of leaves
Max_L	the maximum number of leaves between the two subtrees
P_L	Weight used for number of leaves

3   Application of Structuring Methodology

In the following, we consider some real web pages to which the structuring methodology is applied in order to show how to detect collections using (1), also testing whether structuring results agree with those suggested by intuition.

The first step is the assignment of parameters weights. We start establishing which parameters should have a major and minor weight (table 2), based on some heuristics explained in the following. Considering attributes, the greatest similarity occurs when brother subtrees have roots whose tag has the *same* attributes with the *same* values; similarity decreases when values are different or when some attribute is present in just one root. However, the increase in distance given by attributes present in both roots but with a different value is less than the increase due to attributes present in just one root, e.g. *<td bgcolor="0044AE"* and *<td width=120>* are less similar than *<td bgcolor="0044AE">* and *<td bgcolor="3B4400">*. Hence, the weight for the former contribution is less than the weight for the latter, respectively *medium* and *high* in Table 2 ($P^A{}_{MED}$ and $P^A{}_{MAX}$ in the formula).

Considering the absolute depth and the number of levels contained in the subtree, since they represent the position of the subtree root in the tree with respect to main root and leaves respectively, we assign the same weight to these parameters.

Table 2. Weights order

Parameter	Weight
Attributes	High, Medium
Absolute depth	Medium
# of levels	Medium
# of leaves	Low

Moreover, this weight (P_{POS} in Tab. 5) is less than P^A_{MED} and P^A_{MAX} since absolute depth and number of levels are determined by non primary tags.

Then, we assign a minimum weight (P_L in Tab. 5) to the number of direct leaves since a different number of leaves, even if it affects similarity (the less is the difference, the more similar subtrees will be), it is a structural difference which could not be due to semantic reasons, e.g. two tables with different number of rows to be displayed may still be semantically related. Finally, no weight is given for relative depth (it is indeed just used to select *brother* subtrees).

To quantify weights in order to actually apply (1), we assign values in the range [0,1], in particular the maximum is 1, the medium is 0.5 and the low value is 0.1 (0 would erase the corresponding term).

We choose test web pages among home pages, since they have generally a more complex structure than inner pages, hence they are more significant. In particular, we choose the home page of Texas University (http://www.cs.utexas.edu), whose structure is quite simple, and the home page of Times (http://www.times.com), which is quite complex; we choose such pages since they belong to completely different context. Tables 3 and 4 represent primary tags properties for Texas University and Times respectively. In particular, the first column simply denotes a numeric identifier for each primary tag, all intermediate columns represent tag attributes (except for attributes, which are omitted), and the last column indicate the identifier of the ancestor primary tag (e.g., in table 3 the tag 2 is the ancestor of 3,4,5,6). Note that tags ore ordered based on their ancestor (i.e. corresponding brothers subtrees are actually grouped).

Note that actually dynamic Html is frequently used in real pages; the use of client/server side programming (Java applets, Active-X technologies, scripting) and style sheets indeed affect both the structure and the semantic of the page. To take this into account, in tables 3 and 4 we distinguish leaves in the Html tree into ordinary tags and scripting tags (e.g. those including Javascript code), in order to check whether the importance given to scripting tags is relevant or not for collections extraction when using formula (1). More details about the influence of dynamic Html can be found in [11].

Table 3. Primary tags and their attributes for Texas University home page

Primary tag ID	Relative Depth	Absolute Depth	Number of levels	Number of leaves		Primary tag Ancestor ID
				Ordinary tags	Scripting tags	
1	1	1	3	1		0
2	1	1	7		1	0
3	2	5	3	48		2
4	2	5	3	8		2
5	2	3	3	1		2
6	2	5	3	1		2

Table 4. Primary tags and their attributes for Times home page

| Primary tag ID | Relative Depth | Absolute Depth | Number of levels | Number of leaves | | Primary tag Ancestor ID |
				Ordinary tags	Scripting tags	
1	1	1	5	1	2	0
20	1	1	14	0		0
4	2	4	6	4	1	20
5	2	4	4	4		20
6	2	4	3	16		20
19	2	4	10	1		20
21	2	4	3	35		20
22	2	4	2	1	2	20
2	3	6	4	3		4
3	3	6	4	6		4
8	3	8	8	6		19
10	3	6	7	2		19
12	3	6	6	2		19
17	3	6	7	4		19
18	3	6	3	35		19
7	4	12	3	2		8
9	4	9	3	1		10
11	4	9	3	1		12
13	4	9	4	1		17
14	4	9	4	1		17
15	4	9	4	1		17
16	4	9	4	1		17

To apply the formula (1), we assign $P^A_{MAX}=1$, $P^A_{MED}= P_{POS}=0.5$, $P_L=0.1$ and evaluate the distance for each pair of brothers subtrees. Considering Texas University home page, we start from deepest subtrees 3,4,5,6, whose common ancestror is the subtree 2 getting to table 5 (note that $D(t1, t2)=D(t2, t1)$).

Referring to Fig.2, where the home page is represented together with subtrees highlighting, some considerations can be made. First, subtrees 3 and 4 are structurally similar since both represents a list of links mixed with descriptive text, whereas 5 and 6 are different from each other and from 3,4. This should lead to the conclusion that subtrees 3 and 4 forms a collection, while 5 and 6 represents other two distinct collections.

Table 5. Subtrees distances for Texas University home page

Ancestor ID 2	3	4	5	6
3	-	0.5	0.82	0.84
4	0.5	-	0.82	0.84
5	0.82	0.82	-	0.83
6	0.84	0.84	0.83	-

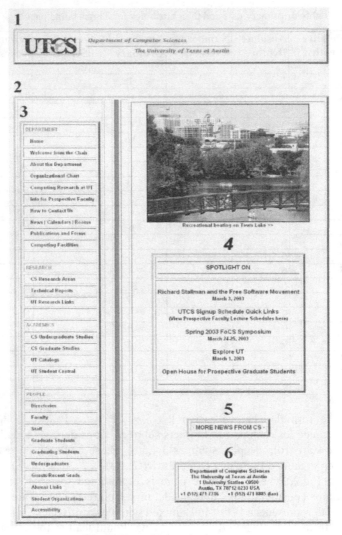

Fig. 2. Texas University home page

To obtain this from distance values, a proper threshold T must be chosen. In particular, since (1) is intended as a measure of the structural difference (or similarity) between subtrees, it must be used to distinguish subtrees pairs with low distance (similar) from those having higher values (different), hence T must be an intermediate value between low and high. Moreover, since (1) is linear, this intermediate value is chosen as the *mean* between such values. In table 5, D(3,4)=0.5 is the the *current* minimum while *current* maximum is 0.84, hence T=(0.5+0.84)/2=0.67; in this way, subtrees 3 and 4 are similar (0.5<T), while others form stand-alone collections.

Note that *current* means that the set of values from which minimum and maximum derive is that of *brothers* subtrees.

Also note that this approach (*relative* threshold) is not suitable when the current set of distances presents a low variance, since this implies that the boundary between similar and not-similar subtrees is not clear. This happens for instance when all distances have the same value (T would coincide with this unique value) or highly similar (e.g. the distances set 1.510, 1.508, 1.512, 1.505, 1.510, 1.513) or finally when just a value is present (i.e. brothers are just *two* subtrees). In all these cases we define an *absolute* threshold T as the mean between the *absolute* minimum and maximum values, i.e. the lowest value of (1) is 0, whereas its maximum is given by $P^A_{MAX} + P^A_{MED} + 2P_{POS} + P_L = 2.6$ (parameters are indeed normalized with their maximum), hence T=1.3. In this way, if distances are less than T, corresponding subtrees will belong to the same collection, otherwise stand-alone collections will arise, regardless of distances distribution.

Referring to Fig.2, next distance concerns with subtrees 1 and 2 (tags at a higher level in the tree), and its (single) value is $D(1,2)=0.92$. Since $D(1,2)<T$ (absolute T is used), 1 and 2 should belong to the same collection. Though, Fig.2 shows that they are very different, hence an additional factor should be included in (1) to detect this. In particular, subtree 2 includes a scripting tag, i.e. a Javascript function used to manage the entire menu (subtree 5), therefore we can highlight this difference by giving scripting tags a higher weight. To do this in (1), we separate scripting from ordinary tags and introduce the additional term $P_{JS} \Delta_J / Max_J$, where $P_{JS}=0.5$ is the weight (instead of 0.1), whereas Δ_J and Max_J have the same meaning of Δ_L and Max_L in table 1 but referred just to scripting tags. Adding this term leads to $D(1,2)=1.62$, while absolute T becomes 1.55, therefore $D(1,2)>T$, accordingly to their appearance in fig. 1. This also shows that scripting tags are relevant when extracting collections.

Considering the Times home page (Fig. 3), several subtrees sets are examined, though some are not considered just to highlight most significant cases. In detail:

- subtrees 13,14,15 and 16 (common ancestor id is 17), present mutual distances always with value 0.5; Using the absolute T=1.55, we conclude that all subtrees belong to the same collection due to their low distance, as it can be also seen in Fig. 3
- Considering subtrees with ancestor 19, table 6 shows their distances. Their distribution allows to use relative thresold $T=(D_{MIN}+D_{MAX})/2 =(0.48+1.24)/2=0.86$. Using this value and referring to Fig. 3, subtrees 8 and 10 are structurally (hence, graphically) similar and form a collection, whereas 12,17 and 18 mutual distances confirm that they are structurally different from each other and from 8 and 10 (all values are indeed greater than T), as also their appearance reveal in Fig. 3: 17 includes 4 tables, 12 includes one table, 18 has no table.
- Table 6 shows distances for subtrees 4,5,6,19,21,22 (ancestor 20). Using absolute T, we get to all separate collections, as their appearances confirm in Fig. 3.
- All subtrees with no brothers (e.g. 7, 9, 11 in table 4) form stand-alone collections, they however will belong to the collection their ancestor will eventually belong to.
- Finally, highest level subtrees 1 and 20 (i.e. whose ancestor is the *<body>* tag) are different, as confirmed both by their distance (1.7 is greater than absolute T=1.55) and by their appearance.

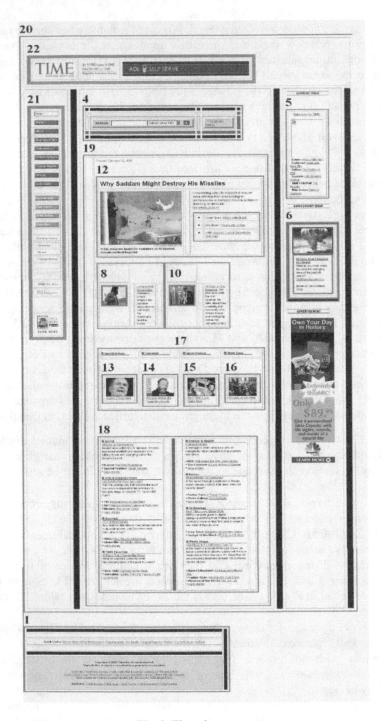

Fig. 3. Times home page

Table 6. Subtrees distances for Time home page

Ancestor ID 19	8	10	12	17	18
8	-	0.48	1	0.95	1.1
10	0.48	-	1	0.95	1.1
12	1	1	-	0.92	1
17	0.95	0.95	0.92	-	1.02
18	1.1	1.1	1	1.02	-

Ancestor ID 20	4	5	6	19	21	22
4	-	1.5	1.56	1.54	1.41	1.39
5	1.5	-	1.56	1.55	1.35	1.43
6	1.56	1.56	-	1.35	1.35	1.46
19	1.54	1.55	1.35	-	1.38	1.46
21	1.41	1.35	1.35	1.38	-	1.40
22	1.39	1.43	1.46	1.46	1.40	-

Ancestor ID 0	1	20
1	-	1.7
20	1.7	-

After distance evalutation, collections can be built based on previous results; fig. 4 shows collections for both examined home pages. The next step is to map these collections onto logical sections cited in the introduction; however, this is out of the scope of this paper. For more details, see [8][9][10].

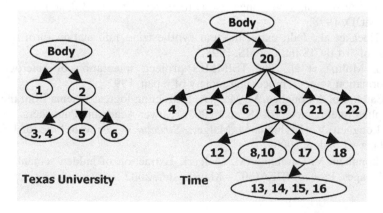

Fig. 4. Collections

4   Conclusions and Future Works

This paper deals with web documents schema extraction, in particular by analyzing HTML source tree. We introduced a set of primary tags actually used to give a structural/logical backbone to the page, classifying them with a set of tree-related properties, in order to divide the page into collections, which represent distinct *structural* page sections; collections will be finally mapped into *logical* sections according to their semantics.

Several future directions can be exploited:

- distance formula (1) and its threshold can be refined, e.g. evaluating for which variance values absolute or relative T must be used, or fuzzy approach may be adopted;
- a significant step is to validate the entire approach through an extensive application of the methodology to a significant set of web pages, both considering home/inner pages, as well as covering different site categories (e.g. commercial, institutional, etc);
- another factor to consider in more detail is the analisys of dynamic HTML pages, here actually limited to the use of scripting tags; in [8] some aspects (client vs server) are examined, but they need to be quantified (i.e. possibly influencing (1)).

References

[1]   P.M.G. Apers, *Identifying internet-related database reasearch*, 2nd Intl. East-West DB Workshop, 1994.

[2]   P.Buneman, Semistructured data, Workshop on Management of Semistructured Data, 1997.

[3]   S. Abiteboul, Querying Semi-structured Data, Proc. of ICDT, 1997.

[4]   S. Abiteboul et al., Data on the Web, Morgan Kaufmann, 2000.

[5]   S. Nestrorov et al., Extracting schema from semistructured data, Proc. of ACM SIGMOD, 1998.

[6]   G. Huck et al., Jedi: extracting and synthesizing information form the web, Proc of 3rd IFCIS Intl CoopIS, 1998.

[7]   H.G. Molina et al., The TSIMMIS project: integration of heterogeneous information sources, processing society of japan, 1997.

[8]   V.Carchiolo, A Longheu, M. Malgeri: Extracting logical schema from the web, Applied Intelligence, Vol 18, no.3 2003, Kluwer Academic Publishers.

[9]   A. Longheu, V. Carchiolo, M. Malgeri, *Structuring the web*, Proc. of DEXA - Takma – London, 2000.

[10]   A. Longheu, V. Carchiolo, M. Malgeri, Extraction of hidden semantics from web pages, Proc. of IDEAL 02 – Manchester, 2002.

Automatically Customizing Service Pages on the Web for Mobile Devices*

Yeonghyo Jeon[1] and Eenjun Hwang[1]

[1]Graduate School of Information and Communication, Ajou University, Suwon
Gyeonggi, Korea
{jeonyh,ehwang}@ajou.ac.kr

Abstract. Recent popularity of mobile devices such as PDA and cellphone has made wireless Internet access very crucial. However, most Web contents and services are optimized for desktop computing environment. Taking different system features of mobile devices such as small display, limited input capability and low power into consideration, an alternative access scheme to the Web has to be invented. On the other hand, personalization plays an important role in the tailored access to the Web contents and services. In this paper, we propose a proxy-based personalizing scheme of Web service pages for mobile users. It automatically provides mobile users with the tailored list of Web services well suited for diverse mobile devices. Eventually, mobile users can access Web service pages with minimum navigation on the small display. In addition, users can be provided with customized services. We have performed several experiments on the prototype system and reported some of the results.

1   Introduction

Due to the increasing demand for ubiquitous Internet access and the advance of mobile technology, wireless Internet access is getting popular. Particularly, mobile Internet access spreads everywhere as supplemental to PC Internet access. According to the survey from comScore Networks Inc, 10 million Americans surf from cell phones or PDAs. And they found that of the 19.1 million users owning a PDA, 5 million accesses the Internet with those devices and among the 67.2 million online users that own a cell phone, 5.8 million accesses the Internet with those devices [1]. Further research comes from Computer Industry Almanac Inc.'s analysis of Internet usage across more than 50 countries indicating that of the 1.12 billion Internet users projected for the end of 2005, a significant number will be using wireless devices such as Web-enabled cell phones and PDAs to go online [2].

However, accessing Web contents and services with mobile devices is inconvenient and restrictive. This is because mobile Internet devices have limited interface and performance. Furthermore, Web contents and services are optimized for desktop com-

---

*   This work was supported by a grant (M1-0219-24-0000) from the National Research and Development Program funded by the Ministry of Science and Technology, Republic of Korea.

N. Bianchi-Berthouze (Ed.): DNIS 2003, LNCS 2822, pp. 53-65, 2003.

puting environment. New PDA series such as Dell Axim^{TM} X5 or Compaq iPAQ H3900 have more memory and faster processor than existing products. In addition, the major microprocessor manufacturers such as Intel, Motorola, and Hitachi are trying to improve those mobile processor. However, small display and limited input capability cannot be overcome easily because there is a trade-off between device size and mobility. Many efforts have been done to get over such handicaps. Power Browser [3] and Digestor [4] summarize Web contents and reconstruct the Web pages for mobile devices. In addition, a number of companies [5, 6] have been providing basic content transformation services. Content transformation can reduce Web contents for mobile devices. However, Web contents and services can be lost during the transformation.

On the other hand, personalization plays an important role in accessing Web contents. Based on the user preference, Web pages can be summarized and reconstructed through the personalization process.

There are roughly two kinds of approaches to provide personalization. Implicit personalization uses the personal information provided by the user such as name, address, phone number, age and so on [7]. Explicit personalization is based on the collection and analysis of Web usage pattern and frequency data. Especially, personalization can be automated if such information can be collected from log data.

However, personalization based on log analysis has following drawbacks: i) It often spoils an original navigation structure. Consequently, users will face difficulty searching or utilizing services from the page. ii) Since it just counts the access frequency, it cannot tell the target page. Not all frequently accessed pages can be target pages. For example, if user usually follows page links $P_1 \rightarrow P_2 \rightarrow P_3$ to access a service page, then three page's access frequencies are all 1. However, P_1 or P_2 is not the target page. iii) It may not be possible to process all data in a real time due to heavy workload of log analysis and content transformation.

To overcome such drawbacks, in this paper, we propose a personalization scheme focused on the service page, which makes it possible to find out service with less navigation. Mobile users want to find services as soon as possible because wireless communication is more expensive than wired communication. Most mobile services provide service-oriented or menu-based interface. Menu-based interface helps user to navigate services with limited input capability. Therefore, if personalization system can provide Web contents and services similar to mobile services, it enables easy search for services.

We have implemented a service-oriented personalization system that provides most frequently accessed service pages. For easy access, service pages and region list similar to mobile service are generated automatically. Also, in addition to the log data, service related features of the page are considered for the correct identification of service.

The structure of the paper is as follows. Section 2 discusses related works. Section 3 describes service page, service region and examples. Section 4 describes overall system architecture and how to detect service page and service region. Section 5 presents some of the experimental results and the last section concludes this paper.

2   Related Works

So far, many efforts have been done for personalizing Web contents and services, mostly focused on log data. In PROTEUS [8, 9], personalized Web pages are created from pattern and preference by analyzing logs stored in the proxy or Web server. It analyzes the access logs, builds a model for each visitor and transforms the site to maximize the expected utility [8]. However, the process cannot be done in a real time due to workload. In addition, there is neither content negotiation nor consideration for the device used. Daily Learner [10] is an intelligent news agent that adopts a content-based machine-learning algorithm. It can learn preference of Palm or desktop users. iMobile [11] provides proxy-based personalized multimedia services. iMobile manages user and device profile for adaptive multimedia file service, but not for general Web contents. WebViews [12] and WebVCR [13] have taken different approach. WebViews is an extended version of the WebVCR. WebViews creates customized views of Web contents and services by recording and analyzing all users' navigation actions. End-users create and maintain simplified views of Web contents and services. However, creating views is manual operation. Once creating customized views, it automatically navigates to the itinerary pages, extracting specified contents from those pages.

Another work related to this topic is Web content summarization and reconstruction for heterogeneous mobile devices. Power Browser [3] and Digestor [4] can dynamically summarize Web pages using transformation proxy. Web Stream Customizers (WSC) [14] are dynamically deployable software modules and can be strategically located between client and server to customize Web contents. Transcoding Proxy [15] is an annotation based transcoding system, where pages are annotated using WYSIWYG annotation tool. Consequently, Web pages are summarized more accurately but not automatically. PageMap [16] performs region-based summarization for Web pages and constructs a page map composed of summarized regions for the small screen.

Web usage mining has been widely studied for Web page personalization system, product recommendation system and Web site optimization. Also, access log mining has been studied to analyze user browsing behavior and preference. J. Srivastava et al. [17] describes process and data source for Web usage mining. B. Mobasher et al. [18] describes how to mine Web usage patterns and Web contents for the personalization from Web access log. He proposes the recommendation system that can recommend new content to the visitor. Fenstermacher and Ginsburg [19] describe weaknesses of server-side monitoring and propose a client-side monitoring system. S. Dua et al [20] proposes an algorithm to extract access sequences from semi-structured Web access log.

3   Service Page Detection for Personalization

In this section, we describe Web page features that are related with service page detection and personalization. Some Web pages provide interaction-based services to the user. Most of these pages contain forms and Web scripts that need data processing at the server side or dynamic service control. We call such page service page. For example, assume we make reservation on the Web. If the user wants to reserve any movie, he or she wants to access only the page containing reservation information directly. Probably reservation service page has some forms for user input. In addition, it causes data processing to the server.

A service page source may has service features such as form tags to take user input and Web script to provide link to server processes or service control. Also, several features can be obtained when the user accesses service pages. Service features usually take long response time due to the extra processing time. Especially, in case the user_requests multimedia services for image, audio and video, large amount of network resource should be allocated. We name such codes or features as service elements.

Some service elements such as the search form or media player for video in HTML and sports news section in a news page take only small portion on the whole page. When users want to use a service, only that portion of the page containing the service element is needed. For example, on accessing *yahoo* or *google* only for Web search, the search form for keyword input will be sufficient. If the user wants to watch music video, link list for video player launches will be enough. All other service elements are unnecessary. Generally, a page author groups services into blocks and locates service elements in a page frame, in a table cell or in a draw layer. We call such a region as service region. A service region is a small part of service page where service elements are clustered. Therefore, service regions can be moved to a mobile device using low network bandwidth by simple transformation process.

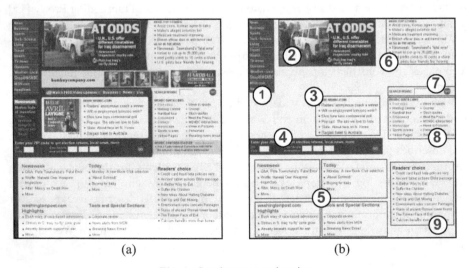

(a)   (b)

Fig. 1. Service page and region

Table 1. Service elements of MSNBC main page

Service element	Number of service elements
Form	3
ASP	120
JavaScript	7
Total link	144

Table 2. Distribution of service elements for each service region

Service element	Service region								
	1	2	3	4	5	6	7	8	9
Form				2			1		
ASP	13	1	6		16	8	1	16	10

Figure 1-(a) shows MSNBC news service page. Some of the service elements contained in the page are: i) link menu for lower-level news category, ii) Web script links for direct service such as live news and highlight news, iii) search forms for local news and entire news search. Table 1 shows the number of service elements that were observed from MSNBC news service page. Figure 1-(b) represents the service regions that are extracted from news service page. Table 2 shows distribution of service elements over service region. Service regions □, □, □, □, □ contain ASP (Active Server Page) Web script link for news or VoD (Video on Demand). Regions □ and □ contain the search form for news.

4   System Architecture

The overall system architecture is shown in Figure 2. Main components of the system are: i) User profile server which performs user authentication as well as maintains personalization data. ii) Access log miner that periodically analyzes log data and identifies frequently accessed pages. iii) Service page and region detector that extracts service pages and region from frequently accessed pages. iv) Service page and region cache, which contain cached service pages and regions. v) Contents converter, which extracts service regions from service pages and performs simple contents conversion.

The access log miner detects frequently accessed sites or pages. After mining, the detector identifies service pages by evaluating service elements. Service regions are extracted from service pages based on the access frequency and the number of service elements. Service page and region data are transferred to profile server. When a mobile user connects to the system, a list of service pages and regions is shown to the user. If a mobile user requests specific service page or region, the contents converter provides it for user as a suitable form. In addition, extracted service page and service region will be cached for the next access. In the following subsections, we will describe some of the algorithms used in the system.

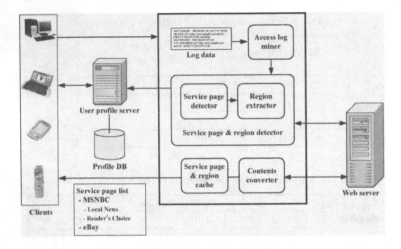

Fig. 2. System architecture

4.1   User Profile Server

In the web personalization, user identification is a challenging problem. Although IP address provides a simple and common solution for user identification, it has a serious drawback. Most ISPs (Internet Service Provider) use the DHCP (Dynamic Host Configuration Protocol) to manage IP addresses. They randomly assign one of several IP addresses to each request from users. Thus, the same IP address might be assigned to two or more users [19]. To identify users, we used a separate profile server to identify the user more accurately and reduce proxy workload. Also, it manages user preference and device profile. When the user first accesses the system, he or she provides simple authentication, preference and device profile for the user profile server. Figure 3 shows the input form for the user profile server. In the figure, preferential factor provides language, sound and other user preference items. Device profile has specifications for Hardware and Software platform. Hardware platform has device specification such as vendor, model, class of device, screen size, bandwidth and so on. Software platform specification includes OS brand, version and level of HTML support etc.

Users send their profile to the user profile server using CC/PP (Composite Capability/Preference Profiles)[21]. A CC/PP profile is a description of device capabilities and user preferences. The RDF (Resource Description Framework)[22] is used to create profiles. We use simple RDF schema and input form for user profile data. The profile DB stores user profile with service page and region data. Authentication profile identifies users uniquely. Device profiles are used for content conversion process. Figure 4 shows a part of CC/PP profile.

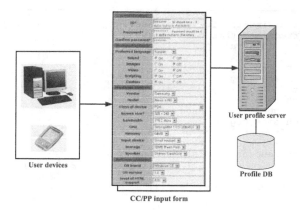

CC/PP input form

Fig. 3. CC/PP input form

```xml
<?xml version="1.0"?>
<rdf:RDF xmlns:rdf="http://www.w3.org/1999/02/22-rdf-syntax-ns#"
         xmlns:ccpp="http://www.w3.org/2002/11/08-ccpp#"
         xmlns:prf="http://adtl.ajou.ac.kr/Schema#">


        . . . . . . . . . . . .

   <rdf:Description rdf:about="http://adtl.ajou.ac.kr/MyProfile">
     <ccpp:component>
       <rdf:Description
              rdf:about="http://adtl.ajou.ac.kr/TerminalHardware">
         <rdf:type
rdf:resource="http://adtl.ajou.ac.kr/Schema#HardwarePlatform"/>
         <ccpp:defaults>
           <rdf:Description
                   rdf:about="http://adtl.ajou.ac.kr/HWDefault">
             <rdf:type
rdf:resource="http://adtl.ajou.ac.kr/Schema#HardwarePlatform"/>
             <prf:cpu>PPC</prf:cpu>
             <prf:displayWidth>320</prf:displayWidth>
             <prf:displayHeight>200</prf:displayHeight>
           </rdf:Description>
         </ccpp:defaults>
         <prf:vendor>Samsung</prf:vendor>
         <prf:model>nexio s150</prf:model>
         <prf:classofdevice>PDA</prf:classofdevice>
         <prf:displayHeight>320</prf:displayHeight>
         <prf:displayWidth>240</prf:displayWidth>
         <prf:bandwidth>115.2</prf:bandwidth>
         <prf:cpu>strongARM 1110</prf:cpu>
         <prf:memory>64</prf:memory>
         <prf:input>small keypad</prf:input>
         <prf:storage>32</prf:storage>
         <prf:speaker>yes</prf:speaker>
       </rdf:Description>
     </ccpp:component>
   .
   .
   .
```

Fig. 4. CC/PP profile

```
Function FindFrequentlyAccessedPage()
ft = frequency threshold value
T = time interval

load changed log
clean loaded log
repeat
foreach user begin
find frequently accessed sites
foreach site begin
   find frequently accessed page
   if ft < frequency then
      enqueue(page urls)
                        //insert page url and frequency
   end
call FindServicePage(queue())
end
sleep(T)
until deamon stop
```

Fig. 5. Find frequently accessed page (Algorithm I)

4.2   Service Page and Region Detection

Service page and region detection is processed in two phases. The first phase is log cleaning and analysis to detect frequently accessed pages. Service page and region information will be extracted during the second phase. Figure 5 shows an algorithm for detecting frequently accessed sites and pages.

To provide personalized service, frequently accessed Web sites and pages are first analyzed for each user. Especially, access logs are analyzed periodically for each accessed user during the period to reduce the workload by the log miner. In our implementation, frequently accessed pages are accumulated into a queue according to the access frequency.

```
Function FindServicePage()
k = sum of weight for each service element
kt= threshold value of k
ri[] = region data
fin = 1

repeat
while page ← dequeue() do {
     download page from web server
foreach page begin
calculate k
if k > kt then {
   ri[] ← call pagemap()
   estimate service elements for each region and rank region
}
end
}
call SavetoProfile()
fin ← 0
until fin=0
```

Fig. 6. Find service page (Algorithm II)

```
Function ServiceList()
foreach login begin
  generate service and region information from profile DB
  provide service list to client
  if request then
    call ContentConverter()
end

Function ContentConverter()
foreach request begin
  if request service page then
    call pagemap()
  else if request service region then
    extract region from service page by region information
    send to client with content conversion by device profile
  end
```

Fig. 7. Service list generation and content transform (Algorithm III)

The service page and region detector downloads frequently accessed pages from the web server using URL in the queue. Then, it identifies service elements and calculates their weights. Each service element is assigned a default weight. During this step, we can give preference to the service page containing specific service elements by assigning different weight. When the weight of a service element exceeds a threshold, the service page and region detector considers frequently accessed page as service page and extracts the service region from the service page using PageMap algorithm [16]. PageMap extracts page regions using <TABLE> tag information. Finally, extracted regions are ranked by their weight and access frequency.

4.3   Contents Transform

Mobile users are provided with a preference service list when they access the system. The lists are organized in a tree structure. When the user clicks a region, the content converter extracts service region from service page. It transfers service region to mobile user through lightweight converting process. Figure 8 shows service list and selected region. Figure 8-(a) shows service page and region list. Each service page has region list as child node. Figure 8-(b) depicts politics region of CNN video service page. Politics region size is small. Therefore, it can be displayed without transformation on the small display.

5   Experimental Results

In this section, we describe some of the experiments we performed to prove its effectiveness. The system is implemented using Squid Web proxy cache [23] running at a Linux-based machine. Squid is a full-featured Web proxy cache designed to run on Unix systems. The Squid provides various log options for the handy analysis of log file. The eXcelon (native XML Database)[24] was used for user profile DB.

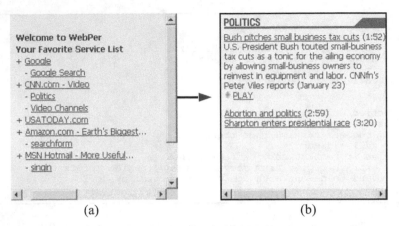

(a)   (b)

Fig. 8. Service list and selected region

In order to produce detailed access log, we arranged every requests to go to its Web server through our system. In general, mobile devices have a small cache, so we ignored it in our experiment. Consequently, all the pages visited and links followed were recorded in the access log. In addition to the preliminary log cleaning, we removed unnecessary information that was generated unintentionally. For example, messenger or adware such as ICQ and MSN are removed since they periodically access web sites for advertisements.

Then, we asked twenty users to answer the following questions: First, what is the most frequently accessed web site? Second, What is the most frequently used service for each site that was answered at the first question? After answering the required questions, users had used the Web for a week. In this period, the system extracted service pages and regions. To evaluate its effectiveness, we measured the recall and precision [25]. Recall is the proportion of relevant service pages retrieved, while precision quantifies the proportion of retrieved service page that are relevant to the frequently used service page. We used following variables.

For each user

(1) All pages: All service pages that were extracted from the system.
(2) Relevant pages: Service pages that were submitted by the users. We removed some service pages that were not included in all pages. Removed pages are caused by users´ wrong answer, popular page becomes unpopular. For example, the user frequently accesses some online stores for shopping. However, after purchasing, the users hardly access shopping sites again for a time.
(3) Retrieved pages: Frequently accessed service pages that were extracted from the system. We increased the number of retrieved service pages from 5 to 20 by 5. In service list, a service page is shown as a line that has a hyperlink. Generally, cell phone has 5-10 line display and smart phone has about 15 line display. PDA can display about 20 lines using browser. Thus, we calculated four precisions for various display size of mobile devices.
(4) Relevant and retrieved pages: The set of service pages that are both relevant and retrieved.

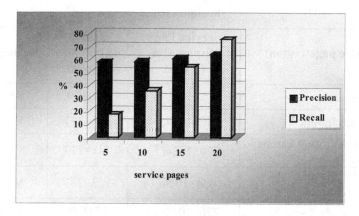

Fig. 9. Average precision of twenty users

Figure 9 shows the average precision of the twenty users. When the system extracts 20 service pages, the average precision was 64.25% and average recall was 76.02%. This precision can apply for PDA that has 320× 240 resolution.

Next, we measured bandwidth saving by comparing the region volume with service page volume. We chose six service page and region randomly from relevant service pages. Table 3-(a) shows bandwidth saving caused by region hit. The average data transfer amount was decreased by 94.04%. Small region volume relieves the low bandwidth limitation of mobile devices. In addition, Table 3-(b) shows the region display size. The average display size can be reduced up to 91.41%. The reduction of display size using service region relieves the small display limitation and scrolling.

Table 3. The comparison of the bandwidth and display size

(a) bandwidth

Service page (region)	Region volume(byte)	Service page volume(byte)	Saving(%)
Google (search)	1213	12578	90.36
CNN Video (politics)	2517	217404	98.84
USATODAY, sport baseball (team index)	3633	155313	97.66
ebay, PDAs/Handheld PC (PDA search)	2863	332547	99.14
Amazon (product search)	2797	121339	97.69
Hotmail (login)	3974	20438	80.56

(b) display size

Service page(region)	Service Page display size (pixels)	Region display size (pixels)	Saving(%)
Google (search)	523×427	419×79	85.18
CNN Video (politics)	770×1024(↑)	307×331	87.11
USATODAY, sport baseball (team index)	770×1024(↑)	141×117	97.91
ebay, PDAs/Handheld PC (PDA search)	1024×1024(↑)	163×287	95.54
Amazon (product search)	770×1024(↑)	171×75	98.37
Hotmail (login)	649×637	316×205	84.33

6   Conclusions

With the popularity of wireless Internet access, an alternative to browse Web contents on mobile devices is required. In addition, due to enormous amount of information, Web personalization was proposed to provide customized information to each user. Mobile personalization system can personalize every aspect of hardware and software. By a using mobile personalization scheme, limitation of mobile devices can be relieved. Also, it can help users to access interesting Web contents and service more easily.

In this paper, we proposed a new personalization system that has focused on service pages. Our system personalizes frequently used service pages by log and service element analysis. Consequently, users are enabled to access Web services as mobile services. In addition, the proposed system efficiently reduces content conversion overhead and overcomes small display of mobile device by region extraction

References

[1]   comScore Networks, Inc. - http://www.comscore.com
[2]   Computer Industry Almanac Inc. - http://www.c-i-a.com
[3]   O. Buyukkokten, H. Garcia Molina, A. Paepcke and T. Winograd, "Power Browser: Efficient Web Browsing for PDAs," Proceedings of the Conference on Human Factors in Computing Systems, pp. 430-437, 2000
[4]   T. Bickmore and B. Schilit, "Digestor: Device-independent Access to the World Wide Web," Proceedings of the 6th International World Wide Web Conference, pp. 655-663, 1999
[5]   AvantGo, Inc. - http://www.avantgo.com
[6]   Earthlink, Inc. - http://www.earthlink.net
[7]   C. Sharma, Wireless Internet Enterprise Applications – A Willey Tech Brief, John Wiley & Sons, Inc, pp.91-93, 2001

[8]   C. R. Anderson, P. Domingos and D. S. Weld, "Personalizing Web Sites for Mobile Users," Proceedings of the 10th World Wide Web Conference, 2001

[9]   C. R. Anderson, P. Domingos and D. S. Weld, "Adaptive web navigation for wireless devices," Proceedings of the 17th International Joint Conference on Artificial Intelligence, 2001

[10] D. Billsus, M. J. Pazzani and J. Chen, "A learning agent for wireless news access," Proceedings of the 2000 International Conference on Intelligent User Interfaces, pp. 33-36, 2000

[11] C. Yih-Farn, H. Huale, R. Jana, S. John, S. Jora, A. Reibman and W. Bin, "Personalized multimedia services using a mobile service platform," Wireless Communications and Networking Conference, 2002

[12] J. Freire, B. Kumar and D. F. Lieuwen, "WebViews: accessing personalized web content and services," Proceedings of the 10th International Conference on World Wide Web, pp. 576 - 586, 2001

[13] V. Anupam, J. Freire, B. Kumar and D. Lieuwen, "Automating Web navigation with the WebVCR," Computer Networks, Vol 33(1-6), pp. 503-517, 2000

[14] J. Steinberg and J. Pasquale, "A web middleware architecture for dynamic customization of content for wireless clients," Proceedings of the 11th International Conference on World Wide Web, Honolulu, Hawaii, USA, 2002

[15] M. Hori, G. Kondoh, K. Ono, S. Hirose and S. Singhal, "Annotation-based web content transcoding," Proceeding of 9th International World Wide Web Conference, pp. 197-211, 2000

[16] D. Song and E. Hwang. "PageMap: Summarizing Web Pages for Small Display Devices," Proceeding of International Conference on Internet Computing, Vol. 2, pp. 506-512, June 2002

[17] J. Srivastava, R. Cooley, M. Deshpande and Tan, P.-N. "Web Usage Mining: Discovery and Applications of Usage Patterns from Web Data," SIGKDD Explorations, Vol. 1(2), pp. 12-23, January 2000

[18] B. Mobasher, R. Cooley and J. Srivastava. "Automatic Personalization Based on Web Usage Mining," Communications of the ACM, Vol. 43(8), pp. 142-151, August 2000

[19] K.D. Fenstermacher and M. Ginsburg. "Mining client-side activity for personalization," Advanced Issues of E-Commerce and Web-Based Information Systems (WECWIS 2002), Proceedings of 4th IEEE International Workshop, pp. 205-212, 2002

[20] S. Dua, E. Cho and S.S. Iyengar. "Discovery of Web frequent patterns and user characteristics from Web access logs: a framework for dynamic Web personalization," Application-Specific Systems and Software Engineering Technology, 2000. Proceedings of 3rd IEEE Symposium, pp. 3-8, 2000

[21] http://www.w3.org/Mobile/CCPP/ - CC/PP (Composite Capabilities /Preference Profiles)

[22] http://www.w3.org/RDF/ - RDF

[23] Squid Web Proxy Cache - http://www.squid-cache.org/

[24] eXcelon - http://www.exln.com/

[25] J. Han and M. Kamber, Data Mining: Concepts and Techniques, Morgan Kaufmann Publishers, pp. 428-433, 2001

Author-$\mathcal{X}$ – A System for Secure Dissemination and Update of XML Documents

Elisa Bertino[1], Barbara Carminati[1], Elena Ferrari[2], and Giovanni Mella[1]

[1] Dipartimento di Informatica e Comunicazione, Università degli Studi di Milano
Via Comelico, 39/41, 20135 Milano, Italy
Fax +39-0250316253
{bertino,carminati,mella}@dico.unimi.it
[2] Dipartimento di Scienze Chimiche, Fisiche e Matematiche, Università dell'Insubria
Como
Via Valleggio, 11, 22100 Como, Italy
Fax +39-0312386119
elena.ferrari@uninsubria.it

Abstract. In this paper we describe the main features of Author-$\mathcal{X}$, a Java-based system providing a comprehensive environment for securing XML documents. The most innovative and relevant features of Author-$\mathcal{X}$ are the support for different dissemination strategies (i.e., push and pull) and for cooperative and distributed updates of XML documents. These functionalities are obtained through the use of digital signature and encryption techniques. In the paper, besides illustrating the general architecture of Author-$\mathcal{X}$, we describe in details the strategies we have devised for the support of both information push and distributed updates

1 Introduction

A key requirement of today web-based applications is related to security of information that are made available and disseminated among users and applications. Even though a large number of techniques are today available to protect data when being transmitted across sites, such as cryptography and electronic signatures, a truly comprehensive approach for data protection must also include mechanisms for enforcing access control policies, based on data contents, on subject qualifications and characteristics, as well as on other relevant contextual information, such as time. It is today well understood also that, in order to specify effective access control policies, one must take into account data semantics. In database systems for example, data semantics is mainly conveyed by schema information and therefore access control policies are expressed against the database schema. Achieving the same level of functionality for web data is today possible because of the widespread use of XML [11] for describing data that are circulated across web sites. The advent of XML has thus pushed the development of access control models and systems. Such models and systems are crucial in order to facilitate a selective dissemination of XML documents

N. Bianchi-Berthouze (Ed.): DNIS 2003, LNCS 2822, pp. 66–85, 2003.

containing information of different sensitivity levels among (possibly large) user communities. An overview of research work can be found in [6].

The development of access control models and systems for XML data poses, however, several requirements. The fact that XML semantic elements, delimited by application-defined *tags*, can be directly and independently retrieved though XML query languages requires a system able to control access at varying levels within the protected documents. In some cases, a single-access control policy may apply to a set of documents; in other cases, different policies may apply to fine-grained portions of the same document. Many other intermediate situations also arise. Therefore, a suitable access control system must have provision for variable protection granularity level. Another relevant requirement derives from the need of supporting a variety of data dissemination techniques, such as for example information push and pull, by yet enforcing the stated access control policies. Such a need may require the adoption of different access control techniques depending on the information dissemination strategy adopted. A comprehensive access control system must thus provide all those techniques in order to adapt to various dissemination strategies. Finally, another relevant requirement is represented by the fact that several new web-enabled applications, such as virtual communities and contract negotiation, require support for distributed cooperative document updates. Therefore, a suitable access control system must not only support read privileges for the disseminated documents, but it must also provide a large variety of update privileges reflecting the various modification operations that are possible on XML documents.

In this paper we discuss how the above requirements can be meet by describing the solutions adopted in the framework of the Author-$\mathcal{X}$ system, a Java-based system, for discretionary access control of XML documents. Author-$\mathcal{X}$ takes into account XML document characteristics, the presence of DTDs/XML schemas describing the structure of documents at a schema level, and the types of actions that can be executed on XML documents (i.e., navigation, browsing, and update), as well temporal constraints, for implementing an access control mechanism tailored to XML. Furthermore, Author-$\mathcal{X}$ supports the specification of *subject credentials* as a way to enforce access control based on subject qualifications and profiles, and two different document distribution policies, namely *push distribution* for document broadcast, and *pull distribution* for document distribution on user demand. Finally, Author-$\mathcal{X}$ supports distributed cooperative updates through a combination of hash functions, digital signature techniques and digital certificates. The Author-$\mathcal{X}$ approach to distributed updates allows a subject to verify a document's integrity without requiring interactions with the document server.

The remainder of this paper is organized as follows. Next section presents an overview of the Author-$\mathcal{X}$ architecture, whereas Section 3 presents the security policies supported by our system. In Section 4 we show how Author-$\mathcal{X}$ supports the push selective dissemination mode, whereas Section 5 presents the management of a collaborative and distribute update process. Finally, in Section 6 the paper presents future work.

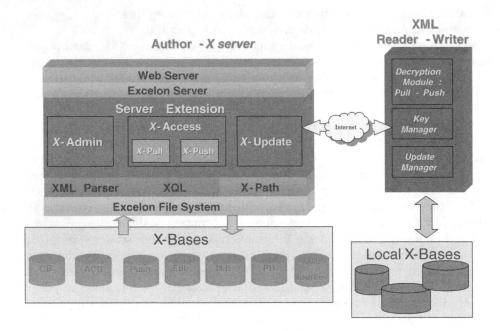

Fig. 1. Author-$\mathcal{X}$ architecture

2 Overview

Author-$\mathcal{X}$ is a Java-based system exploiting a client-server paradigm, that is, it consists of two main components, namely the Author-$\mathcal{X}$ server and the *XML Reader-Writer* client (see Figure 1).

The Author-$\mathcal{X}$ server provides all functions related to services for the selective and distributed dissemination of XML documents and their updates and consists of three main Java server extensions, namely $\mathcal{X}$-*Admin*, $\mathcal{X}$-*Access*, and $\mathcal{X}$-*Update*, described in what follows:

- $\mathcal{X}$-*Admin* is the component by which the Security Administrator (SA) carries out all administration activities: management of credentials and policies, management of the XML Source (i.e., acquiring new documents, deleting documents, or modifying existing documents), and management of subjects (e.g., assigning credentials to new subjects). The main benefit of $\mathcal{X}$-*Admin* is that it provides a graphical interface, which greatly helps the SA in performing these operations;
- $\mathcal{X}$-*Access* supports the selective distribution of XML documents (or portions of it) to subjects, according to the access control policies stated on the source. The main feature of $\mathcal{X}$-*Access* is that it provides two different dissemination modes. Indeed, besides the traditional request-response paradigm (also called *pull distribution*) by which a subject must directly request to the source

the documents of interest when needed, $\mathcal{X}$-*Access* supports also the *push distribution*, according to which it periodically sends (or when some predefined events happen) its documents (or portions of them) to authorized subjects. As shown in Figure 1, $\mathcal{X}$-*Access* consists of two modules, that is, $\mathcal{X}$-*Pull* and $\mathcal{X}$-*Push*, which enforce the pull and push distribution mode, respectively;

– $\mathcal{X}$-*Update* is the component that supports distributed and collaborative updates of XML documents. This means that an XML document can undergo a controlled sequential update process in which a sequence of subjects receive the document and may exercise modification operations, according to the access control policies that apply to it. The key feature is that $\mathcal{X}$-*Update* makes, in most cases, a receiver subject able to locally verify the correctness of the updates performed on the document, without requiring interaction with the document server.

All security information managed by Author-$\mathcal{X}$ are encoded using XML, thus allowing a uniform protection of data and their related security information. XML documents are managed through the eXcelon XML data server [5] and organized into an XML native database, called X-bases, which contains five main repositories:

– *Credential Base* ($\mathcal{CB}$): it contains the subject credentials and the credential types;
– *Policy Base* ($\mathcal{PB}$): it contains the access control policies for the documents stored in the XML-Source;
– *Authoring Certificate Base* ($\mathcal{ACB}$): it contains the certificates generated according to the policies stored in $\mathcal{PB}$;
– *Push*: it contains the XML representation of all the information needed by the push dissemination mechanism;
– *Encryption Document Base* ($\mathcal{EDB}$): it contains the encrypted copy of some of the documents stored in the XML-Source. Such representation is used to enforce information push;
– *Management Information Base* ($\mathcal{MIB}$): it contains all the information required to manage the collaborative update of documents stored in the XML-Source.

Each subject wishing to interact with the Author-$\mathcal{X}$ server needs to be supplied with the proper client called *XML Reader-Writer*. This client provides the following functions: 1) transmission to the server of document access requests; 2) decryption of the copies of documents received by the server, when the push dissemination mode is adopted; 3) management of the collaborative update processes. In order to perform all these tasks, the *XML Reader-Writer* needs to manage a local XML-based database that consists of the following repositories:

– *KeyStore*: it contains the keys received by the server to decrypt the encrypted documents sent by the server itself or by another subject;
– *Certificates*: it contains the certificates received by the server;

– *Document Repository*: it contains the encrypted documents or the document
packages received by the server or by another subject;

The architecture we discuss so far is the final result of several efforts carried
out by our group in the last years. The first version of Author-$\mathcal{X}$, described
in [7], includes only the $\mathcal{X}$-*Admin* and the pull component of $\mathcal{X}$-*Access*. For this
reason, in this paper we mainly focus on the push dissemination mode and on the
collaborative and distributed updates of XML documents, which are the most
innovative features of Author-$\mathcal{X}$. Before doing that, we need to briefly introduce
Author-$\mathcal{X}$ security policies, since these are the building blocks of both the pull
dissemination mode and the collaborative and distributed updates.

3   Security Policies for XML Documents

In general, security policies in a Web environment specify the principles for
the protection and release of data on the Web. According to this definition
it is possible to distinguish two different categories of security policies: *access
control policies* and *dissemination policies*. The former specify the authorization
rules and conditions according to which subjects are allowed to access an XML
document (or portions of it). Whereas the latter state the distribution modes
under which the release of data contents should occur. In the following section,
we illustrate the security policies supported by Author-$\mathcal{X}$.

3.1   Access Control Policies

An access control policy basically specifies *who* can access *which* object and under
which mode. In the following we describe access control policy specification in
Author-$\mathcal{X}$ by focusing on the most relevant features that the Author-$\mathcal{X}$ access
control model provides.

Who – Subject Credentials. Access control policies are based on the notion
of *credential* [10], where a credential is set of attributes, representing subject
properties (either simple or composite) that are relevant for access control purpose, such as for instance the age or the nationality of a subject. To make the
task of credential specification easier, credentials with the same structure are
grouped into *credential types*. A credential is, thus, an instance of a credential-
type, and specifies the set of property values characterizing a given subject
against the credential-type itself. Author-$\mathcal{X}$ provides an XML-based language,
called $\mathcal{X}$-Sec [8], for encoding both credentials and credential types. In particular, in $\mathcal{X}$-Sec a credential-type is modeled as a DTD and a specific credential as
an XML document valid according to the DTD representing the corresponding
credential-type. In the DTD simple properties are modeled as empty elements,
whereas composite properties are modeled as elements with element content,
whose subelements model composite property components. Examples of credential specifications in $\mathcal{X}$-Sec are reported in Figure 2. Each credential contains

```
<Subscriber credID="154">
   <name>Alice</name>
   <surname>Brown</surname>
   <type> week-end</type>
   <supplements> Wednesday </supplements>
</Subscriber>
```

```
<Subscriber credID="155">
   <name>Bob</name>
   <surname>Robbin</surname>
   <type> full </type>
   <supplements> all</supplements>
</Subscriber>
```

```
<Reporter credID="121">
   <name>Tom</name>
   <surname>Smith</surname>
   <section>Sport</section>
   <salary>2000</salary>
</Reporter>
```

```
<Director credID="132">
   <name>Ann</name>
   <surname>Tylor</surname>
   <level>Executive-Director</level>
   <salary>5000</salary>
</Director>
```

Fig. 2. Examples of $\mathcal{X}$-Sec credentials

a `credID` attribute which denotes the credential identifier. Each subject possesses one or more credentials which can be issued by the document source itself, or by a third party credential authority. Moreover, in order to prevent malicious modifications, the credential issuer signs the credential according to the XML signature standard [12]. Access control policies are then specified by imposing conditions (using an XPath-compliant language [13]) on the credentials and credential attribute values. An access control policy applies to a subject only if his/her credentials satisfy the constraints stated in the policy specification.

Where – Protection Objects. By *protection objects* we mean the document portions to which a policy applies. Author-$\mathcal{X}$ provides a wide range of options in that we allow the possibility of specifying access control policies that apply to: 1) all the instances of a DTD/XML Schema; 2) arbitrary collections of documents, not necessarily instances of the same DTD/XML Schema; 3) selected portions within a document, i.e., an element (or a set of elements), an attribute (or a set of attributes), a link (or a set of links). In addition to the this wide range of protection objects, Author-$\mathcal{X}$ supports also content-dependent access control, that is, it allows the specification of policies which apply to a protection object on the basis of its content. This is a useful feature since it may happen that documents with the same structure have completely different protection requirements. In Author-$\mathcal{X}$ all these features are achieved by specifying protection objects through XPath-compliant expressions.

What − Privileges. Access control policies can be divided into two different groups: *browsing policies*, that allow a subject to read the information in a protection object or possibly to navigate through its link, and *authoring policies*, that allow a subject to modify protection objects according to different modes (i.e., update, delete, insert). Since Author-$\mathcal{X}$ supports both browsing and authoring policies, in the following we briefly summarize all the implied privileges.

– *Browsing privileges*. Author-$\mathcal{X}$ supports three different browsing privileges: `view`, `navigate`, and `browse_all`. The `view` privilege allows a subject to read the values of all (or some of) the attributes/elements in a protection object, apart from attributes of type `IDREF/URI`(s). By contrast, the `navigate` privilege allows a subject to see all the links implied by attributes of type `IDREF/URI`(s) contained in a protection object. The view the subject has on the referred elements depends on the authorizations the subject has on such elements. The distinction between `view` and `navigate` privileges makes it possible to grant subjects the access to a protection object without disclosing its links with other protection objects. `view` and `navigate` privileges can also be given on selected attributes within an element. Finally, the `browse_all` privilege subsumes the `navigate` and the `view` privilege.
– *Authoring privileges*. Author-$\mathcal{X}$ supports six distinct authoring privileges. Three of them can be exercised over attributes: [1] `delete_attr`, `insert_attr`, and `update_attr`; by contrast other two, that is, `insert_elemt` and `delete_elemt`, can be exercised over elements, whereas the sixth privilege, called `auth_all`, subsumes all the other authoring privileges, enabling a subject to exercise on a protection object all the authoring privileges supported by our model. The `delete_attr` privilege allows a subject to remove an attribute from an element; the `insert_attr` privilege is used to add an attribute into an element; the `update_attr` privilege is used to modify an attribute value; the `insert_elemt` privilege allows a subject to insert new elements that are direct subelements of the element on which this privilege is specified; finally the `delete_elemt` privilege allows one to remove the subtree rooted at the element on which this privilege is specified.

In the following, we denote with $\mathcal{P}$ the set of browsing and authoring privileges supported by Author-$\mathcal{X}$.

When − Temporal Constraints. Another important feature of the access control model supported by Author-$\mathcal{X}$ is its temporal dimension, in that it is possible to express policies that hold only for specific periods of time (such as for instance a particular day of the week). This feature makes able the SA to state

---

[1] In this paper we also consider the data content of an element as a particular attribute whose name is *content* and whose value is the element data content itself.

Table 1.   Examples of periodic expressions

periodic expression	meaning
Weeks + {2}.*Days*	Wednesday
Weeks + {6}.*Days*	Sunday
Weeks +{5}.*Days* $\triangleright$ 2.Days	Week-end
Weeks + *All*.*Days*	All the days of the week

the set of time intervals in which a policy holds. This is a relevant feature since there are several situations in which subjects should have the right to access a document or a document portion only in specific periods of time. As an example, consider the case of a newspaper company offering several types of subscriptions, which differ for the subscription period (one year, six-month, only the week-end, and so on).

In Author-$\mathcal{X}$ temporal constraints are defined by using the formalism presented in [1]. According to this formalism, a temporal constraint is defined as a pair $\langle$[begin,end], P$\rangle$, where P is a *periodic expression* denoting an infinite set of periodic time instants, and [begin,end] is a time interval denoting the lower and upper bounds that are imposed on instants in P. In the current version of Author-$\mathcal{X}$ temporal constraints can only be specified for browsing policies and are not thus supported for authoring policies. Therefore, update policies have associated **Always** and **All days** as temporal constraints, to denote the fact that these policies always hold from when they are entered until when they are explicitly revoked. Some examples of periodic expressions are reported in Table 1.

A further feature of Author-$\mathcal{X}$ is that it exploits a set of *propagation options* in the specification of access control policies to reduce the number of policies that need to be specified. More precisely, a *propagation option* states whether and how a policy specified on a given protection object *o* propagates to protection objects that are related to *o* by some sort of semantic relationships. The main benefit of the propagation options is that they allow one to concisely express a set of security requirements. In Author-$\mathcal{X}$ two different types of propagation are provided: *implicit* and *explicit propagation*. The first type is applied by default according to the following principles: *i)* policies specified on a DTD/XML Schema propagate to all the DTD/XML Schema instances; *ii)* policies specified on a given element propagate to all the attributes and links of the element. By contrast, the explicit propagations make the SA able to state in the policy specification whether and how a policy specified on a given protection object propagates to lower level protection objects (wrt the document or DTD/XML Schema hierarchy). Author-$\mathcal{X}$ supports three different options for explicit propagations: *i)* no propagation (NO_PROP option), that is, the policy only applies to the protection objects which appear in the specification; *ii)* the policy propagates to all the direct subelements of the elements in the specification (FIRST_LEVEL option); *iii)* the policy propagates to all the direct and indirect subelements (CASCADE option).

Table 2. An example of Policy Base

Identifier	Access control policy
acp_1	([01/01/2003,12/31/2003], All days, //Subscriber/type=''full'', /Newspaper,VIEW,CASCADE)
acp_2	([01/01/2003,12/31/2003], Week-end, //Subscriber/type=''week-end'', /Newspaper, VIEW, CASCADE)
acp_3	([01/01/2003,12/31/2003], Wednesday, //Subscriber/supplements=''Wednesday'', //Financial_supplement, VIEW, CASCADE)
acp_4	([01/01/2003,12/31/2003], Sunday, //Subscriber/supplements=''Sunday'', //Literary_supplement, VIEW, CASCADE)
acp_5	([01/01/2003,12/31/2003], All days, //Subscriber/type=''light'', //Leading_article, VIEW, NO_PROP)
acp_6	(Always, All days, //Reporter[@credID=''121''], //Sport_page/News[@Author=''Smith''], UPDATE_ATTR, FIRST_LEVEL)
acp_7	(Always, All days, //Press-Corrector, //Body, UPDATE_ATTR, NO_PROP)
acp_8	(Always, All days, //director, /Newspaper, DELETE_ELEMT, FIRST_LEVEL)

We are now ready to formally define an access control policy.

Definition 1. (Access control policy). *An access control policy[2] is a tuple (*I*, *P*, sbj-spec, prot-obj-spec, priv, prop-opt), where:* I *is a temporal interval;* P *a periodic expression;* subject-spec *is an XPath-compliant expression on credentials or credential types;* prot-obj-spec *is an XPath-compliant expression denoting the protection objects to which the policy applies;* priv$\in$P *is a privilege; and* prop-opt$\in\{$NO_PROP, FIRST_LEVEL, CASCADE$\}$ *is a propagation option.*

Tuple (I,P,sbj-spec,prot-obj-spec,priv,pro-opt) states that subjects denoted by sbj-spec are allowed to exercise privilege priv on the protection objects identified by prot-obj-spec for each istant in interval I and denoted by the periodic expression P. Moreover, in the remainder of the paper the set of access control policies defined for source $\mathcal{S}$ is called *Policy Base* and denoted as $\mathcal{PB}$. It is important to note that besides the table representation given in the following example, Author-$\mathcal{X}$ encodes all the access control policies into an XML document according to $\mathcal{X}$-Sec language [8].

Example 1. Table 2 presents examples of access control policies defined for the XML document in Figure 3. The considered XML document models a newspaper, consisting of a leading article (modeled through the Leading_Article element). Like traditional paper-based newspapers, the example newspaper contains also

---

[2] We assume that each access control policy is uniquely identified by an identifier generated by the system when the policy is specified.

```
<Newspaper Title=''MyNewspaper'' Date=''04\10\03''>
  <Leading_Article>
    The leading article is inserted here!
    <Sections>
      <Section Author=''Smith'' Title=''...''>
      ......
      </Section>
    ......
    </Sections>
  </Leading_Article>
  <Science_page>
    <Science topic=''Astronomy'' Author=''Brown'' Title=''...''>
    ......
    </Science>
    <Science topic=''Biology'' Author=''Wright'' Title=''...''>
    ......
    </Science>
  ......
  </Science_page>
  <Literary_supplement day_of_issue=''Sunday''>
    <Article topic=''Poetry'' Author=''Lee'' Title=''...''>
    ......
    </Article>
    <Article topic=''Art'' Author=''Low'' Title=''...''>
    ......
    </Article>
  ......
  </Literary_supplement>
  <Sport_page>
    <News topic=''Football'' Author=''Evans'' Title=''...''>
      <Body>
      ......
      </Body>
    </News>
    <News topic=''Basket'' Author=''Smith'' Title=''...''>
      <Body>
      ......
      </Body>
    </News>
  ......
  </Sport_page>
</Newspaper>
```

Fig. 3.   An example of XML document

additional pages related to several topics. Each page is modeled by a different XML element (e.g., Science_page, Sport_page). Additionally, the Wednesday issue contains a financial supplement, whereas the Sunday issue contains a literary supplement. The XML document presented in Figure 3 represents a Sunday issue of the newspaper. All browsing policies are defined for the current year, whereas all authoring policies always hold. By contrast all the access control policies refer to the periodic expressions in Table 1. The first policy represents an annual subscription to the whole newspaper. By contrast, the second policy represents a subscription to Saturday and Sunday issues. The third policy states that subscribers to the Wednesday supplement can access the Financial supplement of the newspaper. Similarly, the fourth policy states that subjects subscribed to the Sunday supplement can access the Literary supplement of the newspaper. The fifth policy represents an annual subscription to the leading article contained into the Leading_Article element. The sixth policy allows the subject with credential identifier equals to "121" to view the News element associated with the author Smith and update all the attributes contained in that element and in its Body subelement. Similarly the seventh policy allows a press-corrector to update the content associated with all the Body elements in the newspaper. Finally, the eighth policy allows a director to delete the whole newspaper or one or more subelements of the Newspaper element. Thus, according to the credentials in Figure 2 and the access control policies in Table 2, Alice can access the whole newspaper during the week-end, and the Financial supplement on Wednesday. By contrast, Bob can read all newspaper issues for the whole year; Tom can always update the sport news whose author is himself, whereas Ann can delete the whole newspaper or one of its portions.

3.2   Dissemination Policies

Once the access control policies for a given source have been specified, XML documents belonging to the source can be released to subjects, on the basis of the specified policies. Author-$\mathcal{X}$ supports two different dissemination policies, which are described in the following:

- *Pull policies*. This is the traditional mode according to which access control usually takes place in conventional DBMSs. If the pull mode is adopted, the subjects explicitly require the XML documents (or portions of documents) when needed. Upon a document request, Author-$\mathcal{X}$ first verifies whether the requesting subject is entitled to access the requested document, according to the specified access control policies. Based on these authorizations, the subject is returned a *view* of the requested document(s), consisting of all and only those portions for which he/she has a corresponding authorization. When no authorizations are found, the access is denied.
- *Push policies*. Besides the traditional pull mode, also a push dissemination mode can be adopted in Author-$\mathcal{X}$. Indeed, this distribution mode is particularly suited for XML documents that must be released to a large community of subjects and which show a regular behaviour with respect to their release. According to the push modality, Author-$\mathcal{X}$ periodically (or when some pre-defined events happen) sends (portion of) its documents to authorized subjects, without the need of an explicit access request by the subjects. Also in this case, different subjects may have privileges to see different, selected portions of the same document based on the specified access control policies. To respect these different privileges, the mechanism enforcing information push must ensure a different view for each different subject.

In the following sections we focus only on the information push mechanism of Author-$\mathcal{X}$ since it represents the most novel approach to data dissemination. We refer the interested reader to [7] for a detailed description of information pull mechanism implemented in Author-$\mathcal{X}$.

4   Selective Dissemination: Author-$\mathcal{X}$ Push

Supporting information push entails generating different physical views of the same document for each group of subjects to which the same access control policies apply. This implies, in the worst case, the generation of a different view for each different subject. Moreover, after the generation of the view, the push

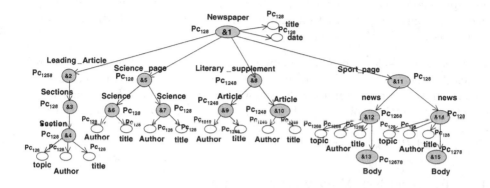

Fig. 4. Policy configurations for the XML document in Figure 3

dissemination mechanism must properly deliver all these views to the interested subjects. In this scenario, we need to take in consideration that due to the possibly high number of subjects accessing an XML source, and the wide range of access granularities provided by Author-$\mathcal{X}$, the number of these views may become considerable large and thus such an approach cannot be practically applied. To efficiently support information push we therefore have adopted an approach based on the use of encryption techniques. More precisely, our approach consists of using different encryption keys for encrypting different portions of an XML document, on the basis of the specified access control policies. According to this approach, all portions of an XML document to which the same *policy configuration* applies are encrypted with the same secret key, where with the term policy configuration we denote a set of access control policies belonging to $\mathcal{PB}$. Then, the same encrypted copy of the document (called well-formed encrypted document, hereafter) is distributed to all subjects, whereas each subject only receives the key(s) for the portion(s) he/she is enabled to access.

In the following to better clarify our approach we first briefly explain the encrypted document generation. Then we describe the key assignment scheme adopted in such a scenario.

4.1 Well-Formed Encryption

The first step to efficiently support the information push is the development of a strategy to generate a correct document encryption. In Author-$\mathcal{X}$ the generation of the document encryption consists of two main steps: first, the XML document undergoes a *marking phase* in which each document node is marked with the access control policies that apply to it; then, all nodes marked by the same policy configuration are grouped and encrypted with the same key. An additional key, called *default key*, is generated to encrypt those portions of the document which are not marked by any policy. The encrypted copy of the document is then placed into the Encrypted Document Base (i.e., $\mathcal{EDB}$), which stores the encrypted copies of all documents to be released under the push mode. In [2] two algorithms are presented for marking and encrypting an XML document, on the basis of the above strategy.

Example 2. Consider the XML document in Figure 3, and the access control policies in Table 2. In the following, to keep track of the policies composing a configuration, we use notation $Pc_{ijk...}$, where the subscript $ijk...$ denotes the policy configuration consisting of policies acp_i, acp_j, acp_k, ... Thus, the policy configurations marking the document are PC_{128}, PC_{1248}, PC_{1268}, PC_{1278}, PC_{1258}, and PC_{12678} as shown by Figure 4.

4.2   Temporal Key Management Scheme

The main issue in the generation of the well-formed encryption is that it could imply the management of a high number of secret keys. For instance, by using a traditional symmetric scheme, in the worst case the well-formed encryption implies the generation of 2^{N_p} different secret keys, where N_p is the number of access control policies in the $\mathcal{PB}$, that is, one for each different policy config-uration that could be generated from N_p policies. To cope with such an high number of secret keys, in [4] we have proposed a flexible key assignment scheme (adapted from [9]) which allows us to greatly reduce the number of keys that need to be managed. More precisely, the number of keys to be generated does not depend on the number of subjects nor on the document size, but it is linear in the number of specified access control policies.

According to our approach, each subject is required to register to the Author-$\mathcal{X}$ server, during a mandatory *subscription phase*. As depicted in Fig-ure 5, this phase is carried out by the *X-Admin* module, which, as result of the

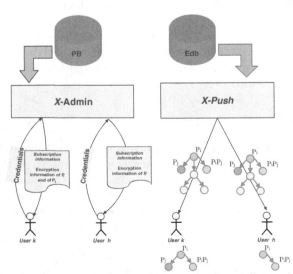

Fig. 5. The Author-$\mathcal{X}$ approach for supporting information push

subscription phase, returns to the subject a unique information, called *encryption information*, for each policy he/she satisfies and an additional set of initial parameters, called *subscription information*. Then, by using only such information the subject is able to derive the set of secret keys that makes him/her able to access all and only the portions of the encrypted document, received by *X-Push*, for which he/she has an authorization, and only for the time instants in which this authorization holds.

To achieve this goal, secret keys are constrained not only by the applicable access control policies but also by their periods of validity. Indeed, Author-$\mathcal{X}$ generates the secret keys by applying an hash function to two different components, called *class information* and *temporal information*, respectively. The first component is an information univocally associated with a policy configuration, whereas the second component binds each secret key to a precise time granule t (that is, the time at which the encryption takes place). Thus, at each time granule t, Author-$\mathcal{X}$ verifies whether a modification occurs in the XML source. In this case, it groups the modified source portions according to their policy configurations. Then, for each group it generates a secret key as a result of the hashing of the class information associated with that policy configuration and the temporal information corresponding to t.

The most relevant aspect of this key assignment scheme is that by using only the *encryption information* received during the subscription phase, a subject is able to generate all the keys associated with the policy configurations he/she satisfies, and to generate all the *temporal information* corresponding to time granules belonging to the interval of validity of the policies he/she satisfies. Indeed, the formula for the generation of the *class information* is defined in such a way that from each *encryption information* associated with a policy acp_i, it is possible to derive all and only the *class information* associated with a policy configuration containing acp_i. For instance, with referring to Figure 4 a subject receiving the *encryption information* associated with policy acp_2, is able to derive the class information associated with PC_{128}, PC_{1248}, PC_{1268}, PC_{1278}, PC_{1258}, and PC_{12678}.

Example 3. According to the access control policies presented in Table 2, Alice receives the encryption information associated with access control policies acp_3 and acp_2 (denoted as $Enc\_Inf(acp_3)$ and $Enc\_Inf(acp_2)$, respectively). Using $Enc\_Inf(acp_3)$ she can derive the class information of policy configuration PC_{123} and the temporal information w_t associated with all the time granules of the acp_3 period of validity. Thus, she can generate all the secret keys used to encrypt the set of nodes marked by PC_{1238}, that is, the subtree of the newspaper rooted at node `Financial_supplement`, at each Wednesday in [01/01/2003,12/31/2003]. By contrast, using $Enc\_Inf(acp_2)$, Alice can generate all the secret keys used to encrypt the set of nodes marked by PC_{128}, PC_{1248}, PC_{1268}, PC_{1278}, PC_{1258}, and PC_{12678} that is, all the issues of the newspaper, for each Saturday and Sunday in the temporal interval [01/01/2003,12/31/2003]. By contrast, Tom receives only the encryption information associated with access control policy acp_6, whereas Ann receives the encryption information associated with access control policy acp_8. Thus, by using $Enc\_Inf(acp_6)$ Tom is able to derive the class information of policy configurations PC_{1268} and PC_{12678} and the temporal information w_t associated with all the time granules of the acp_6 period of validity, that is, all the days. Finally, by using $Enc\_Inf(acp_8)$ Ann can derive the class information of policy configurations PC_{128}, PC_{1248}, PC_{1268}, PC_{1278}, PC_{1258}, and PC_{12678}.

5 Management of Distributed Updates

Author-$\mathcal{X}$ also provides an infrastructure for managing distributed and collaborative updates of XML documents [3]. This is a relevant feature since it is often the case that a document is subject to this type of process that takes place at specific period of times. The subjects involved in such an update process belong to a so-called *collaborative group*, that is, a set of subjects to which the document can be sent for update. Each of those subjects must be able to view and modify possibly different portions of the same document. In this scenario a document is sent by the system to a first subject belonging to the collaborative group, then this first subject chooses the next receiver and so forth until the document concludes its update process and is returned to the server. The path that must be followed by a document, generated according to the collaborative process type, can be either fully specified at the beginning of the process or be dynamically modified by the subjects that receive it. The document sent by the system to the first subject is encrypted following the strategy presented in Section 4.1, in which different portions of the same document are encrypted with the same symmetric key. Portions encrypted with the same key are those marked with the same policy configuration. Due to this encryption method each subject receives all and only the keys that decrypt document portions for which it has a proper authorization according to the policies in $\mathcal{PB}$. Our approach allows a subject that receives a document to check its integrity with respect to the modification operations executed over it till that point, without interacting with the document server. This goal is obtained by attaching to the encrypted document additional *control information* and by generating, according to the access control policies in $\mathcal{PB}$, some *authoring certificates* attesting the rights a subject possesses over a document, that the system takes care of sending to the corresponding subjects. The encrypted document and its corresponding control information form the *document package*.

In what follows we first present the structure of a document package (Section 5.1), and then the protocols for server and client side (Section 5.2).

5.1 Document Package

A document package contains an encrypted document, denoted in the following d^e, and the corresponding control information.

As we described in Section 4.1 to generate a well-formed encryption of an XML document the first step is the execution of a *marking* of the document. We recall that during this phase each portion of the document is marked with the access control policies that apply to it. We introduce at this point the notion of *region*, that is, the set of all document portions to which the same policy configuration applies. The regions of a document can be distinguished in *modifiable* and *non-modifiable* regions according to the privileges associated with the policy configuration of that region. A region is modifiable whether at least an access control policy that apply to it contains a privilege in the set {delete_attr, delete_elemt, or update_attr}, whereas a region is considered non-modifiable otherwise. Note that a region r to which an insert_attr|insert_elemt privilege applies is classified as non-modifiable, because an operation of insertion adds to the document a new region, leaving unmodified region r. Basic portions that compose a region are denoted with the term *atomic elements*. An atomic element can be the start and end tags of an element, the data content of an element, or an attribute. Each atomic element is identified by the identifier of the corresponding document element e,[3] followed by the reserved name: "**tags**", if the atomic element is the pair of tags of e, "**content**", if it is the data content of e or the **name** of an attribute of e otherwise.

Example 4. Example of atomic elements in the XML document in Figure 3 are:
   a) &6.*tags* corresponding to: "$< Science >$" "$< /Science >$";
   b) &4.*Author* corresponding to: "*Author* = "*Smith*"";
   c) &2.*content* corresponding to: "The leading article is inserted here".

Control information, added by the document server to the encrypted document, consists of some hash values and digital signatures computed over document portions. Non-modifiable and modifiable portions are protected region by region, generating proper control data structures, containing control information for each non-modifiable or modifiable region, denoted with the terms NMR_d and MR_d respectively.

Structure NMR_d contains for each non-modifiable region nmr an hash value computed over the content associated with the atomic elements belonging to nmr itself. These hash values are computed at the beginning of the update process, and are not modifiable by any subject that receives the package. They are used by the client protocol to check the integrity of the non-modifiable regions of the document.

To generate structure MR_d it is first necessary to generate for each atomic element, belonging to a modifiable region, an hash value computed over its corresponding content in the document. These hash values, contained in the structure MAE_d, are used to enable the client protocol to check also the integrity of the content associated with each single atomic element. MR_d contains for each modifiable region mr four hash values: 1) the first is computed over the mr content by the last but one subject (s_{last-1}) that operated over mr; 2) the second is computed over the hash values associated with the atomic elements belonging to mr by the last but one subject (s_{last-1}) that operated over mr; 3) the third is computed over the mr content by the last subject (s_{last}) that operated over

---

[3] In this paper element identifiers are represented as &n, where n is a natural number.

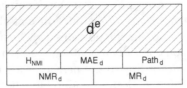

Fig. 6. Graphical representation of a document package

mr; 4) the fourth is computed over the hash values associated with the atomic elements belonging to mr by the last subject (s_{last}) that operated over mr. This is done to have in the package the last two states of the region content and of the hash values computed over the atomic elements belonging to that region.[4] If s_{last} has modified the content of a modifiable region mr, MR_d also contains a *modification declaration*. This declaration contains the set of atomic element identifiers that refer to the atomic element contents, belonging to mr, modified by s_{last}, together with the set of authoring certificates, belonging to s_{last}, involved in the region update. Hash values associated with the updated atomic elements are left unmodified by s_{last}, to enable a subsequent subject to correctly check the integrity of the updated region.

The system also computes a digital signature, stored in the control data structure H_{NMI}, over the structure NMR_d. This signature is used by the client protocol to check the integrity of the NMR_d structure. It is also required that in a control data structure, denoted as $Path_d$, each receiver inserts its identifier to compose the path already followed by the package till that point. When a fixed path is required by the update process the $Path_d$ control data structure is used to check the correct flow of the document, otherwise it is used to rebuild the path followed by the package till that point during a recovery session. Figure 6 shows the graphical representation of a document package.

5.2   Protocols

In this section we explain the protocols supporting the collaborative and distributed update process. Our system provides two main protocols, one at the server side, and another one at the client side.

Server Protocol. The server protocol generates the document packages and the authoring certificates, delivers a generated document package, at the specified period of times, to the subjects belonging to the corresponding collaborative group. It also manages recovery sessions whenever invoked by subjects.

A document package, for a given document, consists of the encrypted copy of the document and the hash values that compose the control data structures associated with the document.

---

[4] More details about how the client protocol checks the integrity of a modifiable region are given in Section 5.2.

The system also generates, according to the policies in $\mathcal{PB}$, and signs proper authoring certificates containing the following information:

- *priv*: it is an authoring privilege;
- *prot-obj*: it is a set of atomic elements belonging to a modifiable region, if *priv* is equal to *delete_attr*, *insert_attr*, *update_attr* or *insert_elemt*, otherwise it is a set of atomic elements belonging to one or more modifiable regions;
- *sbj_id*: it is a subject identifier specifying who can exercise the privilege *priv* over the protection object *prot-obj*.

Authoring certificates are inserted in the corresponding modification declaration by a subject whenever it modifies a portion of a document for which it has a proper authorization. In particular they are used by a subject to determine which authoring privileges it can exercise and over which portions of a document. Moreover they are used to guarantee other subjects, checking the integrity of a document d, that the declared modification operations were executed by an authorized subject and over the correct portions of d.

Example 5. Consider three users Tom (sbj_id=“s_{10}”), Bob (sbj_id=“s_{54}”) and Ann (sbj_id=“s_{102}”) with credentials reporter, press-corrector, and director, respectively. The following three authoring certificates are generated according to the policies in Table 2 and information in Figure 4:

- (update_attr, {&12.topic, &12.Author, &12.title}, s_{10});
- (update_attr, {&15.content}, s_{54});
- (delete_elemt, {&2.tags, &3.tags, &4.tags, &4.topic, &4.Author, &4.title}, s_{102}).

At the beginning of a collaborative and distributed update process the server protocol chooses the subject that must firstly receive the document package and then sends it to this subject. Whenever a subject finds that the received document package is corrupted the server protocol opens a recovery session in which it rebuilds the last correct version of the document package. This is achieved by requiring to the subjects in the collaborative group the last version of that document package that they received. Then the server protocol checks the integrity of the received document versions and chooses the correct received one that contains the longest path followed by the document package, and sends it to the subject that sent the recovery request.

Client Protocol. The client protocol is executed by a subject whenever it receives a document package. Such a protocol enables a receiver to check the integrity of the portions of the document for which it possesses an authorization, to exercise the authoring privileges according to the access control policies in $\mathcal{PB}$, and to send the updated document package to a subsequent receiver.

To check the integrity of a non-modifiable region *nmr* the client protocol locally computes an hash value over its content and then compares it with the one, associated with nmr, stored in the NMR_d structure. If the two hash values match the nmr content is correct, otherwise it is corrupted. Integrity of the hash values stored in NMR_d are checked using the digital signature stored in H_{NMI}. By contrast to check the integrity of a modifiable region mr, the client protocol firstly checks whether the last subject that operated over that region has modified it. We denote with the term *modified* a modifiable region for which a modification declaration is stored in MR_d. A region is denoted as *confirmed* when it results not to have been *modified*.

A confirmed region is checked by locally computing an hash value over its content and another over the hash values that cover the atomic elements belonging to that region. If these two hash values match those stored in MR_d for that region by s_{last-1} and by s_{last}, then the region is considered correct, otherwise it is corrupted.

A modified region is checked first by verifying that the atomic elements declared as modified were updated according to the authoring certificates stored in the modification declaration and that those certificates are *valid*. A certificate is valid if it belongs to s_{last} and its content is not corrupted. Then the client protocol checks that the atomic elements not declared as modified have kept the content they had before the update. This is done by comparing the hash values, stored in MAE_d, associated to these atomic elements with those locally computed over the current content of these atomic elements in the document. The integrity of the hash values in MAE_d is checked using the hash value computed by s_{last-1} over them.

The client protocol after the checking phase enables a subject to modify the document content according to the information contained in the authoring certificates it has received by the system. For each updated region the client protocol inserts in MR_d a modification declaration and the new computed hash values over the new region content and the hash values that cover the atomic elements belonging to that region.

Finally the client protocol allows a subject to choose the next subject to which sending the document package, and then it delivers the package to the chosen subject.

6   Conclusion

In this paper we have presented Author-$\mathcal{X}$, a comprehensive system for securing XML documents, which provides several innovative features, such as the support for different dissemination strategies (i.e., push and pull) and for the cooperative and distributed update of XML documents.

Even though Author-$\mathcal{X}$ is a very comprehensive system, supporting a large variety of functions, there is still room for extensions to the system. An open issue that we aim at addressing in the near future is how to enforce temporal constraints when dealing with distributed cooperative updates. Because a temporal constraint states that a given subject may modify a given document only within a specified time frame, a distributed cooperative update process may easily undergo denial-of-rights attacks by which a malicious subject may hold a document and send it to the legitimate subject only after the specified time frame has expired. Thus, the legitimate subject is denied the right to exercise the privileges it holds. Another direction concerns the development of policies governing the specification of dissemination strategy policies according to subject profiles and contextual information. Thus, by using such policies one can easily tailor the dissemination strategies for different subjects and/or conditions and time of use.

References

[1] E. Bertino, C. Bettini, E. Ferrari, and P. Samarati An Access Control Model Supporting Periodicity Constraints and Temporal Reasoning. *ACM Transaction on Database Systems, TODS*, 23(3):231–285, 1998. 73

[2] E. Bertino, and E. Ferrari. Secure and Selective Dissemination of XML Documents. *ACM Transactions on Information and System Security* 5(3): 290-331 (2002). 78

[3] E.Bertino, E.Ferrari, G.Mella, A Framework for Distributed and Cooperative Updates of XML Documents, *Proc. of the 16th Annual IFIP WG 11.3, Working Conference on Data and Application Security*, Cambridge, UK, July 2002, pp 211-227. 80

[4] E. Bertino, B. Carminati, E. Ferrari. A Temporal Key Management Scheme for Broadcasting XML Documents, *Proc. of the 9th ACM Conference on Computer and Communications Security (CCS'02)*, Washington, November, 2002, ACM Press. 78

[5] The Excelon Home Page. http://www.exceloncorp.com 69

[6] C. Geuer Pollmann. The XML Security Page. Available at: http://www.nue.et-inf.uni-siegen.de/~geuer-pollmann/ xml_security.html. 67

[7] E. Bertino, S. Castano, e E. Ferrari. Author-$\mathcal{X}$: a Comprehensive System for Securing XML Documents, *IEEE Internet Computing*, 5(3):21–31, May/June 2001. 70, 76

[8] E. Bertino, S. Castano, E. Ferrari. On Specifying Security Policies for Web Documents with an XML-based Language. *Proc. of SACMAT'2001, ACM Symposium on Access Control Models and Technologies*, Fairfax, VA, May 2001. 70, 74

[9] Wen-Guey Tzeng. A Time-Bound Cryptographic Key Assignment Scheme for Access Control in a Hierarchy *IEEE TKDE*, 14(1):182–188, 2002. 78

[10] M. Winslett, N. Ching, V. Jones, I. Slepchin. Using Digital Credentials on the World Wide Web. *Journal of Computer Security*, v.5 n.3, p.255-267, Dec. 1997. 70

[11] World Wide Web Consortium. Extensible Markup Language (XML) 1.0, 1998. Available at: http://www.w3.org/TR/REC-xml 66

[12] World Wide Web Consortium. XML Signature Syntax and Processing, 2002. Available at: http://www.w3.org/TR/2002/REC-xmldsig-core-20020212/ 71

[13] World Wide Web Consortium. XML Path Language (Xpath), 1.0, 1999. W3C Recommendation. Available at: http://www.w3.org/TR/xpath. 71

What's Wrong with Wrapper Approaches in Modeling Information System Integration and Interoperability?

Tosiyasu L. Kunii

IT Institute
Kanazawa Institute of Technology
1-15-13 Jingumae, Shibuya-ku
Tokyo 150-0001 Japan
Phone +81-3-5410-5280, FAX +81-3-5410-3057
tosi@kunii.com
http://www.kunii.com/

Abstract. Among the largest impact research themes at the time of world-wide recession, the key subject is how to cope with mega company formations and e-government (digital government) projects that depend on the successes of information system integration. The current information system integration approaches such as wrapper approaches basically create combinatorial interfacing and/or combinatorial data conversion making the integration practically impossible because of interfacing explosion and/or computational explosion. A linear approach to overcome the combinatorial explosion is presented and discussed.

1   What Are Impact Projects at the Time of World-Wide Recession?

It has been a while since I have stated the following: "Web information management systems are emerging as key players in the global society we live [Kunii98]. As a matter of fact, the global society has been driven by cyberworlds on the Web. Cyberworlds are types of information worlds created on the Web with or without design. The major key players of cyberworlds include e-finance that trades a GDP-equivalent a day and e-manufacturing that is transforming industrial production into Web shopping of product components and of assembly factories. We can handle the complexity and the growth speed of such cyberworlds only through Web information management systems by processing them instantly as needed [Kunii2002a]."

However, the international situations have changed a lot in a year. Continued gulf wars, ever prevailing international terrorisms and SARS (severe acute respiratory syndrome) have been spreading economic havoc, forcing companies and governmental organizations to merge for survival as mega corporations and digital governments. Organization-wise merges do not save anything much any longer. It rather simply aims at eliminating further workplaces, resulting in more and more lay-offs to make the economy worse. First of all it does not usually mean organizational

N. Bianchi-Berthouze (Ed.): DNIS 2003, LNCS 2822, pp. 86-96, 2003.
© Springer-Verlag Berlin Heidelberg 2003

operation merge. The main reason is that the current information system technology provides element-by-element operation merge with inevitable combinatorial explosion. It is well known that the combinatorial explosion is the source of sky high cost coupled with almost infinite delay of operation merge after the organizational merge.

Thus, since the expectation of prolonged recession causes more and more organizations to merge, the project that has the largest impact factor is that on non-combinatorial organizational operation merge. As such, the ideal is linear.

2   How the Combinatorial Explosion of Organizational Operation Merge Has Brought in?

Major changes of information worlds are now requiring the world model changes. The combinatorial explosion of organizational operation merge is the result of the individual designers working hard to create their "best" interfaces for the merge. Such "hard work" creates different designs for interfacing of the different information systems in charge of individual organizational operations.

The situation is very similar to that when the relational model was proposed by E. F. Codd in 1970 [Codd]. At that time, commercial database management systems (DBMS) were pointer-based such as CODASYL and IBM IMS. When data changes occurred at some organization, the databases had to be updated manually. At individual customer sites, employees of DBMS companies were sort of sold to the customer sites spending the whole lives for manual data and pointer updates. They did best database design updating the pointers. That tragedy was saved by data independence of the relational model. When I organized Codd's seminar on the relational model in 1970 in Tokyo inviting major DBMS vendors and experts, everybody refused to get it recognized as a DBMS model by the reason the model lacked pointers! The trend to refuse to recognize the value of the relational model in data independence had continued for at least a decade. I myself in supporting data independence had been treated as a foe of the DBMS community by experts, although I have organized Database Technical Committee and Research Group at Information Processing Society of Japan in 1972 and served as Vice-Chairman, and was a member of IFIP Working Group 2.6 on Data Bases soon after (1974 to 1992).

For information system integration, there is no model currently. Hence, the combinatorial explosions. One of the cases causing the combinatorial explosions is what's called "wrappers". Wrappers can wrap anything in any style, creating varieties of "flexible" designs and ending up with remarkable design combinations to explode.

Before going into the detailed analysis of the current and possible world models for information system integration, let us look back the way I was on information system integration since 1974.

2.1   The Inductive Inference Approach for Information System Integration

In 1974, I have discussed with E. F. Codd on the problem of inconsistency in functional dependency when we have time-dependent database systems. The problem

I faced occurred when I was designing an image database for image analysis. It is a typical time dependent database as often seen in active image databases where new image data instances are constantly flowing in. New data instances may destroy existing functional dependency requiring constant data renormalization. The answer he gave me was very firm that the relational model he designed is under assumption of the world model such that the functional dependencies are wholly controlled by one person called a data administrator as typically seen in managing the database of one organization. He also clarified that any model beyond the world model of assuming one data administrator was outside of his interest. So I had to solve the problem myself. To avoid laborious manual work of renormalization, I have devised an automated renormalization scheme based on mechanical inductive inference on cumulative image database up to the point in time [Kunii74]. It is equivalent to joining all the relations to turn them into one relation and mechanically induce functional dependencies for automated renormalization. The same situation arises when we integrate multiple information systems where up to the point in time of integration, we can automate renormalization of integrated database by the same inductive scheme.

2.2   Design Criteria for Distributed Database Systems

In 1977, Tosiyasu L. Kunii and Hideko S. Kunii have started to work on distributed database systems and the design criteria. We have shown that an abstract design approach can avoid the combinatorial complexity [Kunii77]. Since it was before the dawn of the Internet-based databases, it was on a very general modeling.

Starting from the classifications of the current distributed database systems, this work has identified their two major objectives: the database sharing among the subsystems, and the increase of system adaptivity. The design approaches to meet these respective objectives, that is, compositional- and decompositional- approaches are identified.

The design criteria related to these approaches are elucidated: the minimum Upper Bound of Information Translation Amount (UBITA) in database sharing as a criterion for the compositional design approach; the maximum locality as a criterion for the decompositional design approach. Different design models are tested against these design criteria, by taking typical distributed database system environments. In pursuit of highly adaptive design for very general evolving heterogeneous distributed database systems, an abstract design approach is proposed. It is expected that this design also minimizes the system maintenance load which has already taken up with three times more man power than the system development work. In this approach, Applications (A), Data (D), Machines (M), and a system Controller (C) are identified as major logical subsystems of an evolving heterogeneous distributed database system. Two sets of three independences (3Is, that is, Application-, Data-, and Machine- Independences) criteria are proposed for adaptive evolving heterogeneous system design:

1.   3Is for a non-cascading system design to prevent a change in any one of the A-, D-, and M- subsystems from cascading into the other two logical subsystems, and

2. 3Is for an invariant system controller to keep the system controller invariant under any change in the A-, D-, or M- subsystems.

It is also shown that the conventional data independence is insufficient for adaptive system design. A virtualization method is discussed as a way to fulfill the two sets of the 3Is criteria.

3   How to Meet the Application-, Data-, and Machine- Independence Criteria?

It is extremely hard to meet the application-, data-, and machine- independence criteria.

Theorem: Adjunctions spaces represent the information common to all applications, data and machines to meet the application-, data-, and machine- independence criteria.

Proof: We give an intuitive proof. The only way to achieve the goal is to find a very high level of abstraction mechanism to abstract the information common to all applications, data and machines. It has been 26 years to find the answer to meet the criteria by finding the meaning of "common" and what's common as "adjunction spaces in algebraic topology [Kunii2003]. "To be common" means "to be equivalent so that the equivalent information is shared to be common".   Equivalence relations mathematically define the meaning of to be equivalent. Equivalent information forms adjunction spaces via identification functions on quotient spaces that are also called identification spaces. Then, adjunctions spaces represent the information common to all applications, data and machines to meet the application-, data-, and machine-independence criteria.   Q.E.D.

The adjunction spaces also model the common properties of dominant commercial information systems being used by major private and public organizations by abstracting the common properties to be equivalent among different information systems as adjunction spaces, thus serving as a novel data model that can integrate information systems linearly and hence avoiding the combinatorial explosion of the integration workload.   For automated linear interface generation after the linear integration at the adjunction space level, we use an incrementally modular abstraction hierarchy [Kunii2002a] as shown below such that we are interfaced to existing information systems to the extent we realize linear interoperability to perform the integrated system-wide tasks.

1. The homotopy level;
2. The set theoretical level;
3. The topological space level;
4. The adjunction space level;
5. The cellular space level;
6. The representation level;
7. The view level.

The details on this theme require intensive case analysis and case studies after careful theoretical studies.   We are currently working on it with promising perspectives. The major problems we have been encountering are how to work with dominant existing systems that have no clean interoperability provisions.   The relational model is a typical example. We briefly summarize such problems in the following chapter. To be practical, we have to rely on varieties of APIs (application programming interfaces) and tools to achieve the automation goal as much as possible.   Still the relational model-based information systems are the easiest to achieve the automated linear interface generation to integrate them at the adjunction space level by extracting the cellular space level information of different information systems and to achieve the linear interoperability. There are numbers of Java APIs and C++ APIs for us to implement the automated linear integration and linear interoperability. Enterprise Resource Planning (ERP) are also fairly easy to achieve liner automated integration by our approach because in formalism ERP is graph theoretical and easily transformed to process graphs (Figure 1) [Kunii97] supported by the relational model.

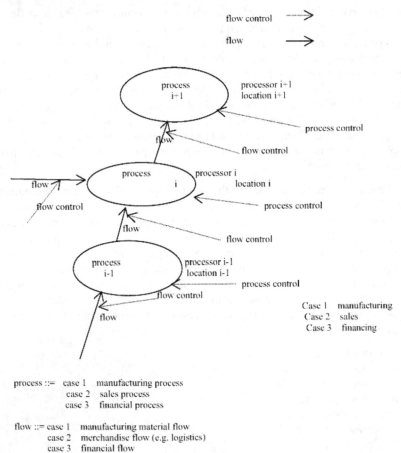

Fig. 1. A process graph

The process graphs are generalized to enjoy the theoretical properties of the incrementally modular abstraction hierarchy by representing them in the adjunction spaces first followed by the cellular spaces as needed.   Abundant ontological properties appear in process graphs, very often with nesting as we worked out in 1980 under the name of recursive graphs [Kunii80]. It also is called conceptual graphs [Sowa84, Sowa2002, Schärfe]. It is being formulated by the incrementally modular abstraction hierarchy.   The recursive graph (conceptual graph) formulation in the incrementally modular abstraction hierarchy obviously requires the topological spaces to be half Hausdorff (T_0). Therefore, since the most of the topological researches are in the Hausdorff topological spaces (T_2), we have to restart the formulation from T_0.

4   Comparison with the Relational Model, the Entity Relationship Model, UML, and XML

As I have proven in the previous DNIS paper [Kunii2002a], none of the currently popular information models such as the relational model, UML, and XML have the information modularity simply because they are not based on the disjoint unions of information.   Hence, modular Web information modeling based on equivalence to identify necessary information does *not* apply to any of them.

Suppose on the Web a company X is searching for a joint venture partner company, say Y. After the successful search, a joint venture (JV) is formed such that $X \square Y / (x \bar{a} f(y) | \cdot y \, \text{R} \, Y_0)$ via an attaching function f An attaching map f where f: $Y_0 \rightarrow X | Y_0 \square Y$. $Y_0 \square Y$ is the part of company Y running the JV with the corresponding part f(Y_0) of company X.   As a model, this JV model belongs to, and is exactly identical with, the adjunction space model explained so far.   Now, let us suppose a company X is searching for a company, say Y, to merge and acquire (M&A) Y. After successful M&A, denoting the part Y_0 of Y ($Y_0 \square Y$) merged to X, we get the union of X and Y joined by the part $Y_0 \square Y$ common to that of Y such that $X \square Y / (x \bar{a} f(y) | \cdot y \, \text{R} \, Y_0)$. In the relational model, the join operation performs M&A, but the relational model fails to support JV. Union by join in manufacturing makes the product parts irreplaceable and makes it impossible to enjoy the advantages of e-manufacturing. The frame of a bicycle in Figure 2 is built by fusing the parts via join operations, and hence the parts are hard to be replaced or interchanged. The entity relationship (ER) model is basically an intuitive graph theoretical model, and the model itself fails to support the identification by equivalence. So is UML.

XML is flexible, born from bibliographic markup language SGML. It consists of nested pairs of brackets, lacking formalisms to validate the ever-expanding and complicated nesting. When the system being constructed becomes very large as usual in any practices, it falls apart by the lack of the formal and hence automated mechanism of validation.   We have to formulate XML in the half Hausdorff spaces T_0.

Fig. 2. The frame of a bicycle made by fusing components via join operations

5   What Has Been Popular in General such as "Wrappers" and What's Wrong with Them?

There have varieties of approaches in information system integration and interoperability. Let us browse through them.

5.1   Standardizing vs. Theorizing

Standardizing is on the assumption for the existing systems to be rebuilt to follow a given specification called the "standard". For information systems as the infrastructure of major social organizations, the cost of the rebuilding is prohibitively high to make the assumption usually invalid.

Posing theorizing as a counter-concept of standardization, let us examine it. If we define theorizing in the following way, it becomes valuable: Theorizing means reasoning on the required features of major information systems followed by abstracting the common features of such systems to find the consistent logical structures called theories.

5.2   Modeling and Designing as the First Phase

Now, suppose we do not standardize. Then, if we make the modeling and the designing the first phase without theorizing, we end up with a combination of the models and designs of different information systems leading us to combinatorial explosions.

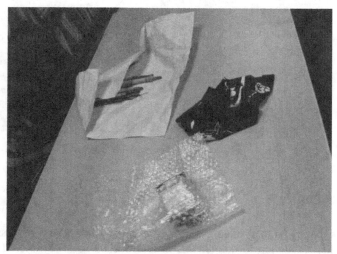

Fig. 3. Varieties of wrappers in the real world

5.3   Wrappers: What's Wrong?

Saying "interfaced by wrappers" does not mean more than "interfaced somehow".

Historically what meant by wrappers have been in more and more varieties including interfaces in general, relational extensions [Stonebraker]. There have been mediated system wrappers and extensive ontological studies by Wiederhold [Wiederhold94, Wiederhold2000] that require our careful attentions. Yet his model is still at the set theoretical level and I view more abundant ontological aspects to be incorporated by reformulating his Domain Knowledge- Base (DKB) model by our incrementally modular abstraction hierarchy. The notion of wrappers is too general and vague, and inevitably leads the information system integration tasks to end up with combinatorial explosion of different wrappers.

6   Conclusions

We have examined the troubles of existing models and approaches in integrating information systems and establishing interoperability, combinatorial explosion in particular. A liner integration model with linear interoperability is presented as the remedy based on the incrementally modular abstraction hierarchy.

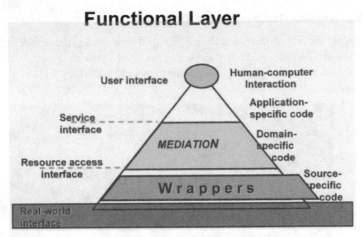

Fig. 4. Wiederhold's wrappers [Wiederhold2000]

Acknowledgements

The author's thanks go to Professor Nadia Bianchi-Berthouze and Professor Subhash Bhalla for their invitation to deliver this at DNIS 2003 as a keynote. I also like to dedicate this research to the memory of my friend Edger F. Codd.

References

[Codd]   Edger F. Codd, "A Relational Model of Data for Large Shared Data Banks. CACM 13(6): 377-387 (1970).

[Kunii74]   T. L. Kunii, S. Weyl and J. M. Tenenbaum, "A Relational Data Base Schema for Describing Complex Picture with Color and Texture", Proc. of the 2nd International Joint Conference on Pattern Recognition, pp.3I0-3I6 (Lyngby-Copenhagen, August 1974) [also available as Stanford Research Institute Technical Note 93, SRI Project 8721 (June 1974); reprinted in Policy Analysis and Information Systems, Vol. 1, No. 2, pp. 127-142 (January 1978).

[Kunii77]   Tosiyasu L. Kunii and Hideko S. Kunii, "Design Criteria for Distributed Database Systems", Proc. of the third International Conference on Very Large Data Bases (VLDB 77), pp. 93I04, (Tokyo, Japan, October 1977), IEEE, New York, NY, USA, 1977.

[Kunii80]   Tosiyasu L. Kunii and Minoru Harada, "SID: A System for Interactive Design", Proceedings of National Computer Conference 1980, AFIPS Conference Proceedings, Vol.49, pp.33-40 (AFIPS Press, Arlington, Virginia, 1980).

[Kunii97]   Tosiyasu L. Kunii, "The 21st Century Manufacturing Automation
                 and the Social Impact", Proceedings of International Conference on
                 Manufacturing Automation (ICMA'97), April 28-30, 1997, Hong
                 Kong, pp.21-29 , A. T .Tan, T. N. Wong and I. Gibson, Editors
                 (Department of Mechanical Engineering, University of Hong
                 Kong).

[Kunii98]   Tosiyasu L. Kunii and Annie Luciani, Eds., "Cyberworlds",
                 Springer-Verlag, 1998.

[Kunii2000]   Tosiyasu L. Kunii, "Discovering Cyberworlds", Vision 2000 of the
                 January/February, 2000 Issue of IEEE Computer Graphics and
                 Applications, pp. 64-65.

[Kunii99]   Tosiyasu L. Kunii and Hideko S. Kunii, "A Cellular Model for
                 Information Systems on the Web - Integrating Local and Global
                 Information -", 1999 International Symposium on Database
                 Applications in Non-Traditional Environments   (DANTE'99),
                 November 28-30, 1999, Heian Shrine, Kyoto, Japan, Organized by
                 Research Project on Advanced Databases, in cooperation with
                 Information Processing Society of Japan, ACM Japan, ACM
                 SIGMOD Japan, pp. 19-24, IEEE Computer Society Press, Los
                 Alamitos, California, U. S. A.

[Stonebraker]   Michael Stonebraker and Paul Brown, "Object-Relational DBMSs –
                 Tracing the Next Great Wave-", Morgan Kaufmann Publishers, Inc.,
                 San Francisco, CA USA, 1999.

[Kunii2002a]   Tosiyasu L. Kunii, "Web Information Modeling: The Adjunction
                 Space Model", Proceedings of the 2nd International Workshop on
                 Databases in Networked Information Systems (DNIS 2002), pp. 58-
                 63, The University of Aizu, Japan, December 16-18, 2002, Lecture
                 Notes in Computer Science, Subhash Bhalla, Ed., Springer-Verlag,
                 December, 2002.

[Kunii2002b]   Tosiyasu L. Kunii, "Cyber Graphics", Proceedings of the First
                 International Symposium on Cyber Worlds (CW2002), November
                 6-8 2002 Tokyo, Japan, pp. 3-7, IEEE Computer Society Press, Los
                 Alamitos, California, November 2002.

[Kunii2003]   Tosiyasu L. Kunii, Masumi Ibusuki, Galina I. Pasko, Alexander A.
                 Pasko, Daisuke Terasaki, and Hiroshi Hanaizumi, "Modeling of
                 Conceptual Multiresolution Analysis by an Incrementally Modular
                 Abstraction Hierarchy", Transactions of Institute of Electronics,
                 Information and Communication Engineers, in press, July 2003.

[Sowa84]   John F. Sowa: "Conceptual Structures: Information Processing in
                 Mind and Machine", Addison-Wesley 1984.

[Sowa2002]   John F. Sowa, "Architectures for intelligent systems", IBM Systems
                 Journal 41(3): 331-349 (2002).

[Schärfe]   Henrik Schärfe, "Online Course in Knowledge Representation using
                 Conceptual Graphs", http://www.hum.auc.dk/cg/index.html.

[Wiederhold94] Gio Wiederhold, "Interoperation, Mediation, and Ontologies", Proceedings of International Symposium on Fifth Generation Computer Systems FGCS94), Workshop on Heterogeneous Cooperative Knowledge-Bases, Vol. W3, pp. 33-48, ICOT, Tokyo, Japan, December 1994.
[Wiederhold2000] Gio Wiederhold, "Mediated Systems", http://www-db.stanford.edu/pub/gio/slides/.

Browsing and Editing XML Schema Documents with an Interactive Editor

Mark Sifer[1], Yardena Peres[2], and Yoelle Maarek[2]

[1] School of IT, University of Sydney
NSW, 2006, Australia
sifer@it.usyd.edu.au
[2] Knowledge Management Group, IBM Research Lab in Haifa
Matam, 31905, Israel
{yardena,yoelle}@il.ibm.com

Abstract. With the advent of the web there has been a great demand for data interchange between existing applications using internet infrastructure and also between newer web services applications. The W3C XML standard is becoming the internet data interchange format, even though the initial XML standard was not well suited to this. The XML Schema recommendation which added more rigorous data structuring and data typing provides much better support for defining such data centric XML documents. While data centric XML documents are typically produced by applications there are still a wide range of situations where manual document creation is required. This paper presents an XML editor design which supports the creation of XML Schema based documents. We show how an interface that uses a tight coupling between grammar and content views facilitates the rapid creation of data centric documents. We show how our interface supports browsing and editing of documents where XML schema specific extensions such as subtyping are present. Our design is realised in the Xeena for Schema tool which we demonstrate.

1   Introduction

With the advent of the web there has been increasing demand for data interchange between existing applications using internet infrastructure and also between newer web services applications. The W3C XML [4] recommendation is becoming the internet data interchange format. Such XML data will typically be produced by applications. However during application development and maintenance there remains a significant need for manual creation, editing and browsing of XML data by application and system developers. XML editors can fill this need.

XML or rather the eXtensible Markup Language defines a standard way to markup data and documents as text files. These files (or data streams) which are referred to as documents may be restricted to comply with a gram-mar -- a Document Type Definition (DTD) or an XML Schema [13], but this is not compulsory. Tags are used to

N. Bianchi-Berthouze (Ed.): DNIS 2003, LNCS 2822, pp. 97-111, 2003.

denote the start and end of elements which are nested, forming a tree of elements. A mid level element may denote a whole purchase order record while a leaf element may capture a numeric cost. Data interchange between applications, in addition to a common data format, requires a data exchange protocol such as the Simple Object Access Protocol (SOAP) [10].

XML was originally developed as a simplified version of the Standard Generalized Markup Language (SGML) [7] for the web. SGML is primarily used for maintaining large technical document collections. SGML grammars are defined with DTDs which include complex features that were not included when XML DTDs were defined. However, a general limitation of DTDs is their poor support for data typing. Recently XML Schema has been defined to add much richer data and structure typing which better supports data oriented applications and data exchange.

Specific applications of XML include MathML (Mathematics Markup language), X3D (XML 3D) and XHTML (XML HTML). These applications define how data intended for display in a web browser should be marked up, where display rules are defined in separate style sheets. Because of the increasing availability of XML software libraries, XML is also being used as a data storage format for persistent data when the overhead of a database is not needed. Such applications of XML can also require a generic XML editor for the creation and editing of XML data and documents.

Because XML documents are human readable text files, a standard text editor can be used as a generic XML editor. For users that are already familiar with XML syntax, using a text editor can the easiest way of creating or modifying small XML documents. Otherwise a dedicated XML editor may be easier to use. In this paper we present our design for an interactive XML editor design for documents which conform to an XML Schema. The benefits of our editor are: (i) users do not need to know XML syntax, (ii) they do not need to remember the schema grammar and (iii) through the use of interactive templates users can rapidly build and alter XML documents.

This paper extends the treatment of our editor in [9] where support for browsing XML documents was de-scribed. It provides a full treatment of editing including operations for changing types and support for W3C XML schema subtyping.

In the second section an example XML document fragment is introduced. Requirements for an editor are established in section three. Browsing and editing of documents is shown in sections four and five, while XML schema specific support is detailed in section six. Validation is covered in section seven. Then finally, related work is described and conclusions given

2   Example

In this section we introduce the main data and schema example used in this paper, a small addressbook document.

```
<?xml version="1.0" encoding="UTF-8"?>
<addressbook xmlns:xsi=http://www.w3.org/2001/XMLSchema-instance>
<person first-name="Robert" family-name="Brown" middle- initial=
  "L." employee-number="A7000">
  <contact-info>
    <email address="robb@iro.ibm.com" />
    <home-phone number="03-3987873" />
  </contact-info>
  <address state="NY" city="New York" street="118 St." number=
    "344" />
  <job-info is-manager="true"  job-description="Group Leader"  em-
    ployee-type="Full-Time" />
  <manager employee-number="A0000" />
</person>
...
</addressbook>
```

The document contains an addressbook which includes multiple person records, one of which is shown. A person record includes name, contact, address, job info and manager information. Names are stored in attributes while contact, address, job info and manager info are stored in sub elements. A contact-info element may contain one or more home or work phone numbers or email addresses. A summary of the address-book element structure is shown in figure one as an BNF based grammar.

```
addressbook  = { person }
person       = ?contact-info + address + job-info
               + manager + ?misc-info
contact-info = { [ home-phone | mobile-phone | email ] }


{A}   zero or more A          [A | B]   choice of A or B
?A    optional A              A+B       sequence of A then B
```

Fig. 1. The addressbook grammar

Some definitions are needed. A document is well-formed when it follows XML tag syntax and element nesting. If a well-formed document also follows all the rules speci-fied in a grammar (whether its a DTD or schema) it is valid. A document is structur-ally valid when it is well-formed and follows all the structure (element typing) rules in a grammar, but perhaps does not follow some data type rules. When documents are manually created they will often be in an invalid state. If a document is structurally valid except for some missing choice elements (alternatives in the grammar) it is par-tially valid. If a document is partially valid except for some missing compulsory ele-ments then it is weakly valid. A weakly valid document is said to *conform to the grammar*, as there are no parent-child element pairs which violate any parent-child rules in the grammar.

3   Requirements for an XML (Schema Instance) Editor

Requirements for an XML editor can be very broad. Editors can be used in a wide variety of roles, such as: assisting with the conversion of text documents into XML, data entry for a database system, ad-hoc creation and editing of specialised applications such as XHTM and the creation and editing of data for data interchange systems. Another dimension is whether the documents to be edited will conform to a specified grammar and if so what kind of grammar. Choices include DTDs (Document Type Definitions), XML Schema, Relax, Schematron and others. The first two are W3C recommendations, while the latter are private proposals which have been widely disseminated. When grammar conformance is required, other dimensions include: the likely size and complexity of the grammar, how familiar users are with the grammar and what level of conformance to the grammar the input documents will have.

Our interface design targets the editing of documents that have an XML Schema grammar and are weakly valid. We wanted to support a spectrum of grammars, from small ones for novice users to large and complex ones for experienced users. In particular, we wanted the interface to make the maximum use of the grammar information, so that a user can create and edit documents with a minimum number of choices and steps, where editing steps that can be inferred are done automatically. Users should be provided with an editing context, so that editing operations proceed by making choices from alternatives that are always visible rather than expecting a user to remember parts of a grammar. This will suit both specialised applications and data interchange, where conformance to a grammar can be expected.

For data interchange, XML Schema or Relax are the best grammar candidates because of their strong support for data typing. Our interface design does not support the conversion of arbitrary text documents into XML, because even if there is a grammar, it cannot be used to accurately guide edit operations. Further such text documents will typically contain sections that are not be well formed.

Once editor requirements are defined, there are still a variety of interface styles that can be used. Content focused and structured focused are two styles. The former typically uses a free form text view of the document supplemented with tag highlighting and perhaps a coordinated tree (structure) overview. The latter typically uses a tree view of the document supplemented with a coordinated views of element content such as attributes and character content.

We choose to use the latter style, and extend it with a coordinated grammar view to provide better support to users that are less familiar with XML syntax and grammars. With our interface user do not need to see markup tags or read an XML schema grammar, rather they are guided by a coordinated tree view of the grammar.

4   Browsing with Coordinated Grammar and Document Views

A key feature of our design for interactive XML editing is the use of a coordinated grammar and instance views of an XML document. Figure two shows a screenshot of our editor browsing addressbook data. Tree representations of the addressbook schema (grammar view) and instance (document view) are shown in the left and right panels respectively. Editing operations are done via the toolbar on the frame's top.

Figure two shows the startup screen (minus an attribute table at the bottom of the frame) where the root document element "addressbook" is selected. Only one level of children is shown in both document and grammar views. The (1) and (*) icons in the

grammar view indicates one addressbook element is required while an arbitrary number of person elements are required. A user browses a document by selecting elements
(by clicking it's title) and by expanding or contracting the element subtrees in the
document view. Figure three shows the result of selecting the first person element in
the document view.

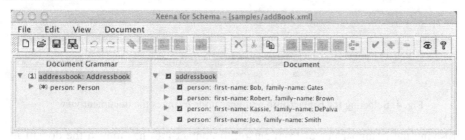

Fig. 2. Our editor interface showing grammar and instance views of addressbook data

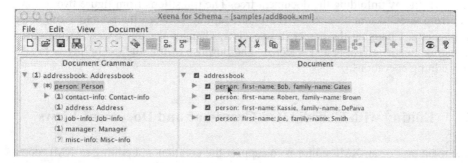

Fig. 3. Selecting the person element in the document view changes the grammar view

Figure three shows a changed grammar view. Selecting a person element in the
document view changed the grammar view automatically, so that the person node and
its children are visible. If the user selects a node in the grammar view there is a similar
effect on the document view. For example, if the contact-info node in the grammar
view is selected, the document view will change to show the corresponding subelement in the first person element, as shown in figure four. However, note that if
another person element subtree (such as for Kassie) were open prior to selecting the
contact-info grammar node, it would remain open after the grammar node selection.
Selections in the grammar view open additional document subtrees, allowing multiple
top-level document nodes to remain open.

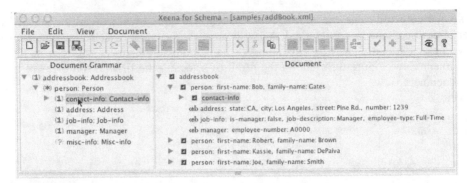

Fig. 4. Selecting the contact-info grammar node changes the document view

Moving the grammar cursor from person to contact-info has moved the document cursor to the contact-info element within the first person element, which has been made visible by unfolding the document tree. The transitions from figure two to three and from three to four show there is a tight coupling between the grammar and document views. Changing the cursor in one view, changes the other view so the corresponding cursor is visible and selected. The purpose of this tight coupling is to support editing operations.

5   Editing with Coordinated Grammar and Document Views

The main task of an XML editor is to support the creation and editing of XML documents. This is done through editing operations such as adding, moving, changing and deleting elements. When an XML document conforms to a grammar, elements can not be added anywhere. Particular elements can only appear in certain contexts which are defined by the grammar. Our interface uses a grammar view panel to provide users with a continuous grammar context to guide editing.

5.1   Adding and Moving Elements

As noted in section four, the grammar view and document share a coordinated cursor which is shown as the selected grammar node and document element in each view. Highlighting is also used to indicate which grammar nodes have been instantiated in the document. For example in figure four, the selected contact-info node and three of its siblings have coloured (dark) icons, while the fourth sibling misc-info has a ghosted icon. Glancing across at the document view reveals the selected contact-info element has only three sibling elements. There is no misc-info element.

The difference in icon colour in the grammar view highlights the misc-info info element could be added into the document at the current document cursor position by selecting the misc-info grammar node then clicking the add element button on the upper toolbar. A misc-info element would then be added in the correct position in the document view. The coordinated grammar view has highlighted via icon colouring what additions can be made to the current document position, so that when a grammar node is chosen, new elements can be created in the correct position automatically.

Another example of editing is shown in figure five. The contact-info grammar node was expanded so its child nodes home-phone, mobile-phone and email were visible, followed by SHIFT-selecting the home-phone grammar node. Alternatively, the user could have selected the home-phone grammar node then clicked the add element button on the toolbar. This creates a home-phone element in the document nested in the correct position within the contact-info element. If there were any intermediate types between the home-phone grammar node and its ancestor contact-info, instances of these would also have been created in the document. If home-phone had any compulsory children they also would have been created by this edit operation. In general, if the grammar requires an element to exist in the document after an edit operation, it is added automatically. This ensures our editor always maintains a document as a partially valid document.

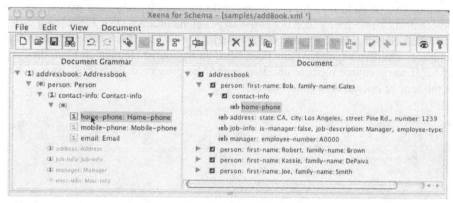

Fig. 5. The result of adding a home-phone element by clicking in the grammar view

While new documents can be rapidly built by just deciding which elements to add and then filling in their attribute and content data. In practice some elements may need to be rearranged. With our interface, elements are moved via cut, copy and paste operations which are done in the document view. These operations are permitted only when they preserve the partial validity of the document. For example an email element can not be copied into a location where a person element is expected. The enabling and disabling of the paste toolbar buttons according to the current cut/copied element and the current document cursor enforces this. Next we show how changing element types is supported via the grammar view.

5.2   Changing an Element's Type by Changing Choices

An XML document can be built by successively adding desired elements from the grammar view. The addition of an element that is optional or can be repeated requires a user decision. The addition of an element that is part of a choice term in the grammar also requires a decision. The decision to add an optional or repeated element can be changed by deleting it. However, changing the addition of a choice element is more complex if it already has content below it which should be preserved.

Recall figure five, which showed the result of choosing to add a home-phone element. To revisit and change this choice, the user selects the home-phone element, which moves the grammar cursor back to the corresponding home-phone grammar node. Next the user changes the choice, by for example selecting the mobile-phone grammar node then clicking the "change" button on the toolbar, so that the home-phone element is replaced by a mobile-phone element. Figure six shows the result.

The editor offers two change element operations. One which preserves children where possible, and another which doesn't. If home-phone and mobile-phone types both contain the same child element types say phone-number and area-code, the former change operation would preserve these, while the latter operation would replace the home-phone element and its child elements with an empty mobile-phone element.

A heuristic is used to preserve as many child elements as possible when a change operations source child element and target child element types do not match. Source child elements that can be added under the target element are added. The sibling order of the child elements is also preserved as much as possible. If the target element has compulsory children which have not been filled in by source element children they are created. If some source element children cannot be preserved the user is warned before the change operation is done.

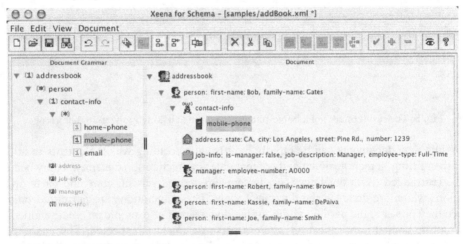

Fig. 6. Result of changing home-phone to a mobile-phone element via the grammar view

6   Support for XML Schema

W3C XML schema has a number of major new additions beyond what was supported in the original XML specification that used DTDs. One of these is support for element subtypes. A subtype extends the content model of its parent type, that is, it may contain extra elements and attributes. To support subtyping the initial grammar view and grammar mapping described in section six need to be extended. Also, support for changing an element's subtype is needed. This is a similar requirement to allowing users to change element types that was covered in section 5.2.

6.1   Presenting and Changing Subtypes

In this section we demonstrate with an example how our interface supports the presentation of subtypes, how subtype changes can be made and revises the grammar view mapping in section six to include support for subtypes. Our example is based on the international purchase order described in the W3C Schema Primer [13]. It includes definitions of element type Address and a subtype USAddress, which we repeat here.

```
<xsd:complexType name="Address">
  <xsd:sequence>
   <xsd:element name="name"    type="xsd:string"/>
   <xsd:element name="street" type="xsd:string"/>
   <xsd:element name="city"    type="xsd:string"/>
  </xsd:sequence>
 </xsd:complexType>
 <xsd:complexType name="USAddress">
  <xsd:complexContent>
   <xsd:extension base="Address">
   <xsd:sequence>
    <xsd:element name="state"   type="USState"/>
    <xsd:element name="zip"     type="xsd:positiveInteger"/>
   </xsd:sequence>
   <xsd:attribute name="country" type="xsd:NMTOKEN"
     use="optional" fixed="US"/>
   </xsd:extension>
  </xsd:complexContent>
 </xsd:complexType>
```

Address element contains three children; name, street and city. USAddress is an Address element which also contains child state and zip elements, and a country attribute. An Address element can appear as part of a PurchaseOrder which we show next.

```
<xsd:complexType name="PurchaseOrder">
  <xsd:sequence>
   <xsd:element name="shipTo" type="Address"/>
   <xsd:element name="billTo" type="Address"/>
   <xsd:element ref="comment" minOccurs="0"/>
   <xsd:element name="items"  type="Items"/>
  </xsd:sequence>
  <xsd:attribute name="orderDate" type="Month"/>
  <xsd:attribute name="completed" type="xsd:boolean"/>
 </xsd:complexType>
```

Note the first and second child elements shipTo and billTo have type Address. An instance of an Address would contain no surprises. It would have three children, elements name, street and city. But a document is unlikely to contains an Address element which is an incomplete address, but rather one of its subtypes such as USAddress or UKAddress. When a subtype is used in place of its base type in a document this must be documented with a "xsi:type" attribute. A billTo element which has been specialised to a USAddress element is qualified with a xsi:type="USAddress" attribute as shown below.

```
<billTo xsi:type="USAddress">
```

```
<name>Robert Smith</name>
<street>8 Oak Ave</street>
<city>Old Town</city>
<state>AL</state>
<zip>95818</zip>
</billTo>
```

Our editor interface hides all the above subtyping detail from a user. Users identify elements which have subtypes by their grammar node title "*" suffix, for example "Address*" in the grammar view. Then select a subtype via a pop-up menu to specialise them. An example of this is shown in figure seven, where shipTo within a purchaseOrder has been selected in the document view followed by a right-click on "shipTo:Address*" in the grammar view to show a pop-up menu of subtype alternatives: USAddress and UKAddress. Figure seven also shows how out editor looks on the Microsoft Windows platform.

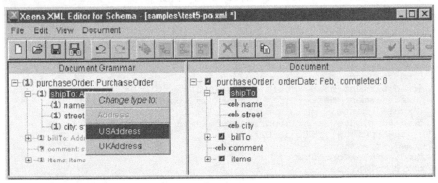

Fig. 7. Viewing the subtype alternatives for a shipTo element

The grammar view shows the corresponding shipTo element has three compulsory children which exist (as their corresponding grammar icons are coloured rather than ghosted). The editor can show both element names and types which is needed once subtypes are used. If the users selected USAddress from the pop-up menu, the selected shipTo element will change to a USAddress, shown in figure eight.

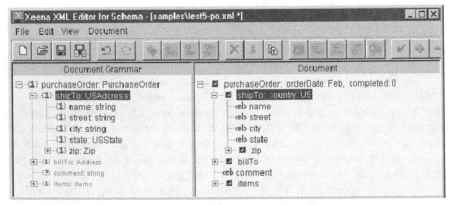

Fig. 8. A shipTo element has been changed to a USAddress type

Figure eight shows two elements have been added to the selected shipTo element in the document view; a state and a zip element. Also the grammar view has changed to show the corresponding shipTo:USAddress template. The effect of the change from Address to USAddress on the document was to add the two additional compulsory elements. If a user wished to change the selected shipTo back to a Address element, Address in the grammar view pop-up menu could be picked. This would remove the recently added state and zip element (after a warning the user). Changing between element subtypes as shown in this section is quite similar to changing between element type choices in section 5.2. The differences are type choices are shown directly in the grammar view tree, while subtype choices are made visible with pop-up menu. The rules for preserving child elements are much more well defined for changes of subtype that for changing a type choice; as a subset relationship exists for the typical case of changing between a base and more specific subtype. While there may not be any structural relationship between types in a choice term.

When the document cursor is set to an elements which is a subtype, the grammar view changes to show the correspond grammar rule, that is, the expected children for that subtype. The design concept used was: when there are subtypes a single grammar node is replaced by a set (the subtypes) which are stacked on behind the other. The document cursor then selects which of these grammar nodes are brought to the front. The "*" suffix for subtyping could be replaced by a 3D shading to such grammar node to indicate the other subtypes behind it, making this concept of stacking in the third dimension more explicit.

6.2   Editing XML Schema

Examples of XML schema in sections 2 and 6.1 show they are also XML documents. Part of creating and maintaining XML documents can include the creation and main-tenance of their schema. Our editor provides additional support for the creation of XML schema. Figure nine shows the purchase order schema used in the last subsec-tion being updated. An additional panel on the right shows the subtype tree.

A close look at the grammar view shows some grammar nodes such as header, body, elements and attributes are shown in italics. Readers who are familiar with the schema would know these do not appear in the W3C XML schema recommendation. These a additional marker types introduced into the grammar to improve its visual structure, to make the grammar view more readable. But, they do not have corre-sponding elements in the document view.

Figure nine also gives a full screen shot of our editor. A message panel on the bot-tom is used for during document validation and in cases where an enabled edit opera-tion can not proceed. The tabbed panel above the messages supports entry of attribute values, character content, notes and application information. This screenshot also shows the benefits of the icon scaling and shading used to create a focus area when large grammars are used. So it is the complexType element and its children which are most visible in the grammar view.

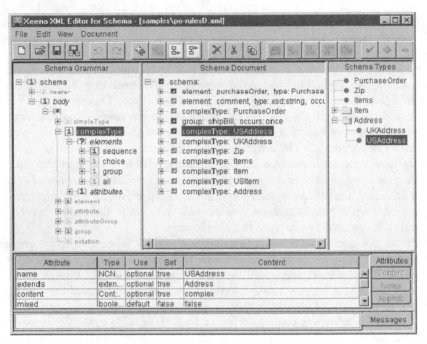

Fig. 9. Updating the purchase order schema in our editor

7   Document Validation

The paper so far, has concentrated on presenting our grammar and document view design, illustrated with screenshots from our XML editor, Xeena for Schema. Our design relies on an edited document conforming to the grammar, so a well defined mapping can be established between the grammar and document views. We use a tool view to enforce this partial validity. A partially valid document may still have missing elements when choices have not been made, missing attributes, wrong data types and other non-structural deviations from what the schema requires. A user makes a document valid by using the editors validation operation which highlights invalid portions of the document, then manually fixes them.

A glance a the toolbar of several editor screen shots reveals one button which is always enabled is the third button from the right whose icon is a red tick. This is the validation check operation button. While our editor does its own structural validation it relies on XERCES an XML parser component, to do full validation. When a user starts validation all invalid elements are highlighted in the document view in red and a summary of the errors is shown in the message panel at the bottom of the editor frame. The plus and minus buttons next to the validate button allows a user to navigate through the list of invalid elements.

Validity here means W3C XML Schema validity. In the introduction alternatives to W3C schema were mentioned. Our editor could be extended to support other grammar based alternatives if the Xerces parser component also supported it. Internally all

Xeena for Schema operations and data structures operate on a simple BNF grammar. When Xeena starts, it converts the document schema it is given, expanding all macro's (groups), unnesting all anonymous types and unfolding all subtypes into a simple flat BNF grammar. This is done by a single conversion class. So other grammars based schema such as Relax (which follows the data type part of the W3C schema definition) could be supported by rewriting this one class.

8   Related Work

Many syntax directed program editors have been developed. Editors such as SUPPORT [16] and Pan [2] sup-ported both structural and content editing. Structural editing proceeds top-down as nodes are elaborated according to grammar rules, while content editing is bottom-up; users directly edit text fragments which are parsed and integrated into the rest of the document.

Grif [5] and Rita [3] are editors for document preparation systems. They use document grammars to provide context sensitive type information to guide editing. They use coordinated content and structure views. The structure view shows the element tree structure. Rita also uses an additional panel which shows the alternatives of a selected element when the grammar contains a choice. Arbitrary cut and paste of element subtrees can require type transformation [1]. This has been added to Grif [8].

Xeena [12], the previous version of our tool provides a content sensitive template for adding types. However the template presents types as an ordered list (by type name) which makes choosing a type and seeing the relationships between them difficult. XML Spy [14] presents a document with a nested tree view. Like the original Xeena it uses a separate panel to show which elements that can be added at the current document position. This interface works well for form based data entry. However changing a document's element structure is difficult without the multi-level grammar view that our editor provides.

Large grammars can result in large and deep grammar trees. Navigating such deep hierarchical trees appears to be difficult for users [15]. TreeViewer [11] uses font, shade, size and animated transitions to help navigate such trees. Many interfaces for information visualisation which use multiple views of data coordinated with synchronised cursors have been built [6].

9   Conclusions

A quick survey of current program editors shows that tree based grammar directed editing has not been adopted by programmers even though many research syntax directed were developed. Such research essentially ended in the late 1980s. Programmers found these editors to be too rigid; cutting and pasting content was often difficult. Experienced programmers did not require grammar guidance, they knew the grammars. For them syntax highlighting was a better solution.

However we argue the situation for XML documents authors is different. Unlike program languages XML document grammars can be very large and varied, so that an author can not reasonably know the full grammars well. Further a diverse range of people may need to create XML documents, some doing so only occasionally. Ideally application specific editors can assist users to create these documents. But in many cases application specific editors will not exist and a generic XML editor will be used. In these later cases, making a user aware of the document grammar as they edit should make using a generic editor easier for them. We presented an editor design targeted at such users, implemented as the Xeena for Schema tool.

We presented a novel design, based on the use of coordinated grammar and document views where the gram-mar view acts as an interactive template which shows what documents changes are possible in any given context, and provides a multi-level document overview. Example uses of our design were given. With our interface, users are able to create and edit XML documents by making choices from presented alternatives, and are able to later revisit and change those choices. Users do not need to remember the grammar . However, the major tradeoff of our design is the requirement that input documents are weakly valid, that is, they follow their grammar element structure rules but may be incomplete. Weakening this constraint remains future work.

Acknowledgements

Mark Sifer was with the IBM Research Lab in Haifa, Israel when this work was done. We wish to thank Roni Raab for her help in programming parts of Xeena for Schema, and the rest of the Knowledge Management group for their feedback.

References

[1]   Akpotsui E., Quint V. and Cecile Roisin.: Type modeling for document trans-formation in structured editing systems. Mathematical and Computer Modeling, Vol 25(4), Feb 1997, 1-19.

[2]   Balance, R.A., Graham S.L. and Van De Vanter M.L.: The Pan language-based editing system. Proceedings of the Fourth ACM SIGSOFT Symposium on Software Development Environments, 1990.

[3]   Cowan D.D., Mackie E.W., Pianosi G.M. and Smit G. V.: Rita – an editor and user interface for manipulating structured documents. Electronic Publishing, John Wiley, Vol 4(3), Sept. 1991, 125-150.

[4]   Extensible Markup Language (XML) 1.0 (Second Edition), W3C Recommen-dation, 6 October 2000, http://www.w3.org/TR/2000/REC-xml-20001006.

[5]   Furuta R., Quint V. and Andre J.: Interactively editing structured documents. Electronic Publishing, John Wiley, Vol 1(1), April 1988, 19-44.

[6]   North, C. and Shneiderman, B.: A taxonomy of multiple window coordinations. Technical Report dCS-TR-3854. University of Maryland, College Park, Dept of Computer Science, 1997.

[7]   Overview of SGML Resources. http://www.w3.org/Markup/SGML.
[8]   Roisin C., Claves P. and Akpotsui E.: Implementing the cut-and-paste operation in a structured editing system. Mathematical and Computer Modeling, Vol 26(1), July 1997, 85-96.
[9]   Sifer, M., Peres Y. and Maarek Y.: Xeena for Schema: creating XML data with an interactive editor. Proceedings of the Second International Workshop on Databases in Networked Information Systems (DNIS), Springer LNCS 2544, Aizu, Japan, Dec. 2002, 133-146.
[10]   SOAP Version 1.2 Part 0: Primer, W3C Working Draft 26 June 2002, http://www.w3.org/TR/2002/WD_soap12_part0-20020626.
[11]   Wittenbug, K. and Sigman, E.: Visual Focusing and Transition Techniques, Proceedings of the IEEE Symposium on Visual Languages, (1997) 20-27.
[12]   Xeena at Alphaworks. http://www.alphaworks.ibm.com/tech/xeena.
[13]   XML Schema Part-0: Primer, W3C Recommendation, 2 May 2001, http://www.w3.org /TR/2001/REC-xmlschema-0-20010502.
[14]   XML Spy. http://www.xmlspy.com/manual.
[15]   Zaphiris P., Shneiderman B. and Norman K. L.: Expandable indexes versus sequential menus for searching hierarchies on the world wide web, (1999) 99-15, http://www.cs.umd.edu/hcil/pubs/tech-reports.shtml.
[16]   Zelkowits, M.: A small contribution to editing with a syntax directed editor. Proceedings of the ACM SIGSOFT/SIGPLAN Software Engineering Symposium on Practical Software Development Environments. 1984.

On-Line Analysis of a Web Data Warehouse

Gilles Nachouki and Marie-Pierre Chastang

IRIN, Faculté des Sciences et des Techniques,
2, rue de la Houssiniére, BP 44322 Nantes Cedex 03, France
{nachouki,chastang}@irin.univ-nantes.fr

Abstract. This paper describes the design of a system, which facilitates Accessing and Interconnecting heterogeneous data sources. Data sources can be static or active: static data sources include structured or semistructured data like databases, XML and HTML documents; active data sources include services which are localised on one or several servers including web services. The main originality of this work is to make interoperability between actives and/or static data sources based on XQuery language. As an example of using our approach, we'll give a scenario for analyzing log files basing on OLAP (On Line Analytical Processing) literature.

1 Introduction

The problem of interconnecting and accessing heterogeneous data sources is an old problem known under the name of Interoperability. As organisations evolve over time interoperability was and is still an important field of current research in both academic and industry. In the past interoperability was limited to structured data sources like databases. Interoperability is the ability of two or more systems (or components) to exchange information and to use the information that has been exchanged. Interoperability can be classified in two approaches [7]: static approach (tightly coupled approach) and dynamic approach (loosely coupled approach). In the static approach, semantic heterogeneity is resolved when a new component database is incorporated in the system. The first stage of this approach uses a Wrapper that translates the database schema from its local data model into a Canonical Data Model. The second stage uses a Mediator that combines multiple component schemes into an integrated schema, in which inconsistencies are resolved and duplicates are removed. In some systems, all component schema are integrated in a single global schema, while in others, multiple integrated schema exist for end-users. In the dynamic approach, semantic heterogeneity is resolved by the end-user at query time. In this approach the end-users are not provided with a predefined view. Instead, they are given direct access to the component schemes at query time by means of a query language or a graphical user interface. This approach uses a metadata resource dictionary that contains descriptions of the component schemes and including conversion information. With the advent of the World Wide Web (WWW) data management has branched out from traditional framework to deal with the variety of information available on the WWW [2]. In the literature many project and

N. Bianchi-Berthouze (Ed.): DNIS 2003, LNCS 2822, pp. 112–121, 2003.

systems are developed in order to connect structured and semistructured data sources; among them we cite Tsimmis [4], Information Mainfold [11], Momix [9], Agora [5], [6]. In such systems (except the Agora system), integration of heterogeneous data sources follows static approach called Global as View (GAV) where query treatment is centric: it chooses a set of queries, and for each such query it provides a procedure to answer the query using the available sources. Given a new query, the approach used in this system consists to try to relate this query to existing ones. AGORA unlike the systems follows another approach called Local As View (LAV). It starts from a global view of data sources expressed with XML data model. Users queries are posed using XML query language (QUILT language), while all the data sources are stored in relational databases. An extension of Agora for the integrating of heterogeneous data sources (including XML and relational database) is proposed in [6]. In this system, relational and XML data sources are defined as view over the global XML schema, by means of an intermediate virtual, generic, relational schema modelling the structure of an XML document. In this approach queries arc translated firstly from Quilt language to the relational integration queries (over the generic relational schema), and then the resulting queries are rewrite using view definitions of data sources (relational databases and XML documents). Recent projects like C-Web [1] and Verso projects [8] provide new approaches for data integration. C-Web proposes an ontology-based integration approach of XML web resources. Like Agora, C-Web start from a global virtual schema (data resides in some external sources) expressed with a given model. The virtual schema allows users to formulate queries (without aware of the source specific structure). The query language is similar to OQL language. Each query can be rewritten to the XQuery expression that the local source can answer. Verso project proposes an extension of XML called Active XML (AXML). AXML is a XML document that may include some special elements carrying the tag <sc> (for service call). These elements embed calls to (web) services. Section 2 gives an overview of our contribution in the domain of interoperability between heterogeneous data sources. Section 3 describes our system based on XQuery language, Corba and Web technologies (XML framework, web services). Section 4 summarises XQuery language, its implementation, and its extension in order to call services. We show in this section some possible scenarios expressed with EXQL. Section 5 gives a concrete example.

2   Overview of Our Approach

Our approach follows a loosely coupled approach where the data sources are under the responsibility of the users. For integration of heterogeneous static data sources our approach is based on the XQuery language in order to extract, interconnect and access heterogeneous data sources such as Relational databases, XML, HTML documents or services. This approach uses metadata (or Canonical Data Model) that contains descriptions of data sources expressed with XML-DTD formalism. The choice of this approach is that data sources on

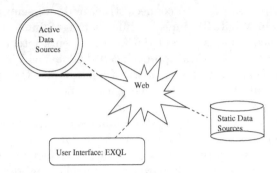

Fig. 1.   Accessing heterogeneous Data Sources based on EXQL

the web are constantly being added, modified or suppressed and the generation of an integrated view of data sources is still a difficult task and requires the intervention of the administrator each time a new query or a new data source is added. Unlike previous approaches proposed in the literature our approach permits the integration of services with static data sources. This integration permits to build a unique view of the integrated sources and facilitates the task to users in their interrogation of data sources using services like existing services web at the WWW. In this work:

1. We have developed wrappers that extract DTDs from data sources and mediators, which offer to users views of data sources expressed with DTDs. DTDs, describe static and/or active data sources. An administrator interface called DSManager permits to describe the data sources (static or active and eventually conflicts existing between them). The administrator provides a description of services accessed by a user (more detail about the description of services is given in section 4). The administrator activates the data sources, which can be accessed by a user;

2. We have extended the XQuery language in order to realise scenarios. A scenario is an EXQL query that integrates services in its body. Services including in a single query are executing sequentially and can be inter-operate with others static data sources necessarily for the realisation of this scenario (fig. 1). Some possible scenarios is given in section 4 and a concrete example is given in section 5.

3   System Architecture

This section describes the design of our system [3]. This system is composed of three components T-Wrappers, Mediators and Interfaces (figure 2):

1. T-Wrappers: this component is a wrapper for data sources of type T. For static data sources we have developed two wrappers denoted SQL-Wrapper

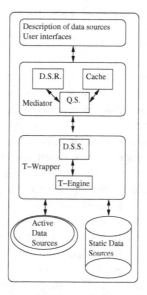

Fig. 2.   Design of the system

and XML-Wrapper that correspond to the most important sources of information existing over the web (e.g. SQL databases, XML and ((X)HTML). For active data sources we have developed a wrapper denoted Service-Wrapper that permits to run services. Services can be local, distant or at the WWW (Web services). In our system the administrator describes each service. A service is considered as any static data source and it offers a schema expressed with XML-DTD. This schema describes the service (name, location, interpreter, parameter). The role of T-Wrappers is to extract automatically DTD from data sources and registers it beside the mediator, then executes queries on data sources and returns results to the mediator.

The design of T-Wrappers is composed of two components: Data Sources Server (DSS) and T-Engine:

Data Source Server (DSS): A DSS is designated as responsible of a data source (static or active). It represents the interface of data sources of any type. There's no way to reach data sources directly in this model, all the communications toward data sources have to go through the DSS. The DSS hides the implementation differences between the different data source types and provides a common prototyping interface for data retrieval.

T-Engine: T-Engine is an engine dedicated to a type T of data source (static or active). It is composed of all the pieces necessarily to extract DTDs, retrieve data from data sources or running services.

2. Mediator: This component offers to users views of data sources expressed with their DTDs. A mediator receives queries from users interfaces, processes queries and returns results to users as XML documents. The mediator has

the knowledge necessary to forward a specific query to the concerned server DSS.

Three components compose a mediator: Data Source Repository (DSR), Query Server (QS) and Cache.

Data Source Repository (DSR): the goal of a DSR is to collect information about the DSSs (references, addresses, names, descriptions and most importantly the DTD of the associate data source). All the DSSs have to register themselves at start-up at the central DSR, providing all the needed pieces of information about the represented Data Source. A Repository therefore has the knowledge of all the main details about the connected data sources, and has also the possibility to share this information with the clients centrally.

Query Server (QS): A Query Server receives complex (Extended) XQuery queries from the client, and processes them. Under processing, we mean analysis of queries first, decomposition of sub-queries, which refer only to one data source, execute those sub-queries, and after collecting the results, join of sub-queries together based on the previous analyses and return the result to the client. Processing of a query is improved by using a cache, which contains data selected from data sources. This mechanism avoids selecting the same data from data sources when it is used frequently. The QS communicates with the DSR in order to obtain more information about data sources and with T-Wrappers in order to execute specific sub-queries.

3. Interfaces: User interface offers to users a list of DTD of data sources. The system provides three distinct interfaces: the first interface permits to familiar users with EXQL language to access data sources by the formulation of queries. The generator interface permits users non-familiar with EXQL language to generate queries starting from their selected attributes. The Administrator interface permits to the administrator of the system to add (or suppress) a data source to (or from) the list of existing data sources. The administrator is able to activate (or stopped) data sources dynamically and users receive a refresh list of active data sources.

4   EXQL Language

We propose in this section an extension of the XQuery language, called EXQL, in order to call services and we show some scenarios that show the integration of services with (or without) static data sources in a single query expressed with EXQL. In this paper, the extension of XQuery consists to define only a new function in the core of the language called 'Service'. This function is incorporated into the library of functions and is defined like the function 'Document' existing in the library function of the XQuery language. This new function defined in the XQuery language permits to run any service, which are localised on one or several servers including Web services. The syntax of this function is given as follows:

service(Interpreter,Name,Arguments,HomeDirectory,Display)

The first argument is the interpreter used by the service at run time. It's optionally and it's specified only if the service needs some interpreter software in order to run it. The second argument is the name of the service. The third argument provides a list of parameters necessary for the execution of the service. The next argument is the 'HomeDirectory' argument. It's the path to the directory homework of the user. 'Display' argument is optionally. It consists to return the result of the execution of the service at the screen of the user.

We show the three principal scenarios:

- The first scenario (A) integrates two services. The result of the first service is used as input in the second service;
- The second scenario (B) is composed of a static data source and a service. This service takes, as input, data from the static data source and produces the final result;
- The third scenario (C) is similar to the scenario (A) but the result of the execution of the service is send toward a static data source.

These scenarios are expressed with EXQL in figure 3 as follows:

AS1, AS2 are the names of two active data sources. These data sources are described in two XML documents having unique DTD (Data Type Document) called service.dtd given in figure 4.

SS1 is a static data source from which we extract its DTD automatically. R1 is the name of a file containing the result of a service and DSLocation describes how to connect to the Data source in update mode.

```
<Scenario–A>
  Let $a := document(AS1)/description
  Let $b := document (AS2)/description
Return
  <sc1>service($a/interpreter /text()/, $a/name/text(),$a/parameter/text(),$a/ HomeDirectory/text())</sc1>,
  <sc2>service($b/interpreter/text(),sb/name/text(),R1,$b/parameter/text(),
  $b/HomeDirectory/text(),Display)</sc2>
</Scenario–A>
- - - - - - - - - - - - - - - - - - - - - - - - - - - - - - - - - - - - - - - - - - - - -
  <Scenario–B>
  Let $a := document(SS1)/path
  Let $b := document (AS2)/description
Return
  <sc1>service($b/interpreter/text(),$b/name/text(),$b/parameter/text(),
  $a/path/text(),$b/HomeDirectory/text())</sc1>

  </Scenario–B>
- - - - - - - - - - - - - - - - - - - - - - - - - - - - - - - - - - - - - - - - - - - - -
  <Scenario–C>
  Let $a := document(AS1)/description
  Let $b := document (AS2)/description
Return
  <sc1>service($a/interpreter/text(),$a/name/text(),$a/parameter/text(),$a/HomeDirectory/text())</sc1>,
  <sc2>service($b/interpreter/text(),sb/name/text(),R1,$b/parameter/text(), R1,DSLocation,
  $b/HomeDirectory/text())</sc2>
  </Scenario–C>
```

Fig. 3.   Scenarios

```
<!ELEMENT description (interpreter,name,parameter,HomeDirectory)>
<!ELEMENT parameter(para*)>
<!ELEMENT interpreter (#PCDATA)>
<!ELEMENT HomeDirectory (#PCDATA)>
<!ELEMENT name (#PCDATA)>
<!ELEMENT para (#PCDATA)>
```

Fig. 4.   Data Type Document of active data sources

Other scenarios are possible and can be deduced from the three one given above. In the following section we show a concrete example using services with static data sources in order to realise a specific scenario.

5   Concrete Example: Web Usage Understanding

In this section we use the approach proposed in [10] in order to test our system. [10] provides an OLAP based approach (called Web Usage Understanding System) to analyze the traffic of users when navigating on the Web. For more efficiency in using this tool, we have made it accessible via EXQL. In this application, we present a concrete scenario using the folowing data sources (Login files for our laboratory doctorants):

the log file covering the period from 24/03/2002 to 31/03/2002.
the log file covering the period from 31/03/2002 to 07/04/2002.
the log file covering the period from 07/04/2002 to 14/04/2002.

This section includes programs to create the database schema, to add log files in the data bases, to update the data warehouse dimensions and to reset the fact table. The administrator interface DSManager makes these data sources accessible by the user and the user interface (called SwingClient) is connected to the DSManager in order to obtain the structure of these data sources. Users not familiar with EXQL language can use the generator interface in order to formulate their queries. Otherwise, users can put directly their queries into the interface and obtain the result from it.

The scenario we suggest is the following: Build a data warehouse for the Web usage understanding from login's log files. In the following we give the structure of the data sources (active and static) :

The active data Source bdcr, which creates the data warehouse multidimensional structure, is given in figure 5(a). The active data Source aclfservice which adds log filescontained in 'logs' to the data warehouse is given in figure 5(b).The active data source 'majdservice' which updates the dimension tables of the data warehouse is given in figure 5(c).The active data source ftiservice which resets the fact table of the data warehouse once dimension tables were updated is given in figure 5(d).The active data source cube which launchs the visualisation of the multidimensional data as an hypercube is given in figure 5(e). The static data source 'logs' which contains logfiles to be added to the data warehouse is given in figure 5(f).

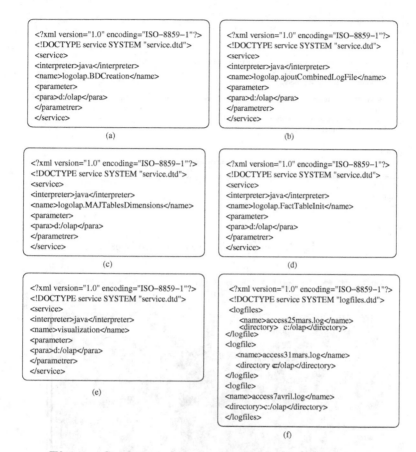

Fig. 5.   Structure of the active and static data sources

The query given in figure 6 builds dynamically the Web data Warehouse and run the visualisation of the multidimensional data as an hypercube (figure 7).

6   Conclusion

Our approach is based on the EXQL language in order to extract, interconnect and access heterogeneous data sources. This approach follows loosely coupled approach where the data sources are of the responsibility of users. We have proposed the design of a system that accepts static and active data sources. We have implemented XQuery language and we have extended this language in order to put services. Services permit to resolve conflicts existing between heterogeneous data sources and realise specific scenarios. In this work services given in a query are executed sequentially. In the future, we plan to study queries where more complex scenarios are possible and queries optimisation.

```
<results>
Let $a := document("bdcr")/service
Return
<Result1>
<crDW>service($a/interpreteur/text(),$a/name/text(),$a/parameter/para/text())</crDW>,
 For $b in document("logs")/logfiles/logfile
 Let $e in document("aclfservice")/service
 Return
        <Aclf>service($e/interpreteur/text(),$e/name/text(),$b/directory/text(),$b/name/text(),$e/parameter/para/text())</Aclf>
 </Result1>
Let $c := document("majdservice")/service
Let $d := document("ftiservice")/service
Return

<Result2>
<Mtd>service($c/interpreteur/text(),$c/name/text(),$c/parameter/para/text())</Mtd>,

<Fti>service($d/interpreteur/text(),$d/name/text(),$d/parameter/para/text())</Fti>
</Result2>
<Result3>
<Visu>service($c/interpreteur/text(),$c/name/text(),$c/parameter/para/text()) </Visu>
</Result3>
</results>
```

Fig. 6.   EXQL: Web traffic analysis

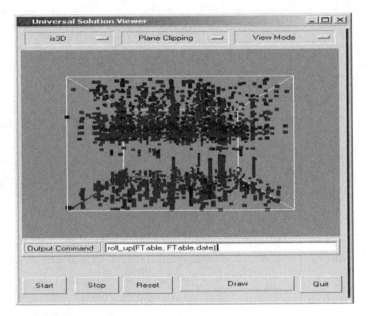

Fig. 7.   Visualisation of the multidimensional data as an hypercube

References

[1] B.Amman & al. Ontology-based integration of xml web resources. In *proceeding of the International Semantic Web Conference*, pages 117–131, 2002.   113
[2] D. Suciu & al. Report on webdb 2000. In *3rd International Workshop on the Web and databases*, 2000.   112
[3] G. Nachouki & al. *Extracting, Interconnecting and Accessing Heterogeneous Data Sources: An XML Query Based Approach*. Springer-Verlag, Iran, 2002.   114

[4] H. Garcia-Molina & al. Integrating and accessing heterogeneous information sources in tsimmis. In *proceeding of the AAAI symposium on information gathering*, California, 1995. 113

[5] I. Manolescu & al. Living with xml and relational. In *in proceedings of the 26th VLDB Conference*, Egypt, 2000. 113

[6] I. Manolescu & al. Answering xml queries over heterogeneous data sources. In *in proceedings of the 27th VLDB Conference*, Italy, 2001. 113

[7] P. Sheth & al. Federated databases systems for managing disributed heterogeneous and'autonomous databases. *ACM Computing Survey*, 22(3):183–236, 1990. 112

[8] S. Abiteboul & al. Active xml: A data-centric perspective on web services. In *BDA 2002*, Paris, 2002. 113

[9] S. Bergamaschi & al. *Integration of Information from Multiple Sources of Textual Data*. Springer-Verlag, 1999. 113

[10] S.Naouali & al. Web rafic analysis. In *proceeding of the Information and Knowledge System (IKS)*, US Virgin Islands, 2002. 118

[11] T. Kirk & al. The information manifold. In *working Notes of the AAAI symposium on information gathering from Heterogeneous Distributed Environments*, California, 1995. 113

Web Information Integration
Based on Compressed XML

Hongzhi Wang, Jianzhong Li, Zhenying He, and Jizhou Luo

Department of Computer Science and Technology
Harbin Institute of Technology
wangzh@hit.edu.cn
lijz@banner.hl.cninfo.net
hzy_hit@sina.com
luojizhou@x263.net

Abstract. Nowadays, information integration to web data sources and XML becomes a favorite information exchange format. New application motivates the problems that massive information is often transmitted in network and must be processed in limited buffer in mediator. To process query on massive data from web data source effectively, we present a method of XML compression based on edit distance for information transmission in information integration. By compressing XML, this method can reduce both the transmission time and buffer space. Two different strategies of XML compression for transmission and process in mediator are designed. Optimization of the combination of these strategies is discussed. We also propose the query execution algorithms on compressed XML data in buffer of mediator. We focus on main operators of data from wrapper in mediator, namely sort, union, join and aggregation. Implementation of these operators on compressed data using two different methods is described in this paper.

1 Introduction

Information integration system aims to integrate autonomy distributed and heterogeneous data sources to form a single data source. There are mainly three information integration methods, federal databases, data warehouse and mediation [1]. Mediation [2] becomes the most favorite information integration form, because of its capability of representing both structured and semi-structured data with semantics tags and XML [3] becomes the most important format of information exchange in information integration system [4].

Nowadays, Internet, which holds massive information, becomes the largest data source (or can be treated as lots of data sources). Information integration is not limited in only traditional known data source but can also be extended to data sources of web. The flexibility of XML makes it adaptive to be used as the format of integration of web data sources. The information integration of web with XML as information exchange format brings new problems:

N. Bianchi-Berthouze (Ed.): DNIS 2003, LNCS 2822, pp. 122–137, 2003.

- Massive information in web makes the information exchange process slow. How to speed up this process of the information exchange in information integration system?
- The web is a dynamic data source with both static web pages and hidden data source with only a query interface [5]. The traversal of the whole web needs long time. How to answer user's query timely?
- The environment of Internet is not stable and the efficiency of various data sources is not the same. How to schedule the execution of the query in various wrappers?

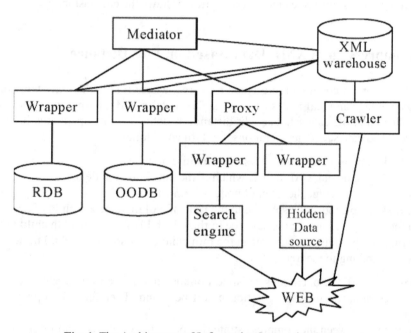

Fig. 1. The Architecture of Information Integration System

To solve the second problem, an XML warehouse is used as a semantics cache for store history information from web. The query to related information could be answered quickly directly from the XML warehouse. The architecture of the information integration is shown in fig.1.

Since the information obtained from web may be massive, XML warehouse need to be compressed. [6] discusses the compression method based on edit distance and the query process techniques on compressed data. Such XML compression techniques could be used to compress exchange information in XML format, thus solves the first problem presented above.

To solve the third problem, query buffer is used in mediator to store the result returned temporarily. In order to make plenary use of the query buffer, the data transferred into the query buffer should be kept compressed and decompressed only when query process needs so.

The contributions of this paper are:

- Various strategies of compressed data in XML format based on edit distance are proposed in various component of information integration system with XML warehouse. The strategies behave differently in a variety of different applications.
- The algorithms of query execution in mediator to integrate data obtained directly from data sources and XML warehouse is presented.

This paper is organized as follows. Section 2 gives the compression method of XML based on edit distance. The algorithms of query execution are presented in section 3 and section 4 sums up related work. Section 5 draws the conclusion.

2   Compression of XML Data Based on Edit Distance

Data in XML format could be represented as a tree, whose root is the outer tag, non-leaf nodes are tags and leaf nodes are values. The data in XML format with just one root is called an XML data set. The edit distance is defined as the operations list between two XML data sets. The operations are defined as follows:

- Insert (n, k, T): insert XML tree T as the kth child of node n.
- Delete (n, k, T): delete XML tree T, which is the kth child of node n.
- Update (n, v, o_v): change the label of node n from v to ov.
- Move (n, k, m, p): move the sub-tree in the pth child of m to the kth child of n.
- Swap (n, k, m, p): exchange the sub-tree in the pth child of m and the kth child of n.
- Copy (n, k, m, p): copy the sub-tree in the mth child of p into the kth child of n.
- Nop (): do nothing to the tree

As proved in [6], the operations satisfied commutative law and integrate law, and for each operation, the inverse operation could be found. Therefore, the operations form a group.

It is different between the compress strategies of XML warehouse and information exchange in XML format.

As for the compression of XML warehouse, XML data items are clustered based on their edit distance and the cost on the operations. Each cluster could be considered as a graph with power with the XML data items as nodes and the edit distance between two XML data items as power, so the minimal spanning tree of this cluster can be generated. For each cluster, a center which makes the total cost of the edit distance in the cluster minimal is chosen. The center is stored as a whole XML document and the other XML data items in the cluster only the base information such as creation time and original location are stored. The edit distance in minimal spanning tree is also stored. Each XML data item in the cluster could be reconstructed by the center and the path of edit distance from center to it in the minimal spanning tree. The detail of compression algorithms and query process for compressed XML warehouse based on edit distance is given in [6]. From each cluster, an XML schema could be extracted as the representation of the cluster, which is defined as represent schema.

The data in information exchange require linear scan, that is to say, the XML data item should be processed one by one. Hence the compression strategy of exchange data needs the information to be compressed as a list with the head a whole XML data item and XML data items are only represented as edit distance. Take future information transmission acceleration into consideration, the operator could be predigested. Only operator Delete and Update could be changed. The results of change are:

- Delete (n, k): delete the kth child of node n.
- Update (n, v): change the label of node n to v.

After such changes, the operations of delete and update need not to contain original values, which will lead to the result that the operations miss reversibility and the list does not support reconstruct former XML data item with latter ones. But the XML data item list is just used in data transmission, which makes reconstruction not a required task.

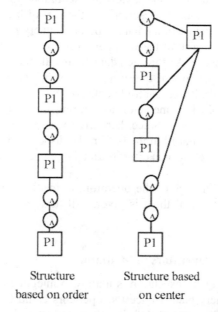

Structure   Structure based

based on order   on center

Fig. 2. The comparison of two compress structures

There are two choices for the design of the structure of the XML data item list, one is to store the center the edit distances between whom to other XML data items to transform and other XML data items are represented as the edit distance between it and the center, as is called structure based on center (SBC in brief), the other choice is that all the XML data items are arranged into a list, the whole first XML data item and the edit distance between each other XML data item and its last XML data item is stored, as is called structure based on order (SBO in brief). The two choices are shown in fig.2. In the figure, a square represents a XML page and a circle represents an edit distance operation.

The selection depends on the relation between the data to be sent by the wrapper. Sometimes, the result to be returned contains the relation of order. In this case, structure based on center should be used. The reason is that the information reaching in such order is easy to process by mediator. The instance that SBO should be used is that the size of XML data item is quite large for the buffer in mediator. In multi sequence algorithms, SBC is preferred because the times of edit distance computation is fewer in SBC than those in SBO. In other instances, the choice depends on the estimation of the query process efficiency based on the predicted parameters of the result returned by the data source.

3   Query Process on Compressed XML Data

The mediator considers data sources as a view in integration system through the wrapper and the capability of wrapper is described as the part of local schema of the data source related to global schema. In mediator, the basic query plan is generated as the integration of the result and task of the wrappers, just like the join or union and scan of tables in relational database. And in each data source, the task assigned by mediator is executed. The query operators of query process in mediator are therefore mainly operators processing the result from multiple data sources.

The buffer size is limited in mediator for storing the result from various data sources temporarily for processing. Since there may be so many data sources to query that the result returned could not fit in the buffer, the disposition of the query to wrapper should be scheduled well to make the buffer large enough for query process in mediator.

In this section, the definitions of the operators in mediator are presented at first. And then the implementation of them is given. All these are based on compressed XML data.

3.1   The Definitions of Operators in Mediator

The task of mediator for query execution is mainly to integrate the result returned by wrapper based on the query plan. Hence the operators could be abstracted from the operations in mediator. The goal of defining these operators is to discuss the implementation of the query in mediator and schedule the query task. These operators are shown as following:

- Join

  Integrate two XML data item together based on some criteria. Since the tree structure of XML data item is more complex than relation, there are various types of join operator, the implementation of which are different. According to the form structure of join, the types and their representation can be classified as followings:

  - Connect join (S1 $\oplus$ [condition][tag]S2)

Connect every XML tree T1 in S1 and T2 in S2 into one XML tree with the tag as the root while S1 and S2 as the two child of root.

– Merge join (S1 $\otimes$ [condition]S2)

Merge every XML tree T1 in S1 and T2 in S2 into one XML tree with the root of T1 as the root and T2 are connected onto the root.

The condition of join permits regular expression and since there may be more than one tag. According to the condition, the types of join are presented as following:

– One-join: if there are more than one objects, only one object satisfies the condition then the condition is true.
– All-join: If there are more than one objects, all the object satisfies the condition, then the condition is true.
– Con-join: If the number of objects satisfying condition is larger than a threshold, the condition is true.

• Union (S1∩S2)

Intersection of XML data item set S1 and S2. It is different from relational operator in that there is no schema limit for two union sets. That is to say, every two XML data item sets could be union.

• Sort (Sort[*condition*]S)

Sort the XML documents in S based on the condition *condition*. *Condition* defines the comparison rules. Since the comparison of complex object is not well-defined, the condition is needed to define the order relation between complex object.

• Group and Aggregationγ[*condition*](S)

Group the XML documents in S based on the rules defined in *condition*. The condition is defined as the object to group with the rules to judge if two objects should be grouped together.

3.2   The Implementation of the Operators in Mediator

In this part, the implementation of the operators join, union, sort and aggregation, which form the main operation in mediator, is described. Since the query plan in mediator may contain more than one operation, the middle result is stored on external memory. The operation should be implemented for both received XML data item sequence from network and those stored on the secondary memory. The algorithms presented in this paper can fit in the two instances.

In order to describe the algorithms, the iterator functions are defined as following. The implementation of these iterators could be operated on accepted data from network and load data from disk.

• Open(s): open a compressed XML data item sequence s.

- Getfirst(s): get the first XML data item of a sequence s.
- Getnextopera(s): get next edit operation in the sequence s. if a complete Δ of a XML data item is accepted, a special symbol is accepted.
- Getpreviousopera(s): get previous operation in the sequence s. It should be noted that the operation the function returns is the inverted operation of the original operation in the sequence.
- output(s): Put next edit operation in the sequence s. if a complete Δ of a XML data item is accepted, a special symbol is outputted.
- Close(s): close a compressed XML data item s.

It is supposed that the two sequences to be processed are $s1=\{x_{11}, x_{12}, ..., x_{1n}\}$ and $s2=\{x_{21}, x_{22}, ..., x_{2m}\}$.

3.2.1 Sort

For the limitation of buffer's space, we assume that the part of the result in compressed XML format could be stored in the buffer could be as little as possible during query process. In order to decrease I/O cost of mediator and distribute the cost to the data source, if sort is needed in any step, the operator could be pre-executed in data source and in mediator and therefore the implementation of sort operator only needs to merge the returned results.

Both of the algorithms of merging SBO sequences and SBC sequences are similar to common merge join while some details are different. The first step of the two algorithms is to compare the head XML data items in the two sequences by the comparison condition and output the smaller one while leave the sorted objects in buffer. For later XML data item represented by edit distance, only the operations related to sort object are considered. The operations are executed on the left sort object. When two XML data item generated symbols are both met, they are compared and the operation sequence of the smaller one is outputted.

It is worth noticing that the output sequence is not the original sequence because the former XML data item in the output XML data item sequence may not be the one in the original sequence. The methods of processing this instance in SBO and SBC are different.

If they are SBO, at first the edit distance between two head XML data items is computed. The edit distances of the XML data items on processing of two sequences are computed when new XML data item flows into buffer. Supposing that the XML data items in buffer are x_{1i} and x_{2j}, and the x_{1i-1} is just outputted by comparison, the edit distance between x_{1i} and x_{2j} is computed as follows:

$$Edit\_distance(x_{1i}, x_{2j})=optim(invert(edit\_distance(x_{1i-1}, x_{2j}))+edit\_distance(x_{1i}, x_{1i-1}))$$

In the formula, function invert() is to compute the inversion of the edit distance, function optim() is to optimize the edit distance and the symbol '+' is overloaded for connecting two edit distances. The implementation of invert() and optim() is in [6]. Since $edit\_distance(x_{1i-1}, x_{2j})$ and $edit\_distance(x_{1i}, x_{1i-1})$ are already computed, the process is effective.

if X1i is smaller, $edit\_distance(x_{1i}, x_{1i-1})$ is outputted.
Otherwise, $edit\_distance(x_{2j}, x_{1i-1})=invert(x_{1i-1}, x_{2j})$ is outputted.

If they are SBC, the edit distance between x_{11} and x_{21} is also computed at first. It is Supposed that the XML data items in buffer are x_{1i} and x_{2j}, the first XML data item output is x_{11}, the last XML data item output is x_{1i-1}. If x_{1i} is smaller than x_{2j} by comparison, edit_distance(x_{1i}, x_{11}) is outputted. Otherwise, edit_distance(x_{2j}, x_{11})= invert(edit_distance(x_{11},x_{21}))+edit_distance(x_{2j}, x_{21}) is outputted, in which edit_distance(x_{11},x_{21}) and edit_distance(x_{2j}, x_{21}) are already know. The other instance could be processed in the method similar to this.

The brief description of the algorithm of merging two SBO sequences together is in algrithm1 of appendix A and that of algorithm of merging two SBC sequence together is in algrithm2 of appendix A.

From these two algorithms, it could be seen that the algorithms of SBO and SBC is quite similar except some details of computing edit distance. In the following discuss, only the algorithms of SBO are described.

3.2.2   Union

The result is assumed to be already sorted by data sources on the object with the most values, as is judged by statistics in catalog. The implementation of union is quite similar to that of sort, except that with the same object value, all of the XML data items should be checked.

For the two sequences S_1 and S_2, x_{11} and x_{21} are compared at first. If they have different sort object, output the XML data item with the smaller one object. If they have same sort object, all the XML data items in the sequences with the sort object should be scanned. It is supposed that $S_1'=\{x_{1i1}, x_{1i1+1},..., x_{1i2}\}$ in S_1 and $S_2'=\{x_{2j1}, x_{2j1+1}, ..., x_{2j2}\}$ in S_2 all have the same sort value. Edit_distance(x_{1i1}, x_{2j1}) is computed at first and if it is nop, they are considered the same and one of them could be eliminated. The XML data items in S_1' and S_2' are checked nest-loop. In order to simplify computing, the edit distance could also be computed with the edit distance computed previously. The course of union S_1' and S_2' in SBC mode is described in algrithm3 of appendix A.

Of course, the extreme instance is that the data source could execute sort and eliminate repetition of the result with all the objects in the XML data item. That is to say, each object in the XML data item should be defined an order relationship. Based on the relationship, the object could be sorted completely. This is an ideal instance because define the order relationship for each object automatically in mediator is a hard work especially for the object permitting repetition in schema and the efficiency of query for data source may decrease a lot.

3.2.3   Join

There are various types of operator join. If the join condition is comparison, sort merge join is considered because the data source could pre-sort the result. The operation sequence is like merge sort with the difference of the process of result because two XML data items in sequence should be connected. In different join mode and XML compress mode, the connect method is various.

For nature join, only the sub-sequences with same join object value should be nest-looped. While for join with unequal object, the sequence will be scanned for many times. External memory must be used to accomplish the operation. Since the compression of XML could shrink the size of XML data a lot, one block brings into buffer may holds many XML data items. The max and min of current block of internal could be used to accelerate the process. The algorithm of nature join is quite like that of union. For x_{1i} and x_{2j} in S_1 and S_2 respectively, if they have equal join value, in connect join the additional root tag is numbered the smallest number and the XML tree x_{1i} and x_{2j} is retraversed for new number. The same process is adaptive for merge join except that only x_{2j} needs to be renumbered as the sub tree of x_{1i}. During the process on compressed XML sequences, the change of number are reflected in the number of tree nodes in operations in sequence. The new number of x_{11} and x_{21} need to be computed by traversal. For each sequence, an offset in number could be defined. The number of node in generated tree by join is the offset added to the offset. When there are sub-tree added or deleted from x_{1i}, the only the offset of x_{2j} is changed. The change of the operation in sequence is to add the offset to the node number in the operation.

The detail of the algorithm for SBC is in algrithm4 of appendix.

3.2.4 Aggregation

As discussed above, as much as work is pushed to the data source, so is the group by and aggregation. The particular instance is the aggregation function avg, as could not be computed directly by the avg value of the XML. To compute this kind of aggregation, the result returned holds two objects of sum and count. The avg could easy to count from the value of sum and count.

The result generating of aggregation is simpler since the merge of two XML data item with the same group object needs only change the value in the operation relevant to the aggregation object. The detail of the algorithm for SBC is in algrithm5 of appendix.

3.2.5 Extension of the Algorithm to Multiple Compressed Sequence

In order to accelerate the process, multiple compressed sequences could be processed together. Join between various sequences relates to different objects and the synchronization is quite difficult for join with limited buffer. The multiple compressed sequence operators are only sort, union and aggregation.

The returned result sorted, the result with the same sort value could be processed together. N sequences $S1=\{x_{11},x_{12},...x_{1m1}\}$, $S2=\{x_{21},x_{22},...x_{2m2}\}$,...., $Sn=\{x_{n1},x_{n2}, ... x_{nmn}\}$ is supposed to be operated together. The implementation of sort in SBO mode is discussed in detail and that of other operators is similar.

The process order is as multi merge sort to output the smallest value each time. The feature of the process in out algorithm is that the XML data item is represented by edit distant. To merge the edit distance in various sequence into one, the edit distances between each on processing one should be kept in buffer. Because of the inversion and connectable properties, supposing current process XML data items are x_{1i1}, x_{2i2}, ..., x_{nin}, only the edit_distance(x_{1i1}, x_{2i2}), edit_distance(x_{2i2}, x_{3i3}), ..., edit_distance($x_{n-1in-1}$, x_{nin}) need to be maintained in buffer. In SBO mode, supposing k is smaller than r if x_{kik} is outputted and the last XML data item outputted is x_{rir-1}, the edit distance between x_{kik} and x_{rir-1} is computed by the following formula:

$$\text{edit\_distance}(x_{ki_k}, x_{ri_r-1}) = optim(\sum_{l=k}^{r-1} \text{edit\_distance}(x_{li_l}, x_{l+1i_{l+1}}) +$$

$$\text{edit\_distance}(x_{ri_r}, x_{ri_r-1}))$$

And in SBC node, based on the same assumption and condition, the edit distance between x_{kik} and x_{rir-1} is computed by the following formula:

$$\text{edit\_distance}(x_{ki_k}, x_{ri_r-1}) = optim(\text{edit\_distance}(x_{ki_k}, x_{k1}) +$$

$$\sum_{l=k}^{r-1} \text{edit\_distance}(x_{l1}, x_{l+11}) + invert(\text{edit\_distance}(x_{ri_r}, x_{ro})))$$

From the two formulas, it could be seen that the cost of computing the edit distance depends on the interval between the sequence of current XML data item with smallest sort value and that of previous outputted XML data item. Hence if there are more than one XML data item contains the same smallest value, the one with the smallest interval between the sequence of last outputted XML data item is chosen. The greedy chose method is not always optimum. The edit_distance(x_{nin}, x_{1i1}) could be stored and elevator algorithm[18] could be used in the cycle to accelerate the computing. If there are too many sequences to merge or the distribution of value is disperse, the cost of optim becomes large.

The implementation of multi sequence union and aggregation is similar. However, it is to be noted that in union, there may be lots of XML data items with the same sort value. The size of buffer should be considered. If buffer is not enough, external memory is to be used and the efficiency decreases.

From the discussion above, the multi sequence operation could not always increase the efficiency of the process. Whether multi sequence operation should be used or not and how many sequences should be operated on by multi sequence operation is the problem for query process scheduling.

4   Related Work

XML becomes a general format of information integration because of its adaptiveness and extensibility. Famous information integration system tsimmis[10] uses OEM as their data model and information integration based on XML is just like it. [10] discusses query process and optimization techniques of information integration based on OEM. Prototype systems of information integration based on XML include Tukwila[11], Xyleme[12], Niagara[13]. Xyleme focuses on maintaining an XML warehouse and loading data from data of external data source into the warehouse without scanning the data source directly to answer user's query. Niagara indexes remote data in known data source. Tukwila is designed for the web data source with unpredictable data transfer rate and absence of statistics information.

[4, 9] are papers in this research field. They focus on the query conversion for the information integration system.. However, none of these works consider the efficiency

of query processing in mediator especially when in the open web environment there are many data sources and massive returned results.

There are also many studies of query process of the information integration techniques of relational database in distributed environment. [14] provides a survey of query process technologies for heterogeneous data sources. [15] gives a dynamic query plan generating method and adaptive query operators, dynamic collector and pipelined join, considering the memory limit. [16] gives the techniques for dynamic query schedule in mediator including pipeline and materialization strategies. All of these studies are based on relational database without considering XML.

There are several papers about compression of data in XML format. XMILL[7] is a compressor for XML document. By splitting of XML document and compressing the parts respectively, it gains higher compression ratio than gzip. [8] describes an online XML compression algorithm ESAX. Although the compression ratio of this algorithm is high, it is inefficient and unable to be applied to XML warehouse with a large amount of XML documents. The fatal shortcoming of these methods is that the query processing of XML data is not considered at all. And if they are used in the communication, the efficiency of query process could be so low as not to be accepted. [17] presents a XML document compression strategy based on edit distance. But the method is limited to storage of the history data with the same original document and DTD in XML warehouse.

5   Conclusions and Future Work

In this paper, we focus on the problem of massive information communication and process in information integration system facing web. The compression method of XML data based on edit distance is presented. The compression of XML data could save the time of communication and the times of I/O so that the efficiency increases.

The operators of mediators are abstracted in this paper in order to design the implementation of the operations in mediator and schedule the query position and process order. The algorithms of implementing operators Sort, Union, Join and Aggregation are also given in this paper. The algorithms are designed for the instances of both information received from network and the data loaded from external memory. The process of edit distance operations is considered in the algorithms in order to accomplish the query process without decompressing XML data items.

In this paper, it could be found that different operation order and the number of the sequences process in one operator result in quite different query process efficiency. In the near future, the problem of scheduling the query process will be considered. Especially in the dynamic distributed environment such as internet, the query response time and the result transfer speed should be considered during the generation of query plan.

The operation of the returned result could form a pipeline. But the size limit of buffer in mediator will limit the capability of the pipeline. The design of pipeline is another research problem to study in future.

References

[1]   H. Garcia-Molina, J. D. Ullman, J. Widom: Database System Implementation. Prentice Hall. 2000.

[2]   G. Wirderhold: Mediators in the Architecture of Future Information Systems. IEEE Computer□ 25:38-49.

[3]   T. Bray□ J. Paoli□ C. M. Sperberg-McQueen: Extensible markup language (XML) 1.0.   W3C Recommendation. Feb.1998.http://www.w3.org/TR/REX-xml.

[4]   V. Christophides, S. Cluet, and J. Simeon: On Wrapping Query Languages and Efficient XML Integration. In Proc. of ACM SIGMOD Conf. on Management of Data, Dallas, TX., May 2000.

[5]   S. Raghavan H. Garcia-Molina: Crawling the Hidden Web. In 27th International Conference on Very Large Data Bases. 2001. Rome, Italy.

[6]   H. Wang, J. Li, Z. He: An Effective Storage Strategy for Compressed XML Warehouse. In Proc. of National Database Conference of China 2002.

[7]   H. Liefke and D. Suciu: XMill: an ecient compressor for XML data. In Proceedings of the 2000 ACM SIGMOD International Conference on Management of Data.

[8]   J. Cheney: Compressing XML with Multiplexed Hierarchical Models. in Proceedings of the 2001 IEEE Data Compression Conference, pp. 163-172.

[9]   Manolescu, D. Florescu, D. Kossmann: Answering XML Queries over Heterogeneous Data Sources . SIGMOD2001.

[10]   Papakonstantinou, S. Abiteboul, H. Garcia-Molina: Object Fusion in Mediator Systems. VLDB'96.

[11]   Z. Ives , A. Halevy , D. Weld: Integrating Network-Bound XML Data. Data Engineering Bulletin 24(2) 2001

[12]   L. Xyleme: A dynamic warehouse for XML data of the Web. IEEE Data Engineering Bulletin. 2001.

[13]   J. Naughton, et al: The Niagara Internet Query System. IEEE Data Engineering Bulletin, 2001.

[14]   D. Kossmann: The state of the art in distributed query processing. ACM Computing Surveys 32(4), December 2000.

[15]   Z. G. Ives, D. Florescu, M. Friedman, A. Levy, D. S. Weld: An Adaptive Query Execution System for Data Integration, Proceedings of the SIGMOD Conference, Philadelphia, Pennsylvania (1999).

[16]   L. Bouganim, F. Fabret, P. Valduriez, C. Mohan: Dynamic Query Scheduling in Data Integration Systems. 16th International Conference on Data Engineering. February 28 - March 03, 2000.San Diego, California.

[17]   Marian, S. Abiteboul, G. Cob´na, L. Mignet: Change-centric management of versions in an XML warehouse. VLDB 2001.

[18]   Silberschatz, P. Baer Galvin, G. Gagne: Operating System Concepts(Sixth Edition). John Wiley & Sons,Incl. 2001.

[19]   H. Wang. Research of Information Integration in distribute Environment. Thesis of Bachelor Degree of Harbin Institute of Technology. 2001.

Appendix - Descriptions of Algorithms in the Paper

Algorithm 1: Merge SBO XML Sequences

Input: SBO XML sequence s_1, s_2
Output: SBO XML sequence
open(s_1);open(s_2);x1=getfirst(s_1); x2=getfirst(s_2);
if compare(x_1,x_2) then x=x_1; b=true;else x=x_2; b=false;
v1=get_sort_value(x_1); v2=get_sort_value(x_2);
output(x);
Δ_0=edit_distance(x_1,x_2);
while (not reach the tail of s_1 OR not reach the tail of s_2) do
  Δ_1=NULL; Δ_2=NULL;
  while(not reach the data item end in s_1) do
      Δ=getnextopera(s_1);
      if (change of value of v_1 occurs in Δ)
          v_1 changes based on Δ;
      Δ_1+=Δ;
  end while
  while(not reach the data item tail in s_2) do
      Δ=getnextopera(s_2);
      if (change of value of v_2 occurs in Δ)
          v_2 changes based on Δ;
      Δ_2+=Δ;
  end while
  if(b)Δ_0=optim(Δ_1+Δ_0);
  else Δ_0=invert(optim(Δ_2+invert(Δ_0)))
  if(v_1<=v_2 AND b) then output(Δ_1);
  else if(v_1<=v_2) then output(optim(Δ_2+Δ_0));
  else if(v_1>v_2 AND b) then
      output(optim(Δ_1+invert(Δ_0)));
  else output(Δ_2);
end while
if the tail of s_1 or s_2 is not reached then output left part
close(s_1);close(s_2);

Algorithm 2: Merge SBC XML Sequences

Input: SBC XML sequence s_1, s_2
Output: Input: SBC XML sequence s
open(s_1);open(s_2);x1=getfirst(s_1); x2=getfirst(s_2);
if compare(x_1,x_2) then x=x_1; b=true;else x=x_2; b=false;
v_{10}=get_sort_value(x_1); v_{20}=get_sort_value(x_2);
output(x);
Δ_0=edit_distance(x_1,x_2);
while (not reach the tail of s_1 OR not reach the tail of s_2) do
  Δ_1=NULL; Δ_2=NULL;
  while(not reach the data item end in s_1) do
      Δ=getnextopera(s_1);
      if (change of value of v_{10} occurs in Δ) v_1=v_{10} changes based on Δ;
      Δ_1+=Δ;
  end while
  while(not reach the data item tail in s_2) do
      Δ=getnextopera(s_2);
      if (change of value of v_{20} occurs in Δ) v_2=v_{20} changes based on Δ;

$\Delta_2 += \Delta$;
    end while
    if($v_1 <= v_2$ AND b) then output(Δ_1);
    else if($v_1 <= v_2$) then output(optim($\Delta_2 + \Delta_0$));
    else if($v_1 > v_2$ AND b) then
    output(optim($\Delta_1 + invert(\Delta_0)$));
    else output(Δ_2);
end while
if the tail of s_1 or s_2 is not reached then output left part;
close(s_1);close(s_2);

Algorithm 3: Unoin SBC XML Sequences

Input: SBC XML sequence s_1, s_2
Output: SBC XML sequence s
open(s_1);open(s_2);x1=getfirst(s_1); x2=getfirst(s_2);
if compare(x_1, x_2) then x=x_1; b=true;
else x=x_2; b=false;
v_{10}=get sort_value(x_1); v_{20}=get_sort_value(x_2); output(x); Δ_0=edit_distance(x_1, x_2);
while (not reach the tail of s_1 OR not reach the tail of s_2) do
    r=false;
    Δ_1=NULL; Δ_2=NULL;
    while(not reach the data item end in s_1 AND r==false) do
      Δ=getnextopera(s_1);
      if (change of value of v_{10} occurs in Δ) then r= true;$v_1=v_{10}$ changes based on Δ;
      $\Delta_1 += \Delta$;
      if(r==false) store Δ to buffer B;
    end while
    while($v_2 < v_1$) do
      Δ=getnextopera(s_2);
      if (change of value of v_{20} occurs in Δ) $v_2=v_{20}$ changes based on Δ;
      $\Delta_2 += \Delta$; output(Δ)
    end while
    if($v_2 > v_1$) thenΔ_0=optim(invert(Δ_2))+Δ_0; output(Δ_0); output B;$\Delta_0=\Delta_0+\Delta_1$;
    else while ($v_2 == v_1$) do
      while (the end of XML data item in s_2 is not reached) do
        Δ= getnextopera(s_2);
        if (change of value of v_{10} occurs in Δ) then r=true; break;
        $\Delta_2 += \Delta$;
      end while
      if(r==false) then for each XML data item in B represented in Δ_i do
        if(optim($\Delta_i + invert(\Delta_2)$)!=nop) then
          Δ_2=NULL;
          if it is the first XML data item in the loop to output output(optim(($\Delta_2 + invert(v_0)$));
          else output(optim(Δ_2 without the symbol of item's end));
        End if
      End if
    End if
End while
if the tail of s_1 or s_2 is not reached then output left part;
close(s_1);close(s_2);

Algorithm 4: Nature Join of SBC XML Sequences

Input: SBC XML sequence s_1, s_2
Output: Input: SBC XML sequence s
open(s_1);open(s_2);x1=getfirst(s_1); x2=getfirst(s_2);
offset1=the number offset of x1(if connect join offset1=1 otherwise offset1=0);
offset2=the number offset of x2(offset1+the number of nodes in x1);
v_1=get_join_value(x_1); v_2=get_join_value(x_2); Δ_0=edit_distance(x_1,x_2);
x=connect(x1, x2);output(x);
while (not reach the tail of s_1 OR not reach the tail of s_2) do
    r=false;
    //searching s2 until its value equal or over that current XML data item in x_1
    while(not reach the data item end in s_1 AND r==false) do
        Δ=getnextopera(s_1);
        renumber(Δ, offset1);
        if(there are nodes added or deleted) then offset2+=the number of node added to x1;
        if (change of value of v_1 occurs in Δ) then r= true;v_1 changes based on Δ;
        Δ_1+=Δ;
        if(r==false) store $\Delta$to buffer B;
    end while
    //searching s2 until its value equal or over that current XML data item in x_1
    while(v_2<v_1) do
        Δ=getnextopera(s_2);
        renumber(Δ, offset2);
        if (change of value of v_{20} occurs in Δ) v_2 changes based on Δ;
        Δ_2+=Δ;
    end while
    if(v_2>v_1) output B;Δ_0=Δ_0+Δ_1;
    else while (v_2==v_1) do //if they could be joined
    //obtain the XML data items with equal value in s_2
        while (the end of XML data item in s_2 is not reached) do
            Δ= getnextopera(s_2);
            if (change of value of v_{10} occurs in Δ) then r=true; break;
            Δ_2+=Δ;
        end while
    //join two XML data items together
        if(r==false) then for each XML data item in B represented in Δ_i do
            output(Δ_1+Δ_2);
        End if
        Δ_1=NULL; Δ_2=NULL;
    End if
End while
close(s_1);close(s_2);

Algorithm 5: Aggregation SBC XML Sequences with Function SUM

Input: SBC XML sequence s_1, s_2
Output: Input: SBC XML sequence s
open(s_1);open(s_2);
x1=getfirst(s_1); x2=getfirst(s_2);
if compare(x_1,x_2) then x=x_1; b=true;
else x=x_2; b=false;
v_1=get_group_value(x_1); v_2=get_group_value(x_2);
a_1=get_aggregation_value(x_1); a_2=get_aggregation_value(x_2);
output(x);
Δ_0=edit_distance(x_1,x_2);
while (not reach the tail of s_1 OR not reach the tail of s_2) do

```
Δ₁=NULL; Δ₂=NULL;
 if(b==true) then
    while(not reach the data item end in s₁) do
        Δ=getnextopera(s₁);
        if (change of value of v₁ occurs in Δ)v₁ changes based on Δ;
        if (change of value of a₁ occurs in Δ)a₁ changes based on Δ;
        Δ₁+=Δ;
    end while
 else
    while(not reach the data item end in s₂) do
        Δ=getnextopera(s₂);
        if (change of value of v₂ occurs in Δ) v₂ changes based on Δ;
        if (change of value of a₂ occurs in Δ) a₂ changes based on Δ;
        Δ₂+=Δ;
    end while
 end if
 if(v₁<v₂ AND b) then output(Δ₁); b=true
 else if(v₁<v₂) then output(optim(Δ₂+Δ₀)); b=true
 else if(v₁>v₂ AND b) then output(optim(Δ₁+invert(Δ₀))); b=false;
 else if(v₁<v₂)output(Δ₂);b=false;
 else if(b)
    output(Δ₁);
    add operation update(the position of aggregation object in x1,a1, a1+a2);
    add XML data item end symbol;
 else
    output(Δ2);
    add operation update(the position of aggregation object in x2,a1, a1+a2);
    add XML data item end symbol;
 end while
 close(s₁);close(s₂);
```

Supporting the Conversational Knowledge Process in the Networked Community

Toyoaki Nishida

Graduate School of Information Science and Technology, The University of Tokyo
7-3-1 Hongo, Bunkyo-ku, Tokyo 113-8656, Japan
nishida@kc.t.u-tokyo.ac.jp

Abstract. Communities play an important role for knowledge creation in the knowledge society. Conversational communications play a primary means for supporting a collective activity of people for knowledge creation, management, and application. In this paper, I propose a framework of the conversational knowledge process for supporting communities, and present the knowledge channel approach featuring knowledge cards for representing conversational units, the knowledge lifecycle support, and the strategic control of information stream. I show some implemented systems to show how these ideas are implemented.

1   Community as a Ground of Knowledge Creation

Community is a collection of people who build and share the common context. A community serves as a ground for creating both tacit and explicit knowledge, which might be called the community knowledge process. Communities of practice, a group of people who share common work practice, develop informal networks of relationships cutting across organizational boundaries in search for better cooperation[1]. Those social networks not only enable the organization to accomplish tasks faster or better but also create novel knowledge.

The purpose of this research is to develop a suite of technologies to facilitate community knowledge creation. Special care should be taken for designing the communication infrastructure for supporting activities of vital communities in order to meet community-specific nature of communication.

First, informal communication is critical for building and maintaining a shared understanding of the nature of potential knowledge sources in the community. By exchanging informal evaluation of the knowledge sources with respect to the coverage and reliability, the community as a whole establishes its own context that serves as a ground for building task-oriented, intensive human relations.

Second, the designer should take into account the fact that each unit of community-oriented communication are rather of the secondary importance than the primary, for the community-related information is more about the ground of people's activity, such as making new human relations or maintaining existing ones, than urgent mission-oriented subjects such as those for team collaboration or workflow execution. Community-oriented interactions can be easily interrupted by more urgent formal

N. Bianchi-Berthouze (Ed.): DNIS 2003, LNCS 2822, pp. 138-157, 2003.

interactions.   Community-oriented interactions are characterized as a background process that is executed when no foreground process runs.   Accordingly, the communication infrastructure for communities need to pay a lot of attentions to increase the incentive for using the system. Unlike the users of team-group support systems who are requested to use the system as a means for fulfilling their mission, the users of community support systems are less motivated due to the lack of such external force.

There are several heuristics for such community communication channel to effectively function. The cost-effect ratio is improved by increasing merits or decreasing the cost of accessing the community communication channel.   Firstly, there is an opportunities for the background communication channel to be accessed when people are released from the tasks, such as at the break time or differ time. Radio broadcasting programs and quite often TV broadcasting programs in Japan are effectively designed to attract people when people are relaxed.   Secondly, the community communication channel might be embedded into the background, or "ground" in terms of Gestalt psychology, of cognition, so that people can concentrate on the primary task.   Thirdly, the incentive of publishing information might be increased by enhancing the we-feeling of the community or providing enough reciprocity for the submission.

In addition, a community is a collection of people with potentially conflicting goals and interests. The community support system need to have functions for mediating or arbitrating conflicts in the community and decision making based on community wide discussion. The communication support systems should be fair in terms of message collection and delivery, for a community medium might have a much potential power for consensus making.

Certain difficulties are known in social psychology such as spiral of science or minority effect that might have community-wide discussion run into disastrous situations or lead to inappropriate conclusions [2,3]. The designer should carefully avoid pitfalls of collective silliness.

2   Requirements
for Facilitating Community Knowledge Process

We address to build a powerful communication facility for effectively supporting community knowledge process. In order for this goal to be satisfied, the following requirements need to be met.

2.1   Supporting Reality Sharing

Competitive knowledge contains much tacit knowledge; enough description may not be given, or knowledge contains much incompleteness and inconsistency or the idea might be very hard to articulate. In such circumstances, linguistic means of encoding information or knowledge is hard to apply. The reality should be communicated by weaker means so that the tacit idea is transferred without being verbalized. Knowledge and information need to be substantiated in the user's daily living space so that the user can understand the meaning from her/his own viewpoints. A virtual reality using a large immersive display will help the user understand the reality. It should noted, however, that perceptual information need to be combined with verbal information to give the user a clear and structured message about the subject.

2.2   Supporting Social Awareness

Awareness is critical to support collective intelligence. Awareness is information that enables people to act. Social awareness provides with information about other agents' activities and knowledge. Awareness is partial information that enables people to monitor critical events in the environment while shifting primary attention away from the subject. Information and computational support (ICS) for social awareness is critical for a network communities whose members are geographically distributed.

2.3   Supporting Context and Knowledge Sharing

In order for a collection of people to be a community, they share a common context: social rules and principles, the discourse of universe, human relations, the background, and so on. Those propositions are often tacit, and hardly spoken explicitly in the community, which frequently puzzles new comers, and even have community members misunderstand each other's claim. ICS should be able to help community members build and maintain the shared context.

2.4   Supporting Collaborative Work

Even though the primary function of a community is to develop and maintain human relations, collaborative work is necessary from time to time. Traditionally, CSCW (computer-assisted collaborative work) is the area for designing a number of useful tools that help people collaborate [4]. Seamless transition between the community oriented support and the more group or team oriented support are needed.

2.5   Supporting Knowledge Cycle

Today's knowledge is dynamic in the sense that it changes quickly and soon becomes obsolete. Knowledge should accompany proper process of keeping it fresh by incorporating new pieces of knowledge. In other words, knowledge is not like a durable good that sustains its value once it is built, rather it becomes more like a consummatory goods that quickly loose its value after it is introduced. Accordingly, he knowledge cycle in the community need to be sustained properly.

The more knowledge is applied, the more opportunity arises as for knowledge creation. Through exercises of knowledge applications, people build an expertise about when and where to apply the knowledge, what are the expected benefits and underlying risks, and what are the limitations of the knowledge. Through applications, the learners raise questions or comments, urging instructors to reply. ICS should integrate the knowledge creation, application, and maintenance phases.

2.6   Supporting Dispute Resolution

It is quite probable that one community member's interest may be inconsistent with another member in the community. It is desirable that the community has a means for predicting, preventing, and resolving disputes in the community without resorting to the external authority. In particular, ICS should facilitate mutual understanding by circulating enough information to tame ignorance and remove sources of misunderstanding.

2.7   Supporting Large Scale Arguments

The potential of a community can be fully exploited by enabling the community-wide discussion. The goal is quite a challenging problem when a community is as large as a city. ICS should permit the user to be aware of arguments that are relevant to her/his own problem, understand its structure, raise questions, submit proposals, and take a leadership when appropriate.

3   Conversational Knowledge Process

Conversations play a critical role in the community knowledge process. The conversational knowledge process is a term we coined to refer to a collective activity for knowledge creation, management, and application where conversational communications are used as a primary means of interaction among participating agents. It refers to the collection of community-wide concurrent process of conversations that contributes to community knowledge creation. The conversational knowledge process allows for the accumulation and use of very high density information about a given subject which is invaluable for understanding not only issues related to the subject but also people in the community.

3.1   The Role of Conversations in Knowledge Creation

Conversations not only provide the most natural communication means but also facilitate the functions of knowledge creations, heuristic production of stories from different points of view, tacit-explicit knowledge conversion, and entrainment to the subject.

(1) Heuristic Production of Stories from Different Points of View

Conversations allow a heuristic composition of stories in a style agreed by a community. In each conversation, attempts are made to structure fragments of knowledge pieces, either tacitly or explicitly possessed by participants into a larger pieces of knowledge in search for possible viewpoints, connections and clusters to encompass the given collection of pieces.

Conversation is an improvisational social process in which agents from different viewpoints collaborate and negotiate from time to time in search for the social and personal satisfaction. The flow of conversation changes dynamically according to micro-macro interaction of participants' thought.

(2) Tacit-Explicit Knowledge Conversion

Messages communicated with conversations are on the boundary of tacit and explicit knowledge. Conversations give a good opportunity and motivation to externalize tacit knowledge. In discussions, each participant tries to Fig. out the idea into expressions that have an intended effect, such as propose, counter propose, support, challenge, negate, etc, in the conversational discourse. In debate, participants try to be the most expressive, in search for new points to win the game.

On the other hand, people can make conversation or discussion to examine the given subject from different points of view. Exercises of applying knowledge may allow people to find and socialize how pieces of knowledge are associated with each other and identify a critical cluster of knowledge that is most relevant to the discussion.

(3) Entrainment to the Subject

In order to understand the given subject deeply, one should be involved in the subject and capture the problem as her/his own. Conversations tend to entrain the audience by providing enough sympathy, facilitating to simulates the role of a playing character.

Conversations will facilitate reality sharing, for they reflect how people articulate the world. Conversations will support social awareness, for they provide a handy means for communicating references to other people and events that the speaker consider worth communicating. It will help context sharing in the community, for conversations often encourage people recheck issues in a community that are tacitly shared in the community but not written in anywhere. Even though conversations may not directly address dispute resolution or supporting large scale arguments, they contribute to establishing a firm ground for mutual understanding with a dense collection of daily thoughts.

In the meanwhile, conversations have limitations as well. Logically precise arguments or visual information are not well communicated by spoken language alone. Furthermore, conversations are volatile. Both the content and the context may be lost quite easily, for it is difficult to reproduce the same mental state as the situation where the conversation was made. Even though conversations are recorded, it is pretty hard to recover the implications of conversations after the conversation session or correcting the transcript is time consuming, tedious task. These weakness should be somehow compensated by advanced information and communication technology.

3.2   Conversation-Story Spiral

In order to exploit the benefits of conversation and compensate for its limitations, I propose a model called the conversation-story spiral. The model shown in Fig.1 suggests that we use two modes of knowledge representation. The story archive is a media-oriented representation of knowledge. It is suitable for representing the static aspects of knowledge, such as the structure or relation. In contrast, the conversation process is the interaction-oriented representation. It allows for representing how components of knowledge interact with each other. These two modes of knowledge representation are related to each other by a couple of conversion processes: conversation making and story making.

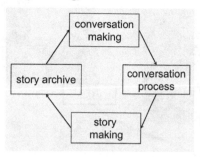

Fig. 1. The Conversation-Story Spiral

Conversation making is a process for adapting story pieces into utterances that are suitable for each scene of a conversation. Various types of transformation are needed to tailor each piece of information so that it can conform to what is allowed in the context.

Story making is a process of composing well-structured stories from a given sequence of utterances. It involves seeking for an optimal story structure that can incorporate conversation fragments, changing the tacit conversational knowledge into explicit representation, transforming components of information representation into those with a uniform grain size, and so on.

4   The Knowledge Channel Approach
to Conversational Knowledge Process

In order of implement the conversational knowledge process, we need to design appropriate representation and mechanism for conversation. The knowledge channel approach we introduce in this section consists of three ideas. First, we use what we call knowledge card as a component for representing conversation. A knowledge card is a data structure that encapsulates a narrative and its references for representing the content of a conversational unit. Each knowledge card is relatively self-contained package of tacit and explicit knowledge, enabling one to implement a rather robust conversational system without introducing a complex discourse generation algorithm. Second, we support the lifecycle of knowledge cards to encourage people to create, edit, share, and utilize knowledge cards. This will bring about a evolutionary system of knowledge cards where a population of knowledge cards evolve by absorbing knowledge and information possessed by community members under selection and mutation. Third, we introduce a mechanism for strategically controlling the flow of knowledge cards. This will contribute to designing long-term interaction by controlling the flow of knowledge cards.

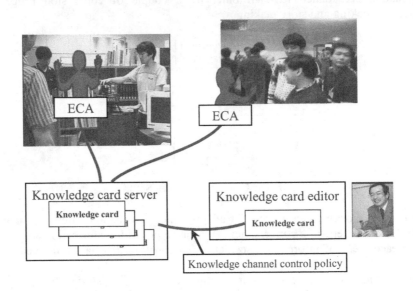

Fig. 2. A general framework of the knowledge channel approach

4.1   The Architecture of the Knowledge Channel Approach

The knowledge channel approach uses the data structure called knowledge card as a representation of the conversation unit (Fig.2).   A knowledge card is a data structure that encapsulates a narrative and its references for representing the content of a conversational unit.   Another data structure called a story is used to represent a discourse structure consisting of one or more knowledge card. A knowledge card server stores knowledge cards and provides them for knowledge card clients. Embodied conversational agent take knowledge cards to generate utterances in conversations. Knowledge channel is a conduit connecting the server and the client where knowledge card flow is controlled strategically. Both the knowledge card server and the knowledge card client can control the knowledge card flow using the knowledge channel control policy.

This approach can approximate the conversational knowledge process even with a simple mechanism, and better with a more sophisticated dialogue engine. Tacit knowledge can be embedded into each knowledge card such as visual images or sound, even though it cannot be encoded into knowledge representation. The current natural language processing techniques such as document classification or summarization may be applied to turn the collection of knowledge cards into a structured knowledge.

I illustrate how the conversational knowledge process is implemented in (a) the public opinion channel, which is a participatory broadcasting system that collects small talks and broadcasts stories reorganized from the archive of small talks, (b) EgoChat which is a conversational agent system based on the talking-virtualized-egos metaphor, and (c) S-POC which is an integrated communication support system.

4.2   Public Opinion Channel

POC (Public Opinion Channel) is a participatory broadcasting system based on the knowledge channel approach [5,6]. We implemented a prototype of POC. The POC prototype implements a knowledge card as a simple data structure consisting of a plain text and possibly a static image. Only a sequential order of knowledge cards are permitted in a story.

POC TV is an STB(Set Top Box)-based POC client that can be directly connected to an ordinary TV set. POC TV takes knowledge cards and translates them into a conversation by two characters, as shown in Fig.3. Given a POC message, one agent (the caster agent) introduces the subject, and another agent (the announcer agent) talks about the content. From time to time, the first agent may interrupt the second by inserting comments or questions. We have found that even a simple conversation generation mechanism (Fig.4) helps the user understand messages. According to our preliminary experiments, the user prefers conversational presentation of the content to monologue presentation by a single agent.

The audience may normally receive the broadcasting just like s/he is watching multiple-channel TV broadcasting. On occasion when an interesting subject appears on a screen, s/he might switch to the on-demand mode and download related programs as much as s/he likes. In addition, s/he can respond with a question or a comment if s/he likes. POC accumulates those reactions into the message archive and dynamically updates programs.

In addition to knowledge card storage and delivery functions, the knowledge server supports community maintenance and analysis functions. The community maintenance function allows for maintaining communities and their members. The community analysis function called the POC analyzer allows researchers to investigate the activities of communities on the server. The POC analyzer permits the user to use social network analysis to investigate both explicit message relations based on reference relationship among knowledge cards and implicit message relations based on similarity between messages calculated based on TFIDF (Term Frequency and Inverse Document Frequency). A sample screen image is shown in Fig. 5.

Furthermore, the POC prototype supplies a voting function. The user can easily vote for a program s/he is watching by pressing a button. The result is reflected in the ranking channel. The knowledge card channel policy was not implemented.

The POC broadcasting can be characterized as an ambient medium, in the sense that it is embedded in the background of the environment, just like radio broadcasting, so that people need not pay complete attention at all times. The advantage of background casting is that it can continually provide people with information without much intervention.

POC was evaluated in the FTTH trial sponsored by KDDI, which took place with participation of 443 families in the Tokyo area from March to September in 2002. During the period for the FTTH trial, two services were provided using POC. One was "my town stream" provided by my group. It consisted of nine channels containing three types of information (messages, stories in chronological order, and stories with the ranking information). They were specialized to three areas: Shinjuku-ku and Bunkyo-ku in Tokyo where the participating families lived (378 families in Shinjuku-ku and 85 families in Bunkyo-ku), and the Kansai district, about 300 miles away from the first two areas, where the service providers lived. The other service was "speaking BBS" provided by KDDI to discuss issues about the FTTH trial.

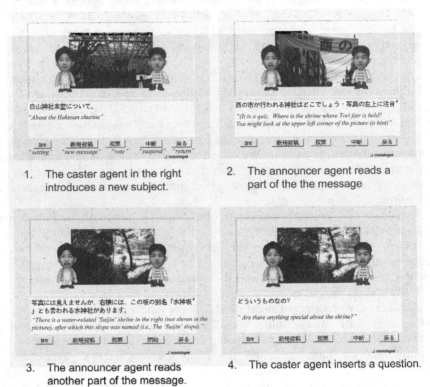

1. The caster agent in the right introduces a new subject.

2. The announcer agent reads a part of the the message

3. The announcer agent reads another part of the message.

4. The caster agent inserts a question.

Fig. 3. A knowledge card presented as a conversation between conversational agents

For the "my town stream" service, we hired part time workers and prepared about 2300 knowledge cards and 700 stories as an initial content. We did so because we knew from previous experiences that users tend to hesitate to submit a content until they see enough preceding examples. We also prepared an agreement for using POC with advices by a lawyer. The agreement was about the policy of submitting messages to POC in the FTTH trial, consisting of four sections: general principles, the policy for publishing messages from POC, the copyright policy, and the liability exemption. The unique feature of this agreement was about the ownership of the copyright. We specified that the copyright of each knowledge card was collectively possessed by the entire community and every community member was allowed to copy knowledge cards originally created by other members and create modified ones.

Fig.6 shows how many accesses have been made during the FTTH trial period (about 190 days). The number of accesses in the first half was so many as maximally 40 IPs a day, 1046 in total from 366 families, while the less access was made the second half, less than five IPs a day, 110 in total, from 46 families. The 43 families of the 46 families who accessed the POC in the second half were repeaters who continually accessed POC from the first half. People tended to access POC in weekends. People clearly preferred to watch service about their residential area. For example, 39% of the residents in the Shinjuku-ku area accessed the Shinjuku-ku channel, but only 5.6% accessed the Bunkyo-ku channel and 3% accessed the Kansai channel.

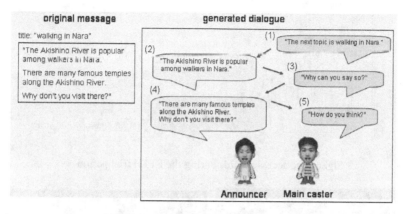

Fig. 4. Conversation Generation Mechanism for POC TV

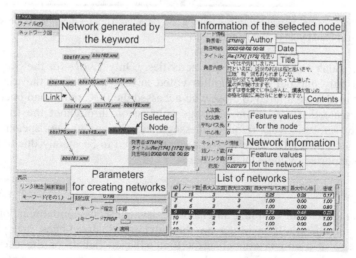

Fig. 5. A sample screen image of the POC analyzer. The graph on the up left corner shows the extracted relations among messages. Messages and their relations are denoted by nodes and directed arcs, respectively. Each arc represents how each message is followed by a more recent message

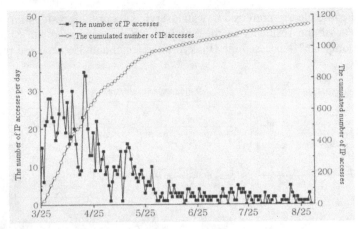

Fig. 6. The access records during the FTTH trial period

Fig. 7. EgoChat: normal presentation mode by a single agent (left), Question mode where the user's question is read by an avatar (right).

The users didn't exhibit much voting activities. Only 17.6% for the Shinjuku-ku channel and only one out of 17 families voted in the first half of the trial period. Those who voted were limited to those who accessed the POC more than once. It was quite unfortunate that we had no message submission throughout the trial period, though there were relatively frequent message submissions to the "speaking BBS" service provided by KDDI. The reason was considered to be mainly due to a strong reciprocity supported by the KDDI personnel.

4.3   EgoChat

EgoChat is a system for enabling an elaborate asynchronous communication among community members. It is based on the talking-virtualized-egos metaphor. A virtualized ego is a conversational agent that talks on behalf of the user. Each virtualized ego stores and maintains the user's personal memory as a collection of knowledge cards and presents them on behalf of the user at appropriate situations. It not only helps the user develop her/his personal memory but also better understand other members' interest, belief, opinion, knowledge, and way of thinking, which is valuable for building mutual understanding. We use a powerful dialogue engine that permits a virtualized ego to answer questions by searching for the best match from a potentially large list of question-answering pairs prepared in advance (Fig. 7).

EgoChat provides a couple of unique features. First, it integrates personal and interpersonal knowledge life cycles [7]. At earlier stages of the lifecycle when knowledge is not well captured, the user might want to describe her/his idea as one or more knowledge card and have the virtualized ego to present them for personal review. After a while when the knowledge becomes clear and evident to the user, s/he might want to delegate her/his virtualized ego to her/his colleagues to present the idea and ask for critiques. The automatic question answering facility of EgoChat will encourage the audience to ask questions or give comments. The virtualized ego can reproduce the question-answering session with the audience so the owner can review the interactions. It will highly motivate the owner to supply more knowledge or improve existing knowledge for better competence.

Second, EgoChat allows for describing a channel policy that is used to define the control strategies of the sender and the receiver. Four types of strategies are identified depending on whether the strategy is about the order of programs in a single program stream or about the way multiple program streams are mixed, and whether the program scheduling is static or dynamic, as shown in Table.1. The skeleton of the actual flow structure of knowledge cards for a given pair of the sender and receiver is determined by resolving constraints of their channel policies. It can be visually presented to the user by the dynamic program table, as shown in Fig.8 [8].

4.4   S-POC

S-POC was designed to serve as an integrated communication environment for a multi-faceted community activities such as risk communication. S-POC supports reality sharing based on visual images, knowledge sharing, and community-wide discussion for decision-making (Fig.9).

Table 1. Four strategies in the knowledge channel policy

	Static scheduling	Dynamic scheduling
Intra-channel arranging	**Order strategy** Giving the outline of the content (messages and channels) in a channel ·course <[message | channel | (a set of content, sorting [by title | category | length | rating | activity | author | date | keyword | ...], order [ascendant | descendant])], ... >	**Access strategy** Changing the stream of the content depending on the interaction and the situation ·browsing [{(behavior [play | skip | ...], condition [always | in events | ...], permission [all | members | owner | ...]), ... } | null] ·contribution [{(action [post | query | rate | create | ...], condition [always | in events | ...], response [agent replies | content changes | never | ...], modification [add the message | change the rating | never | ...], permission [all | members | owner | ...]), ... } | null]
Inter-channel arranging	**Link strategy** Giving a connection with other channels ·loopback [loopback | null] ·channels [{(channel, elements [channel name, ...]), ... } | null]	**Interchange strategy** Navigating channels ·navigation [{(target channel, behavior [branch | merge | parallel | ...], condition [always | in events | ...], permission [all | members | owner | ...]), ... } | null]

<x1, x2, ... > represents ordered elements, {x, y, ...} represents unordered elements, [x \| y \| ...] represents x, y or other elements and (x, y, ...) represents a set of elements, where elements x and y are defined contextually.

Fig. 8. Example of dynamic program table

The S-POC uses the POC system as a knowledge sharing engine and extends it in several respects. First, S-POC allows for sophisticated presentation mechanism using an embodied conversational agent. Second, it supports video editing and presentation. Third, it allows a community discussion support system to be plugged in [9,10].

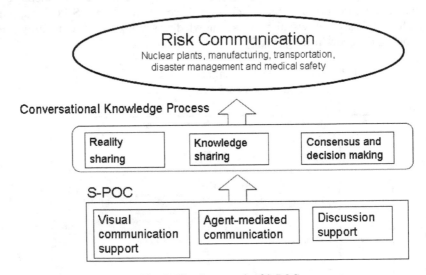

Fig. 9. The framework of S-POC

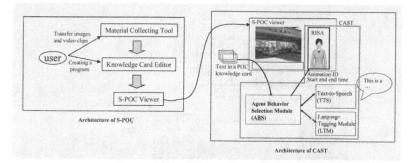

Fig. 10. RISA-CAST subsystem for generating ECA presentation

(1) The Presentation Mechanism Using ECA

The RISA-CAST component allows for automatically generating from plain text as a presentation featured with an animated agent. It selects and generates appropriate gestures and facial expressions for a humanoid agent according to linguistic information in the text. An agent animation system called RISA can draw animations of natural human behaviors on web-based applications. The ECA subsystem called CAST (The Conversational Agent System for neTwork applications) generates agent's nonverbal behavior automatically based on theories of human communication (Fig.10).

(2) Video Editing and Presentation Tools

The S-POC system allows for video presentation, using streamed video clips and camera works, such as zoom and pan, applied to graphic images. In order to help the casual user to create and review the video contents, the following tools are incorporated.

1. tools for collecting and accumulating materials (e.g. pictures, graphics and videos)
2. tools for creating video contents by assembling components of various kinds (Fig.11)
3. a viewer for converting a knowledge card into a synchronized presentation with the ECA and multimedia materials.

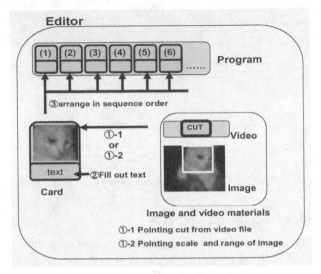

Fig. 11. The overview of the video editor

(3) Discussion Support System

S-POC allows CRANES (Coordinator for Rational Arguments through Nested Substantiation) to be plugged in, which supports discussions in the community for consensus making [11] CRANES uses a probabilistic approach to selectively identify "stirring arguments" that have stimulated the entire group processes. Two random-tree models are developed for the purpose of defining an indicator of noteworthiness. In the perfect random tree, the probability for a new comment to be associated with a certain existing node is assumed to be the same among all existing nodes. A biased random tree model is a more elaborate model that inflates the probability of the last node's producing a new child compared to other existing nodes. It reflects an intuition that when readers of a BBS consider which comment they respond to, they are more likely to choose the last node in the whole thread or those with some specific features. CRANES was applied to a community conflict over a regeneration scheme in London, to result in an augmented social construction of the conflict with multiple dimensions.

4.5   Towards Communicative Intelligence

A five-year research project "Intelligent Media Technology for Supporting Natural Communication between People" sponsored by Japan Society for the Promotion of Science (JSPS) addresses communicative intelligence as a generalization of the idea of conversational knowledge process. The term "communicative intelligence" reflects the idea of communicative intelligence implies a view that communication plays a critical role in both individual and collective intelligence. a more at establishing a technology for creating and utilizing conversational contents.   The project encompasses the environmental medium technology for embedding computational services in the environment, the embodied conversational agent technology for having computers interact with people in a social context, and the communication model of conversations that serves as a theoretical basis of the intelligent media research (Fig.12).

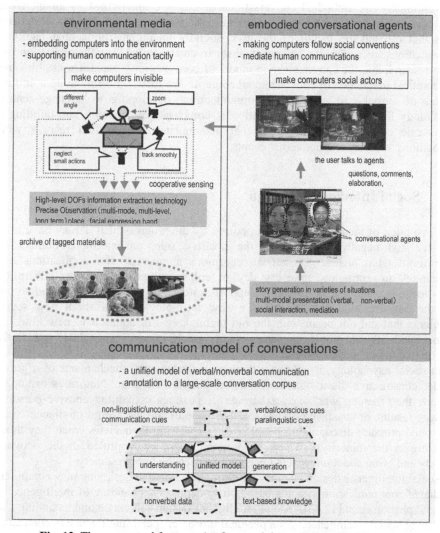

Fig. 12. The conceptual framework of research into conversational content.

The environmental medium technology is based on the "making-computers-invisible" approach, aiming at embedding computers into the everyday environment so that they can assist people in pursuit for their goals without enforcing them to pay special attention to computer operations. We attempt at developing cooperative intelligent activity sensors, automatic analysis of nonverbal communication with high-resolution scene analysis, personalization of environment medium, and intelligent editing of audio-visual streams.

The embodied conversational agent technology is based on the "making-computers-social-actors" approach, aiming at developing embodied conversational agents that can make conversation with people by following various social conventions. The embodied conversational agent is characterized as an interface between people and conversational content. We attempt at developing virtualized egos that can talk on behalf of the user, socially intelligent robots that facilitate conversations among people, and agents that can create stories from their experiences.

In research into the communication model of conversations, we aim at establishing a theoretical foundation of conversational content. We focus on formulating a unified model of verbal and nonverbal communication, developing a language-centric technology for editing and summarization of conversational contents and building a large-scale corpus of conversations that accumulates conversation records with annotations to verbal and nonverbal events.

5   Social Intelligence Design

The evolution of media technology supported by the progress of ICT may have both positive and negative sides.   On the positive side, an enormous number of opportunities has arisen.   In fact, an enormous number of new applications and businesses are springing up every day in collaborative environment, e-learning, knowledge management, community support systems, digital democracy, and so on. On the negative side, the advent of a new technology brings about new social problems that did not occur with the old technology.   In addition to new kinds of crimes and ethical problems, some effects of ICT are very subtle, yet fairly destructive to our spiritual world.

In social psychology, it is known that some fundamental mechanisms of a group hinder constructive discussions and rational decision-making.   Notorious examples include the "flaming war" (i.e., a barrage of postings containing abusive personal attacks, insults, or chastising replies to other people) and the "spiral of silence" (i.e., the social pressure discouraging people from expressing their views when they think they are in the minority).   These phenomena might be amplified in the network society and bring about unexpected negative impacts on human society.

Social intelligence design is a new research area aimed at designing new computer-mediated communication systems based on in-depth understanding of intelligence as a social phenomenon [12,13]. Social intelligence design centers on understanding and designing social intelligence. As a personal attribute, social intelligence is contrasted with other kinds of intelligence such as problem-solving intelligence (ability to solve logically complex problems) or emotional intelligence (ability to monitor one's own and others' emotions and to use the information to guide one's thinking and actions).

Alternatively, social intelligence might be attributed to a collection of agents and defined as an ability to manage complexity and learn from experiences as a function of the design of social structure. This view emphasizes the role of social conventions that constrain the way individual agents interact with each other. A good social culture will allow the members of the community to learn from each other.

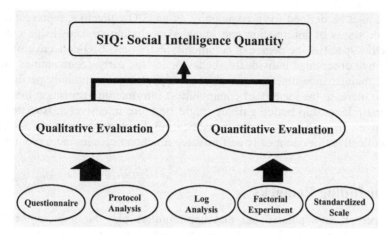

Fig. 13. The framework of Social Intelligence Quantity

Social intelligence design is an interdisciplinary field. On the one hand, it involves engineering approaches concerning the design and implementation of systems, ranging from group/team-oriented collaboration support systems that facilitate intimate goal-oriented interaction among participants to community support systems that support large-scale online discussion. On the other hand, it involves scientific approaches addressing cognitive and social psychological understanding of social intelligence, and provides a means for predicting and evaluating the effect of a given communication medium on the nature of discussions and conclusions. In addition, it encompasses pragmatic considerations from economics, sociology, ethics, and many other disciplines, for social intelligence design has a direct relation with the society.

The central idea underlying the evaluation is to define a standardized measurement of social intelligence of people. Should such a measurement be introduced, it is also applied to measure the effect of a given information system with respect to the degree of improvement of social intelligence of people.

Social Intelligence Quantity is a framework of standardized quantitative measurement of social intelligence. Our approach combines qualitative evaluation consisting of questionnaire and protocol analysis and quantitative evaluation consisting of network log analysis, factorial experiment, and standardized psychological scale, as shown in Fig.13 [14,15].

SIQ can be defined for an individual as an SIQ-personal, representing a standardized psychological measurement that specifies the individual's social information processing activities such as information acquisition and publication activities, interpersonal relationship building desire, and monopolized information possession desire. We made an experiment of partially measuring SIQ-personal by using a suite of questionnaires to measure the strength of each individual's desire of acquiring and publishing information. From psychological experiments, we have found that POC made a significant contribution to satisfy information acquisition desire, though there was not a significant contribution to the satisfaction of information publishing desire, which conforms to observation obtained in the POC FTTH trial.

SIQ can also be defined for a community as an SIQ-collective, representing the community's status of information and knowledge sharing or knowledge creation. SIQ-collective specifies the degree of community activities. SIQ-collective might be measured by observing individuals' behavior.   In early communities where community maintenance functions are more dominant than community performance functions to increase the identity of communities, information acquisition desire and interpersonal relationship building desire might be more intensively associated with SIQ-collective. In contrast, information publication desire might be more associated with SIQ-collective, for community performance function becomes more prominent.

6   Concluding Remarks

In this paper, I have pointed out that communities play an important role for knowledge creation in the knowledge society and conversational communications play a primary means for supporting a collective activity of people for knowledge creation, management, and application.   I have proposed a framework of the conversational knowledge process for supporting communities, and present the knowledge channel approach featuring knowledge cards for representing conversational units, the knowledge lifecycle support, and the strategic control of information stream. I have shown some implemented systems -- POC, EgoChat, and S-POC -- to show how these ideas are implemented.

References

[1]   Etienne Wenger. Communities of Practice -- Learning Meaning, and Identity, Cambridge University Press, 1998.

[2]   Noelle-Neumann, Elisabeth *The Spiral of Silence: Public Opinion--Our Social Skin*. 2d edition. 1984, 1993

[3]   Janis, I. L., *Groupthink, 2nd Edition*, Houghton Mifflin Company, Boston, 1982.

[4]   S. Kelly and M. Jones, "Groupware and the Social Infrastructure of Communication," Comm. ACM, Dec. 2001, pp. 77-79.

[5]   T. Nishida, ed., Dynamic Knowledge Interaction, CRC Press, Boca Raton, Fla., 2000.

[6]   T. Fukuhara, M. Chikama, and T. Nishida. A Platform for Investigating a Knowledge Creating Community: Community Analysis and Maintenance Functions in the Public Opinion Channel. to be presented at Social Intelligence Design SID 2003, 6-th – 8th July 2003, Royal Holloway University of London, Egham, Surrey U.K.

[7]   Hidekazu Kubota, Koji Yamashita, Toyoaki Nishida, Conversational Contents Making a Comment Automatically, Best PhD paper award, In: E. Damiani, R. J. Howlett, L. C. Jain, and N. Ichalkaranje (eds.): *Proc. KES 2002*, pp. 1326-1330, KES'2002 Sixth International Conference on Knowledge-Based Intelligent Information & Engineering Systems, 16, 17 & 18 September 2002, Crema, Italy, 2002

[8]   H. Kubota and T. Nishida. Channel Design for Strategic Knowledge Interaction. to be presented at: *KES'2003 Seventh International Conference on Knowledge-Based Intelligent Information & Engineering Systems*, University of Oxford, United Kingdom 3, 4 & 5 September 2003.

[9]   Y. Nakano, T. Murayama, D. Kawahara, S. Kurohashi, and T. Nishida. Embodied Conversational Agents for Presenting Intellectual Multimedia Contents. to be presented at: *KES'2003 Seventh International Conference on Knowledge-Based Intelligent Information & Engineering Systems*, University of Oxford, United Kingdom 3, 4 & 5 September 2003.

[10]   T. Murayama, Y. Nakano, and T. Nishida. Participatory Broadcasting System Using Interface Agent and Multimedia, to be presented at Social Intelligence Design SID 2003, 6-th – 8th July 2003, Royal Holloway University of London, Egham, Surrey U.K.

[11]   M. Horita and N. Iwahashi. On Discovery of Stirring Arguments: A Random-Tree Approach to Collaborative Argumentation Support, to be presented at Social Intelligence Design SID 2003, 6-th – 8th July 2003, Royal Holloway University of London, Egham, Surrey U.K.

[12]   T. Nishida. Social Intelligence Design for Web Intelligence, Special Issue on Web Intelligence, IEEE Computer, Vol. 35, No. 11, pp. 37-41, November, 2002.

[13]   Toyoaki Nishida. Social Intelligence Design -- An Overview, in: Takao Terano, Toyoaki Nishida, Akira Namatame, Yukio Ohsawa, Shusaku Tsumoto, and Takashi Washio (eds): Exploring New Frontiers on Artificial Intelligence - Selected Papers from the First International Workshops of Japanese Society of Artificial Intelligence -, Lecture Notes on Artificial Intelligence LNAI2253, Springer Verlag, December 2001.

[14]   Koji Yamashita and Toyoaki Nishida: SIQ (Social Intelligence Quantity): Evaluation Package for Network Communication Tools, APCHI 2002 -- 5th Asia Pacific Conference on Computer Human Interaction - Beijing, China, 1-4 November 2002.

[15]   Ken'ichi Matsumura. The factors to activate communication in the network community –New comers or Messages? -, to be presented at Social Intelligence Design SID 2003, 6-th – 8th July 2003, Royal Holloway University of London, Egham, Surrey U.K.

Intelligent Management of SLAs
for Composite Web Services

Malu Castellanos, Fabio Casati, Umeshwar Dayal, and Ming-Chien Shan

Hewlett-Packard
1501 Page Mill Road, MS 1142, Palo Alto, CA, 94304, USA
{malu.castellanos,fabio.casati,umeshwar.dayal,ming-chien.shan}@hp.com

Abstract. For every business, managing the Service Level Agreements (SLAs) stipulated with its customers is a crucial activity. Failing to meet an SLA may lead to contractual penalties and in loss of revenues generated by customers resorting to other providers to obtain the services they need. In this paper we present a framework and an infrastructure for intelligent SLA management, applicable when services are delivered as Web services. The goal of the platform is that of assisting service providers in monitoring SLA violations, in predicting SLA violations before they occur so to try corrective actions, and in analyzing SLA violations to understand their causes and therefore help identify how to improve operations to meet the SLA.

1   Introduction

One of the most intriguing and neglected aspects of Web services is their capability of linking IT operations with business operations. In fact, Web service technology is designed with the purpose of automating B2B interactions. Furthermore, Web services offer operations that are typically at a high level of abstraction (i.e., at the level of business operations such as orderGoods or makePayment, rather than at the level of IT operations such as getID or incrementCounter).

The combination of these two factors makes it natural to use Web services for coarse grained B2B interactions, so that there is a close performance and quality relationship between a business exchange (e.g., a customer ordering a product from a service provider) and a Web service operation (e.g., the orderGoods operation mentioned above). This close relationship makes it possible and even necessary to manage IT operations based on business goals and, conversely, makes it possible to monitor, control, and optimize business operations by monitoring, controlling, and analyzing IT operations [2,3].

A particularly important aspect in the relationship is related to the management of Service Level Agreements (SLA) [8]. An SLA defines the quality of the service offered by a provider to a customer and the circumstances under which this quality is guaranteed. For example, an SLA could state that 90% of the operations executed between 9AM and 5PM should complete within 3 seconds, or that orders of silk ties over 1000 pieces should be received within 15 days of the order or within 10 days from the payment.

It is essential that service providers are able to meet the SLAs stipulated with their customers, as SLAs are one of the main metrics by which customers judge the quality

N. Bianchi-Berthouze (Ed.): DNIS 2003, LNCS 2822, pp. 158-171, 2003.
© Springer-Verlag Berlin Heidelberg 2003

of the services offered by service providers, not to mention that SLAs are often part of a contract. Therefore, missing SLAs not only implies the risk of losing a customer, but comes with consequences such as payments of penalties. For example, the above mentioned SLA about the time to deliver silk ties could be associated to a penalty stating that the customers should be refunded in part or in full if the SLA is not met.

From the examples and considerations above, it is clear that service providers will greatly benefit from the capability of monitoring SLA violations, of understanding why (e.g., under which conditions) SLAs are not met and to predict whether an SLA will be met or not. Explanations of why SLAs are missed can help providers either in correcting the problem (e.g., adding more resources, changing the shipping company, or ordering products from a different supplier) or in revising the SLA for future interactions if the problems cannot be corrected with acceptable costs. Predictions of SLA violations can help providers in taking corrective actions on the fly, where possible, or at least can enable providers to promptly inform customers about the potential problem (e.g., delay in the order). Although this may not avoid payments of penalties, it goes a long way towards improving the relationships between customers and suppliers.

This paper presents a set of techniques and outlines the architecture of a system, partially implemented at HP Labs, that allows service providers to manage SLAs for Web services. In particular, we argue that thanks to the above mentioned relationships between Web services and business interactions, SLAs stipulated with customers can be monitored by looking at Web service execution data, logged by the Web services platform. Furthermore, we show how SLA can not only be monitored, but also explained and predicted by using data mining techniques.

We focus in particular on a specific class of Web services, that of *composite services*, i.e., Web services implemented by composing other services by means of a process flow. The reason for focusing on composite services is twofold: first, as service composition technologies continue to improve, as standardization efforts move forward, and as the service oriented paradigm becomes widely accepted, more and more Web services are expected to be composite. Second, the fact that a service is composite allows visibility into its definition and execution. This characteristic makes composite services particularly suited to analyzing and predicting SLA violations. This work has been developed in the context of the Business Process Intelligence work developed at HP Labs [1].

2   Approach

2.1   A Sample Composite Service

In this section we introduce an example related to supply chain management (SCM). This example will be used throughout the paper to illustrate the concepts. The example is about a Web service named buy_ties. This service is in charge of all the operations related to the processing of silk tie orders placed by customers. Those operations available to the customers are specified in an interface described in WSDL[4]. Next we show a possible customer interface for the buy_ties, abstracting from any particular description language. The operations are prefixed with *in* or *out* qualifiers to denote whether the operation is invoked by the customer or is initiated by the provider:

in quote_request (product id, quantity, city)
out quote (quote #, product id, quantity, city, price)
in order_request (quote #)
out confirm_order (order #, product id, quantity, city, price)
out cancel_order (order #)
out confirm_shipment (order #, date)

The interface lets a customer know how to interact with the **buy_ties** service in the business exchanges with the company offering it. The interface is all a customer sees about this service, but internally **buy_ties** service is implemented by composing a set of simpler services which are orchestrated by a business process depicted in Figure 1 (this process is a simplification of a real one).

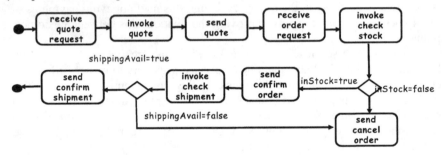

Fig. 1. Buy_tie composite service

A customer invokes the operations of the **buy_ties** service with some expectations on the service quality. These expectations, based on different aspects of the service, are formalized in an SLA in order to obtain a guarantees from the service provider. In our approach we assume that SLAs are defined by business users, typically by means of sentences expressed in natural language and possibly written in a contract. Once such an SLA has been defined, an IT manager maps the definition performed in natural language into definitions expressed in a programming language, so that they can be executed by a management system to monitor SLA compliance. In our system we assume that SLA clauses are mapped to SQL queries that can be then run on top of composite service execution data. Some example SLA clauses for our example could be the following (here we assume that the provider's name is "Ties & Ties"):

- Clause A: *Provider "Ties & Ties" guarantees that the time to deliver ties to customer "ABC" cannot exceed 48 hours from the time the order is received by the provider to the time the goods arrive to the customer.*
- Clause B: *Provider "Ties & Ties" guarantees a response time of 5 minutes for sending a quote from the time the quote is requested by customer "ABC" to the time it is sent to this customer.*
- Clause C: *Provider "Ties & Ties" guarantees not to cancel more than 3% of the orders placed by customer "ABC".*

- Clause D: *Provider "Ties & Ties" guarantees an availability of 99% of the service when customer "ABC" places orders.*

These clauses stipulated in the SLA between provider "Ties & Ties" and customer "ABC" are mapped to conditions over composite service execution data. In fact, for each clause there is a corresponding metric that is computed on composite service execution data. The SLA clause defines a Boolean condition on this metric that has to be satisfied in accordance to the terms of the clause for the SLA not to be violated. Next, we show the correspondences for the clauses defined above.

- Clause A: the corresponding metric is *duration* which is computed on the time interval from the receive_order_request step to the send_confirm_shipment step. The condition on the value measured is not to exceed 48 hours. In this case the composite service execution data are the start time of the step receive_order_request and the end time of the step send_confirm_shipment for process instances of customer "ABC".
- Clause B: the corresponding metric is duration again, but in this case it is computed on the time interval from the start of the receive_quote_request step to the end of the send_quote step. The condition is that this interval does not exceed 5 minutes for process instances of customer "ABC".
- Clause C: for this clause there is metric percentageOfCancellations where the condition is that its value does not exceed 3. The data on which it is computed is the outcome (i.e., accept, reject) of the process for each order_ request.
- Clause D: the metric that corresponds to this clause is availability which is computed on the status of the resources in charge of receiving the order, checking the stock and confirming or canceling the order in the process instances for customer "ABC".

As can be perceived from these example clauses, SLAs are in fact Boolean conditions. They can be measured by looking at the external interactions, but as we will see they can be better analyzed if we have knowledge about the internal implementation of the service, as in the case described above. (Note that in this paper we do not consider the problem related to different perceptions of whether an SLA is violated that customers and providers could have because the system is distributed. We assume that all measurements are made at the service provider's site.)

Once SLAs have been measured, process instances (corresponding to execution of a Web service) can be annotated with the values of these measurements (i.e., satisfaction or violation). This allows business managers to constantly monitor SLAs, which in turn gives them the opportunity to make changes on the IT infrastructure or the process itself to achieve the quality of the service promised to their customers. Furthermore, annotating process instances with SLA measurements makes it possible to detect patterns for explanation and prediction on the behavior of SLA clauses, as will be seen in section 3.2.

2.2   Classification of SLAs

Now that we have introduced some sample SLA in a concrete domain, we try to bring some structure to the problem by classifying the different kinds of SLAs according to several dimensions. This classification is used by the SLA Manager (SLAM) to facilitate SLA definition and management.

SLAs can be broadly divided into *business* SLAs and *IT* SLAs. IT SLAs are related to system or application-level metrics (such as response time of an individual operation or availability) that are applicable to virtually all services. For example, an IT SLA could state that 90% of the operations executed between 9AM and 5PM should complete within 3 seconds. Business SLAs refer instead to agreements on how a specific service is delivered, and refer to the semantics of the service rather than to system- or application-level metrics. For example, a business SLA could state that orders of silk ties over 1000 pieces should be received within 15 days of the order, or within 10 days from the payment.

A contract between businesses can in general include both business and IT SLAs. Although in general these can be independent, in practice they are often correlated, since for example a failure in the system is likely to affect both the performance of the system in terms of response time, but also the performance of the overall service delivery process, thereby endangering business SLAs as well.

Another classification of SLAs is related to the characteristics of the condition that is evaluated over process execution data to assess whether the SLA has been violated. Specifically, we classify SLAs as follows, based on the nature of the SLA clause:

- *Duration (distance)*: the clause requires that the distance between the two steps of the process flow is equal, less than or more than a certain threshold. For example, it may require that no more than N number of hours pass between the *receive_order* step and the *confirm_shipment* step.
- *Data*: the clause is mapped to a condition on the service composition variables. For example, it may require that at least three quality assurance consultants are named for order that are above a certain amount X. X and the number of quality assurance consultants are assumed to be measurable from service composition variables.
- *Path:* the SLA clause is mapped to a condition that involves the execution taking a certain path or executing a certain node. For example, an SLA may require that certain orders be shipped express, which means that the path in the flow corresponding to arranging for the express shipment is executed.
- *Count:* The clause requires that a certain node is activated a specified number of times. For example, an SLA can be mapped to a condition stating that a project should be reviewed at least 3 times (corresponding, from an implementation perspective, to stating that step *projectReview* should be performed at least 3 times).
- *Resource:* The clause is mapped to a condition requiring that a given step of the flow is executed by a certain resource. For example, an SLA could require that projects submitted by certain employees be first reviewed by strategy team members.

Note that some SLA conditions can be of more than one type. For example, a clause could state that the delivery time for orders over 1000$ is at most 20 days. This involved both data and duration conditions.

Besides typing based on the kind of condition being monitored, SLAs can be classified based on their complexity. In particular, we distinguish between basic and composite SLAs. Basic SLAs are defined by a boolean condition over service execution data, as described above. Basic SLAs are sometimes called SLA clauses or Service Level Objectives (SLOs) in the literature. Composite SLAs are defined in terms of conjunction of SLOs or even other SLAs.

A final classification is based on whether the SLA is specific, that is, it is defined on each process instance (i.e., the SLA condition can be evaluated by looking at the execution data of a process instance) or involves instead the aggregated analysis of many instances (we call these *generic* SLAs). The examples above are all related to SLAs for one instance. An example of SLA on aggregate execution data is "at least 95% of the orders should be delivered within 3 days, and no order should be delivered in more than 30 days". Note that while in instance-based SLA whether an SLA is violated or not can be computed at the end of the process instance and the result of the computation never changes, for generic SLAs whether an SLA is violated or not can change with time.

3   Architecture and Implementation

The SLA Management (SLAM) platform offers three main features: SLA monitoring, SLA explanation, and SLA predictions. In the following we describe the architecture and give some implementation details on the SLAM platform, showing how it can provide these features.

3.1   SLA Monitoring

Figure 2 shows the architecture of the proposed SLA management system. SLA clauses and SLAs are specified to the system through the SLA definer. SLA clauses can be specified in two ways: the first consist in defining an SQL query over process execution data that returns the list of process instances that violate that clause.

The second is to reuse one of the functions built into the SLA management systems. In fact, SLAM comes with a large set of predefined, parametric functions that enable the computation of most SLAs. The functions are grouped according to the types of SLAs identified in the previous section, to facilitate the user in quickly identifying the appropriate function to be used for a certain SLA clause. For example, one of these functions is *distanceGreaterThan(N1,N2,T)*. The function returns a list of process instances for which the time elapsed between the completion of node N1 and node N2 is greater than the threshold T. N1 can assume the special value 'start', denoting the start of the process, while N2 can take the special value 'end', denoting the completion of the process. Many SLAs of the *duration* type, that involves conditions on the time elapsed between the execution of certain nodes in a process (or on the duration of the whole process) can be specified using this function. This is for example the case of clauses A and B of our simple case study.

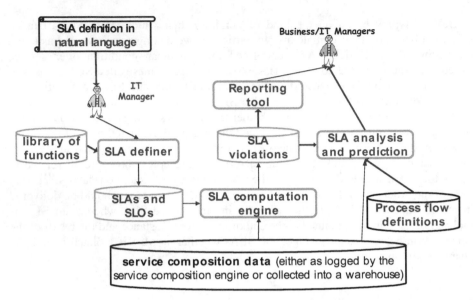

Fig. 2. Architecture of the SLA management platform

Once such functions are available, SLA clauses (corresponding to basic SLAs) are specified by

- referencing one of the predefined functions (e.g., *distanceGreaterThan*)
- specifying the function's parameter (e.g., receive_order, receive_order, 2),
- defining the process type to which the SLA should be applied (e.g., Buy_tie)
- defining the customer with which the SLA should be applied (e.g., ABC)

Once the functions are available, then SLA clauses can be specified without writing any code. SLAs then can be defined in terms of a conjunction of SLA clauses. The SLA computation engine executes the functions over *completed* processes, to compute SLA violations for each process instance. This is typically done when process execution data is loaded into a data warehouse.

Once violations have been computed, SLAM can show a wide variety of statistics such as number of violations by process type, by customer, by time, and the like (Figure 3).

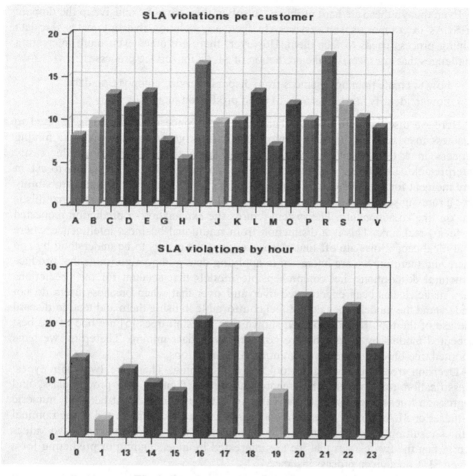

Fig. 3. Sample reports on SLA violations

3.2   SLA Explanation and Prediction

Data mining discovers interesting patterns buried in massive amounts of data. Discovering such patterns for SLAs can respond to two different needs:

a)   the need to understand when SLA violations take place (explanation)
b)   the need to predict when an SLA violation will occur (prediction).

The origins of our work can be found in [8] where SLA exception prediction was demonstrated for a process using decision trees. Now, we want to generalize and automate the approach which imposes several interesting challenges:

–   how to identify the best mining algorithm
–   how to select relevant features (attributes)
–   how to compose new predictive features
–   how to tune the parameters of the mining algorithms

Even though these are hard problems to solve, they are not exclusive to the domain of SLAs in composite web services. In fact, any solution that automates the data mining process needs to face them. However, there are other even more interesting challenges that are special to the prediction of SLAs for service processes:

- how to create training instances from disperse service composition data
- how to identify at which stages to build prediction models

Here we discuss some of these hard problems. Since our solution is targeted to business managers and not data mining experts, our goal is to automate the mining process in a transparent way, while at the same time make the results easily interpretable. The idea is to provide business managers with the capability to ask at any moment for explanations on violations of a given SLA, or request the probability that a running service has of violating a given SLA. It is important to stress that this is an "on-line" functionality. The system returns the explanation or prediction requested in (near) real time. This is a distinction from traditional business intelligence where analytical capabilities are off-line. Also, we want the results to be understood by end users and therefore we are interested in applying data mining algorithms that produce structural descriptions, i.e. comprehensible models that account for the predictions they make. It has been experienced over and over that when business users do not understand the models, they do not feel comfortable in using them and tend to discard the use of the tool. It has also been shown that decision trees [5] are one of the best accepted models by users who are not experts in data mining. Therefore, we have adopted tree-based techniques for mining SLA violations.

Decision trees are a versatile tool for data mining. There are two main types: classification trees which label records assigning them to the proper class, and regression trees which estimate the value of a target variable that takes on numeric values. For SLAs we use classification trees because we are interested in the nominal values resulting from measuring an SLA: satisfaction or violation. These two values are in fact the two classes that we are interested in understanding or predicting for a given SLA on a given process instance.

Since a decision tree is an intuitive structural description model, it serves to explain what has been learned, to explain the basis for new predictions, to gain knowledge about the data, as shown in Figure 4. The tree in this figure shows the patterns found in the buy_ties process data that lead to a violation on an SLA that imposes a limit on the duration of the process shown in Figure 1 to a maximum of 48 hours. By traversing each branch of the tree we obtain a decision rule for the class ("violation" or "satisfaction") assigned to its leaf. One such rule according to this tree is that if the order is placed on a Friday, the SLA will be violated with probability of 0.7. Another rule says that for any day that is not Friday, and for a quantity less than 1000, if the type of ties ordered is T-12, the SLA will be violated with probability of 0.8. By analyzing these rules (explanations), business managers can identify the causes of the violations and make changes to business processes accordingly. For example, a business manager may find out that the reason why orders placed on Friday take more than 48 hours is because a majority of employees leave early on Friday, in which case he should give some incentives to employees to avoid the situation.

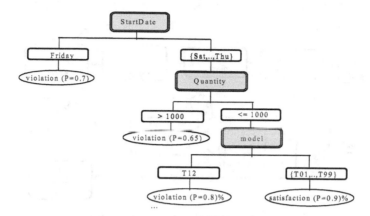

Fig. 4. Decision tree for process duration SLA violation

We also use decision trees for predicting the outcome of SLAs for running process instances. In this case the tree model is retrieved and applied to the instance on which the prediction is to be done. The instance flows through the tree along a path determined by a series of tests on the values of its fields until the instance reaches a leaf of the tree. There, it is given a class label based on the class of the records that reached that node in the training set. If the instance data matches a pattern of SLA violation in the tree, then with probability P the service instance will violate the SLA.

When decision trees are used for explaining SLA violations, a decision tree is learned from a training set composed of execution data generated during the whole lifecycle of complete process instances. In order to monitor SLAs compliance, SLA measurements are taken on complete process instances which are labeled with the resulting measurements (i.e., satisfaction or violation). A classification model (decision tree) of the labels of each SLA can then be learned from all the instances tagged with its labels. Whereas when decision trees are used for prediction of SLA violations on running instances, several decision trees have to be learned corresponding to different stages of execution of the process. In this case, a training set consists of only part of the execution data of complete process instances (i.e. given that predictions need to be done while instances are still running, prediction models have to be learned only on the data that existed up to a given point of the execution process). Different stages of prediction have to be identified so that when a running instance reaches one such stage, the corresponding prediction model is retrieved and applied to that instance. Figure 5 shows a possible stage partitioning of the buy_ties process given in section 2.1. As this figure shows, there is a different decision tree for each prediction stage. Each such model is learned only from the composite service execution data that is available at the corresponding stage. For example, we could have a prediction model for a given SLA for process instances that are in the START state, where nothing is known about their execution except the date and time when they started. This model could be able to predict whether the SLA would be violated or not based on the day of the week and the time of the day.

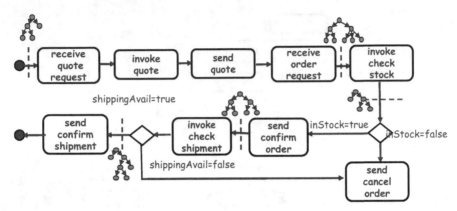

Fig. 5. SLA prediction stages for Buy_Tie process

In general it is difficult to determine at which stages to build prediction models. On one hand the confidence increases as we get closer to the end of the process flow, but on the other hand the ability to take corrective action diminishes at the same time. So, there is an interesting tradeoff which constitutes a hard research problem. The problem can be addressed at different levels of automation:

- let a human specify the stages where it is interesting for him to have predictions on a given SLA
- an expert in the domain identifies the stages where more confident predictions on other metrics can be used as predictors of the outcome of an SLA. For example, he might identify a stage where there is enough data to predict the duration of a given step of the process which can be used to predict the final duration of the process.
- The system has to identify the stages without human intervention and using only process data.
- The system identifies the stages as well as auxiliary metrics that can be predicted with more confidence at those stages and used as predictors of the SLA.

Another problem special to this domain is the creation of training instances. Data about a process instance execution is spread in different tables, and the nodes through which a process instance goes differs from process to process. Furthermore, cycles may exist where a node may be executed more than once for a same process instance. Consequently, process instances differ in the type and number of their node instances. Data mining algorithms require only one record per training instance and training instances have to be of the same length . Thence, data belonging to a flow instance have to be joined and decisions about which iterations of a loop to include have to be made. Determining which iterations to include is not trivial and it may be different from one process type to another. It is necessary to find automatic ways to determine which are the most relevant iterations for a given process.

Among the main factors that affect the success of a classification task, is the quality of the data, i.e., if information is irrelevant or redundant, or the data is noisy and unreliable, then pattern discovery during training is more difficult. Feature subset selection is the process of identifying and removing as much of the irrelevant and redundant information as possible. Regardless of the fact that decision tree inducers try to focus on relevant features by testing their values, feature selection prior to learning is beneficial. Reducing the dimensionality of the data reduces the size of the hypothesis space and allows algorithms to operate faster and more effectively, even accuracy can be improved in some cases, and the result is a more compact, easily interpreted representation of the concept learned. In our approach we use correlation-based feature selection [6] because it can handle both, discrete and continuous features and discrete and continuous classification problems and has been shown to outperform and do more feature selection than other popular attribute estimators particularly for decision trees. The hypothesis behind this method is that "good feature subsets contain features highly correlated with the class, yet uncorrelated with each other".

The task related to features is not only about selection, but also about deriving new features from existing ones. Just as in semantic feature selection, constructing new features is totally dependent on semantics. For example, it seems important to derive a new feature that indicates how many times each node was executed even though we won't capture features for each such iteration. Analogously, it seems meaningful to break down the timestamp features into new components, like day of the week, week of the month, day of the month, and so on. A pattern could be found that indicates that a given SLA is often violated when an order is placed during the last week of the month. Feature selection and feature construction comprise the feature engineering task.

Given that we know the semantics of the process data model used in our platform and the semantic of the SLA classes defined in section 2.2, we are able to do some manual filtering to discard some irrelevant features which otherwise could be found as relevant but that are uninteresting for an explanatory model. This is what we called semantic feature selection, which unfortunately is not possible when the semantics of the data is unknown, as is the case when the feature set is enriched with business specific data like customers or orders. The rest of the attributes are left in the hands of correlation-based feature selection which eliminates attributes that are found irrelevant or redundant. To illustrate the idea, let us suppose that we have the following partial process schema and that we want to obtain an explanation model for orders that violate a *duration* type SLA:

PROCESS (ID, Name, Description, AvgTime, Status)
PROCESS_INSTANCE (ID, Process, StartTime, EndTime, Status)
NODES (ID, Process, Name, Type)
NODE_INSTANCE (ID, Process, Node, StartTime, EndTime, Status, Resource)

Joining all data related to each flow instance is not the right approach. Repeating the same data about the 'order' FLOW for each order flow instance is useless given that the corresponding attribute values will be the same for all instances, i.e., irrelevant data. The same happens with the data about the NODES for each node instance. Also, ID data is not a relevant feature, in fact, since it is unique for each instance it is not predictive at all. For those nodes that are involved in a cycle, only the first and last iteration are captured but the number of iterations is computed and added as a feature. Also each StartTime and EndTime of a flow instance and a node instance are broken down into derived components like those mentioned above and added as new features of a flow instance. Then, these new flow instances are processed by the correlation based feature selection algorithm to select a relevant subset of attributes. The flow instances are then projected on this subset and the result constitutes the training set to be mined by the decision tree inducer.

The configuration of the mining algorithm is also challenging. Decision trees have several parameters that need to be set to achieve the best performance. These parameters are typically related to the splitting criteria, pruning criteria and node or leaf size. An automatic way to tune this parameters needs to be found. The key is in finding a good strategy to explore the search space efficiently. Currently we are investigating the use of some ideas from design of experiments that have previously been applied on other learning methods at HP Labs [7].

4   Conclusions

This paper has presented concepts, techniques, and an architecture for measuring and predicting business SLAs defined on Web services. We have motivated why Web services naturally enable the measurement of business SLA and has shown how SLA can be monitored and predicted in the case of composite Web service, a class of Web services likely to gain importance in the near future.

Although the results presented in this paper are useful in their own right, there are several other aspects of SLA management that need to be addressed to provide a comprehensive solution. Specifically, an SLA specification language is needed so that users can easily define SLAs, possibly through a GUI. These specifications need then to be mapped to a condition on service execution data, so that the SLA can be measured by the tool.

Another interesting area of research is that of SLA analysis focused on providing intelligent explanations about which are the causes of SLA violations. Finally, to completely address all the issues related to SLA management, we plan to address the problem of advising users on how to take corrective actions so that a service execution that is at risk of missing an SLA can be corrected. In a few cases, it is even possible to envision that the system automatically takes corrective actions.

References

[1]   D. Grigori, F. Casati, U. Dayal, M. Castellanos, M. Sayal, and M.C. Shan. Business Process Intelligence. Computers in Industry, special issue on workflow mining. To appear.

[2]   F. Casati and V. Machiraju. Business Visibility with Web Services. Making sense of your IT operations and of what they mean to you. Proceedings of the UMICS workshop. Velden, Austria. June 2003

[3]   F. Casati, U. Dayal and M.C. Shan. Business-oriented Management of Web services. ACM Communications, October 2003.

[4]   Erik Christensen et al. Web Services Description Language (WSDL) 1.1. W3C Note. March 2001

[5]   J. R. Quinlan. Induction of decision trees. Machine Learning, 1:81--106, 1986.

[6]   M. Hall. Correlatioin-based Feature Selection for Discrete and Numeric Class Machine Learning. *Proceedings of the Seventeenth International Conference on Machine Learning*, Stanford University, CA. Morgan Kaufmann Publishers.

[7]   C.Staelin. Parameter Selection for Support Vector Machines. Technical report HPL-2002-354. Hewlett-Packard Laboratories, Palo Alto, CA, December 2002.

[8]   A. Sahai et al. Automated SLA Monitoring for Web Services. IEEE/IFIP DSOM 2002, Montreal, Canada, October 2002.

[9]   D. Grigori et al. Improving Business Process Quality through Exception Understanding, Prediction, and Prevention. VLDB 2001, Rome, Italy, September 2001.

PC Cluster Based Parallel Frequent Pattern Mining and Parallel Web Access Pattern Mining

Masaru Kitsuregawa and Iko Pramudiono

Institute of Industrial Science, The University of Tokyo
4-6-1 Komaba, Meguro-ku, Tokyo 153-8505, Japan
{kitsure,iko}@tkl.iis.u-tokyo.ac.jp

Abstract. The need for scalable and efficient frequent pattern mining has driven the development for parallel algorithms. High cost performance platforms like PC cluster are also becoming widely available. Modern algorithms for frequent pattern mining employs complicated tree structure. Here we report the development of the tree based parallel mining algorithms on PC cluster: Parallel FP-growth and an extension to mine web access patterns called Parallel WAP-mine.

1 Introduction

Frequent pattern mining has become one popular data mining technique. It also becomes the fundamental technique for other important data mining tasks such as association rule, correlation and sequential pattern.

FP-growth has set a new standard for frequent pattern mining [4]. FP-growth compresses transaction database into on-memory data structure called FP-tree and then decompose mining tasks into smaller ones in the form of conditional pattern bases. Conditional pattern bases is a subdatabase of all patterns that co-occur with a particular itemset. FP-growth shows better performance than previously reported algorithms such as Apriori [1].

Further performance improvement can be expected from parallel execution. Pioneering works on parallel algorithm for frequent pattern mining were done in [3, 5]. Those algorithms are based on Apriori [1]. Particularly, development of parallel algorithms on large scale shared nothing environment such as PC cluster has attracted a lot of attention since it is a promising platform for high performance data mining. A better memory utilization schema for shared nothing machines called Hash Partitioned Apriori (HPA) was proposed in [7].

Here we develop parallel algorithms based on modern tree based mining algorithms: Parallel FP-growth and an extension to mine web access patterns called Parallel WAP-mine. We verify the efficiency of our algorithms through real implementation on a PC cluster. We also examine the bottlenecks of the parallelization and also methods to balance the execution efficiently on shared-nothing environment.

N. Bianchi-Berthouze (Ed.): DNIS 2003, LNCS 2822, pp. 172–176, 2003.

2   Parallel Execution of FP-Growth

Since the processing of a conditional pattern base is independent of the processing of other conditional pattern base, it is natural to consider it as the execution unit for the parallel processing.

The basic idea is each node accumulates a complete conditional pattern base and processes it independently until the completion before receiving other conditional pattern base.

It is obvious to achieve good parallelization, we have to consider the granularity of the execution unit or parallel task. Granularity is the amount of computation done in parallel relative to the size of the whole program.

When the execution unit is the processing of a conditional pattern base, the granularity is determined by number of iterations to generate subsequent conditional pattern bases. The number of iteration is exponentially proportional with the depth of the longest frequent path in the conditional pattern base. Thus here we define *path depth* as the measure of the granularity.

Since the granularity differs greatly, many nodes with smaller granularity will have to wait busy nodes with large granularity. This wastes CPU time and reduces scalability. It is confirmed by Fig. 1 (left) that shows the execution of the trivial parallel scheme given in the previous subsection. The line represents the CPU utilization ratio in percentage. Here other nodes have to wait node 1 (pc031) completes its task.

To achieve better parallel performance, we have to split parallel tasks with large granularity. Since the path depth can be calculated when creating FP-tree, we can predict in advance how to split the parallel tasks. So we can control the granularity by specifying a *minimum path depth*.

After employing the path depth adjustment we get a more balanced execution as shown in Fig. 1 (right).

3   Parallel Execution of WAP-Mine

The web access pattern is essentially a sequential pattern. The problem of mining sequential pattern was first addressed by AprioriAll algorithm [2]. It is an extension of well known Apriori algorithm for association rule mining to handle time order constraint.

WAP-mine inherits a mining framework of FP-growth [6]. WAP-mine records all information needed to generate web access patterns in a data structure called WAP-tree. While other sequential pattern mining algorithm can also handle time ordered transaction data, WAP-mine is designed solely for web access pattern mining.

In a web access sequence there are many occasions where a same page is visited more than once. For example in the sequence *abacad*, the page *a* is visited three times. However the support of the event in the sequence is only one. To avoid double counting, WAP-mine devises *unsubsumed count property*. To compensate the excessive count, WAP-mine also decrements the count of sequences

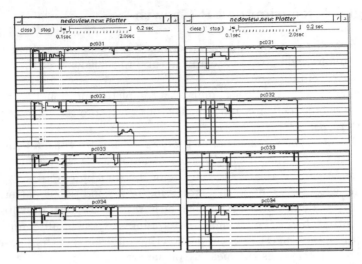

Fig. 1. Trivial execution (left) with path depth (right) (T25.I10.D100K 0.11%)

in conditional pattern bases when it finds duplicate nodes. However original WAP-mine insert additional sequences to decrement the count. Thus the size of conditional pattern bases is multiplied by the number of duplicate items.

Since our parallel framework exchanges conditional pattern bases among nodes, the larger conditional pattern bases will certainly increase the intercommunication overhead. Thus we also propose a method to compress the conditional pattern bases. Our method is based on the observation that the excessive sequences in the conditional pattern base can be eliminated if we directly modify the count of the nodes in the WAP-tree.

4   Implementation and Performance Evaluation

As the shared nothing environment for this experiment we use PC cluster of 32 nodes that interconnected by 100Base-TX Ethernet Switch.

For the performance evaluation, we use synthetically generated dataset as described in Apriori paper for frequent pattern mining [1]. For the evaluation on web access pattern mining, we use the dataset described in AprioriAll paper[2]. The number of transactions is one million.

4.1   Evaluation of Parallel FP-Growth

We have varied the minimum path depth to see how it affects performance. The experiments are conducted on 1, 2, 4, 8, 16 and 32 nodes. The execution time for minimum support of 0.1% is shown in Fig. 2 (left) The best time of 40 seconds is achieved when minimum path depth is set to 12 using 32 nodes. On single node, the experiment requires 904 seconds in average.

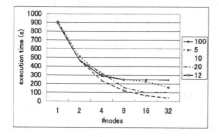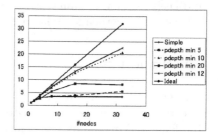

Fig. 2. Execution time(left) Speedup ratio(right) for T25.I20.D100K 0.1%

Fig. 2 (right) shows that path depth greatly affects the speedup achieved by the parallel execution. The trivial parallelization, denoted by "Simple", performs worst since almost no speedup achieved after 4 nodes.

When the minimum path depth is optimum, sufficiently good speedup ratio can be achieved. For "pdepth min = 12", parallel execution on 8 nodes can gain speedup ratio of 7.3. Even on 16 nodes and 32 nodes, we still can get 13.4 and 22.6 times faster performance respectively.

However finding the optimal value of minimum path depth is not a trivial task yet, and it is becoming one of our future works.

4.2   Evaluation of Parallel WAP-Mine

We have varied the minimum support to see how it affects performance. The experiments are conducted on 2, 4, 8 and 15 nodes. The execution time for minimum support of 0.0003%, 0.00005%, 0.001% and 0.003% is shown in Fig. 3 (left).

Figure 3 (right) shows that good speedup ratio is achieved for all minimum support. When the minimum support is set to 0.0003%, 15 processing nodes gain

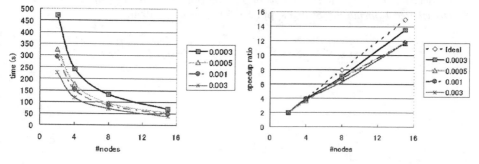

Fig. 3. Execution time (left) Speedup ratio (right) for T20.I10.D1M.i10K

13.6 times faster performance. Our algorithm suitably balances the processing load and keeps the intercommunication overhead low. When the minimum support is lower, the overhead is relatively smaller, thus the speedup is improved.

5   Conclusion

We have reported the development of parallel data mining algorithms that designed to run on shared-nothing environment. Two tree based algorithms have been implemented on top of a PC cluster system : Parallel FP-growth to mine frequent patterns and Parallel WAP-mine to mine web access patterns.

Although the tree data structure is complex and naturally not suitable for parallel processing on shared-nothing environment, the experiments show our algorithms can achieve reasonably good speedup ratio.

References

[1] R. Agrawal and R. Srikant. "Fast Algorithms for Mining Association Rules". In *Proceedings of the 20th International Conference on VLDB*, pp. 487–499, September 1994. 172, 174

[2] R. Agrawal and R. Srikant. "Mining Sequential Patterns". In *Proc. of International Conference of Data Engineering*, pp. 3–14, March 1995. 173, 174

[3] R. Agrawal and J. C. Shafer. "Parallel Mining of Associaton Rules". In *IEEE Transaction on Knowledge and Data Engineering*, Vol. 8, No. 6, pp. 962–969, December, 1996. 172

[4] J. Han, J. Pei and Y. Yin "Mining Frequent Pattern without Candidate Generation" In *Proc. of the ACM SIGMOD Conference on Management of Data*, 2000 172

[5] J. S.Park, M.-S.Chen, P. S.Yu "Efficient Parallel Algorithms for Mining Association Rules" In *Proc. of 4th International Conference on Information and Knowledge Management (CIKM'95)*, pp. 31–36, November, 1995 172

[6] J. Pei, J. Han, B. Mortazavi-asl and H. Zhu "Mining Access Patterns Efficiently from Web Logs" In *Proc. of fourth Pacific-Asia Conference in Knowledge Discovery and Data Mining(PAKDD'00)*, 2000. 173

[7] T. Shintani and M. Kitsuregawa "Hash Based Parallel Algorithms for Mining Association Rules". In *IEEE Fourth International Conference on Parallel and Distributed Information Systems*, pp. 19–30, December 1996. 172

NetIsle: A Hybrid Peer-to-Peer Groupware System Based on Push Technology for Small Group Collaboration

Roman Shtykh[1] and Qun Jin[2]

[1] Research and Development Division, Access Co., Ltd.
2-8-16 Sarugaku-cho, Chiyoda-ku, Tokyo 101-0064, Japan
roman@access.co.jp
[2] Department of Human Informatics and Cognitive Sciences
School of Human Sciences, Waseda University
2-579-15 Mikajima, Tokorozawa-shi, Saitama 359-1192, Japan
jin@waseda.jp
http://www.f.waseda.jp/jin/

Abstract. This paper describes small group collaboration solutions based upon push technology, which provides awareness for collaboration, reduces efforts for necessary information discovery, and makes users collaboration initiators, active information providers and new values creators. The push technology-based tools, i.e. File Pusher, Scheduler, NetIsle Mailer, etc., are implemented in a hybrid peer-to-peer general-purpose groupware system, called NetIsle, which has been developed by using Java RMI and sockets and can be run on any platform where Java VM is available.

Keywords: Push technology, peer-to-peer, groupware, collaboration in small groups, active information provider.

1 Introduction

Work in groups has always been an interesting and, at the same time, difficult topic for research. Since the birth of computers and networks, Computer-Mediated Communication (CMC) has become the center of attention. Collaboration took new forms, and new problems arose at the same time.

Many software giants and researchers have proposed their solutions for work in groups to speed up information flow and ease group collaboration. Here are several examples of them:

- IBM Lotus Notes, IBM Lotus QuickPlace [1]
- Microsoft Exchange Server [2]
- Novell GroupWize [3]
- GroupServe's GroupPort [4]

All the above products are pursuing similar goals – provide dynamic collaboration solutions. Various existing technologies have been used, and new ones are

N. Bianchi-Berthouze (Ed.): DNIS 2003, LNCS 2822, pp. 177–187, 2003.

being created to success at market. Moreover, every developer has his/her own point of view on how to contribute to smooth online collaboration, so that every product has its original characteristics and concepts that serve the basis for every project.

We have been developing our own groupware system called NetIsle that is based on our vision of what the group collaboration is and how to facilitate it, combining old well-known technologies, such as push technology, distributed computing, and new promising ones, such as peer-to-peer (P2P) technology.

We have created a number of tools for online collaboration and integrated them into a single framework, so that the tools can be easily accessed and used when they are needed. The system can be configured in no time and used on any platform that has a Java Virtual Machine (JVM) [5]. The system is mobile – no special administration is necessary. Therefore, the group members can change their place on the Internet, re-organize the group painlessly, and no one has to do a hard job for group administration (if anybody wishes, he/she can though). Doing this, we have been trying to ensure that the system will be flexible and compatible to the dynamic process of group collaboration.

NetIsle targets uniform open groups, where anyone can join a group and leave it freely – only a good leadership and the will of members to work together are important in such a system to collaborate efficiently. The groupware is for task-oriented users who know what problems they need to solve, and by using the integrated tools they can create a high-grade group that possesses the functions outlined by McGrath and Hollingshead [6]: production, well-being and member support.

NetIsle is a general-purpose system, which can be used for Intranet cooperation inside companies or educational institutions, or by any groups that want to create their online community on the Internet. Some modifications of the system to use it for specific purposes can be done though [1].

The aims of our groupware system are as follows:

- to support collaboration and cooperation of uniform open groups, and quick navigation within the information space by providing an environment with a number of tools for users to interact;
- to help solve common problems at shorter time;
- to ensure fast information transfer in shared space; and
- to provide an equal opportunity for all members to participate.

By making use of push technology, we believe that in such a system a user can be not only a passive information receiver (as it happens in many cases when we are watching TV, listening to the radio), but also can be an active information provider. If we take a look at many present applications that are based on push technology, most of them are used mainly by big corporations and the mass media to send pieces of information to the recepients. In our system,

---

[1] Presently, we are developing NetIsle-EM that is a modified NetIsle groupware system for educational purpose by integrating NetIsle with MOO (Multi user dimension Object-Oriented) environments.

we try to provide equal opportunities for all users of the system to create and share information, to be an active creator of community values in real-time collaboration process.

In this paper, we make a focus upon push-type tools and functional units of the system; all the other tools are described in [7]. The rest of this paper is organized as follows. Section 2 explains why small groups are targeted for our groupware system. Section 3 provides an overview of push technology, and describes our view of new media community that transforms users from passive information receivers to active senders, by using push technology. Section 4 discusses design and implementation of the NetIsle push-type tools: File Pusher, Scheduler, NetIsle Mailer, and other functional units. Finally, Section 5 summarizes the results of this paper, and gives future research direction.

2 Small Groups

Process of collaboration in small and large groups is different. Due to this, system design for different kinds of groups is also different. As we mentioned above, NetIsle groupware system is for collaboration within small groups. Let us try to explain why such small groups are targeted.

Actually, if we take a look at some groupware definitions, we can say that groupware is typically for usage within purpose-oriented small groups. For instance, here is a definition given by Johansen [8] – "Groupware is a generic term for specialized computer aids that are designed for the use of collaborative work groups. Typically, these groups are small project-oriented teams that have important tasks and tight deadlines. Groupware can involve software, hardware, services and/or group process support."

So why small groups are targeted in our groupware system? Small groups are quite stable, productive and flexible units of society. Usually they do not subgroup – in case of not more than 12 or 18, as we know from teaching practices. However, if a key member changes in a really small group, the group development has to start all over again. That is the main disadvantage of small groups.

Smaller size groups contribute to the sense of groupness because they allow for greater mutual awareness to take place among group members and, as a result, create greater opportunities for affiliative interactions to take place. Conversely, larger groups normally produce less of a sense of groupness because they foster less perception of mutual awareness. As the number of group members increases beyond a certain point, the ratio of individual interactions will decrease, along with the perception of groupness.

"Humans form effective, coordinated, division-of-labor groupings at several levels of aggregation. At each level, there is a problem of metasystem transition." [9] "At each level, there is also not only competition between other groupings at the same level, but also competition between the interests of the smaller incorporated units and the interests of the larger encompassing unit." [10] Small groups are not likely to subdivide and competition in them is directed for achieving something that will be a mutual benefit for every group member.

3   Push Technology and New Media Community

Push technology is not new, and it has been generally limited to information transmission from one big source of information (such as a news site, customer support center, etc.) to its users or customers. But if we enable all users to send and share information, it makes them not just passive information recepients, but also active participants in information creation. Anybody can become an information provider in this case.

3.1   Short Overview of Push Technology

Push technology is a set of technologies that deliver information directly to a user, automate the search and retrieval function. "The term push technology can be used to describe anything from Webcasting to selective content delivery using sophisticated evolutionary filtering" [11] "Push technology has been touted as an alternative to the way the World Wide Web currently operates, where users go online to search for information." [12]

Push technology is not as new as peer-to-peer technology. It drew attention of many software developers and companies, and many of them started developing push-type systems in mid-1996 to help users retrieve only the information they specify as relevant. For this purpose, a number of HTTP protocol enhancements and multicast protocols for push distribution were developed. The good examples of software products that have been created by using push technology are Keryx Notification System by Keryxsoft (a group in Hewlett Packard Laboratories) [13], Webcanal [14], PointCast [15], ANATAGONOMY [16]. Nowadays push technology is used in reseach on combination with new technologies like XML [17], and wireless data broadcasting [18], [19].

Many companies use this technology to deliver information to employees, collaborate, update their clients' software, and for many other purposes. The modern software representatives of push technology software can be Netpresenter [20] and BackWeb e-Accelerator [21].

Push technology speeds up the process of obtaining information, saves time of many people. Repeatedly searching the Web for information on a particular topic can be both time-consuming and frustrating. Push technology can help by delivering or pushing information directly to one's desktop. Not much effort will be made to obtain the information wanted.

Traditionally, pushing is done by the following way. On getting a certain user's information, a vendor's server will search the Web for it, and the retrieved information is filtered and sent to the user's desktop. It is different from "pull" when a user has to search necessary information and download it himself/herself.

The main disadvantage of using push technology is the quality of information received, and its relevance. This kind of problem arises because the filtering is done at server side by some special algorithms that can overlook some things and it is difficult to provide necessary information just taking keywords from user profiles.

NetIsle is designed for a small group of task-oriented users, so that irrelevant information is unlikely to be sent, since the collaboration community members are interested in producing a good result in a short period of time. We expect it can eliminate the main disadvantage of using push technology and its best features will be mostly utilized.

In push-type systems, some technical problems, like network overload and decreased performance on the client side, can be observed. But as far as testing is being done, we have not experienced any serious problems with it, since our targets are small-scale groups.

3.2 Using Push Technology to Transform User from Passive Receiver to Active Sender

At the days of the first introduction of new media like TV and radio, media were almighty and general public was powerless to influence the media. There were no interaction between them – people were just passive receivers of uni-directional information flow. Nowadays, things are changing – people want to make influence upon many things and information flow becomes bi- and multi-directional. People choose interactivity and participation instead of passiveness and unidirectionality.

Similar things are happening in the computer world due to the rapid popularization of the Internet, a new media community. Today computer is not only a machine for calculating complex equations and perform industrial tasks, but it is also a human-oriented tool to help solve individual problems. Nevertherless, in many cases people are just information recepients when they are accessing Web through their PC browsers, and even if some information is exchanged or renewed it happens slowly and its discovery can take from several minutes to several days.

Applying push technology to groupware enables users to exchange information fast and share it in many forms. By enabling collaborative group members to push information, we believe that they become not only passive information receivers, but also active initiators of collaboration, information senders and, finally, participants in new values creation.

4   NetIsle Push-Type Tools

NetIsle is a hybrid-type peer-to-peer groupware solution for collaboration in small groups. It was started from creating a peer-to-peer collaboration environment with our big concern about push technology [7]. NetIsle provides support for cooperative work on the process level, i.e. focuses on tools by using which users can cooperate, and provide little support on content level [22]. It gives users a shared workspace with a number of tools for synchronous and asynchronous communication. We hope that those who use the groupware find the utilities flexible, easy to learn and applicable in many ways familiar to team members.

In this section, we give a description about the design and implementation of these push-type tools.

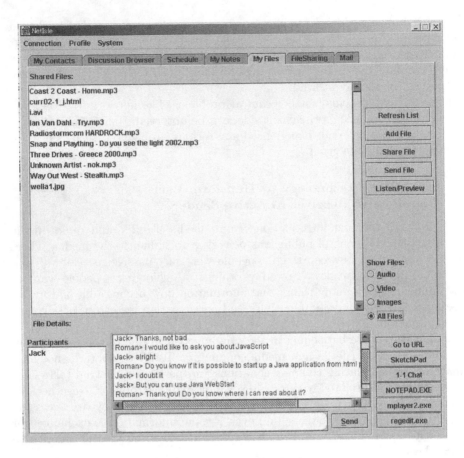

Fig. 1. NetIsle File Pusher

4.1   File Pusher

NetIsle File Pusher, as shown in Fig.1., is a functional unit of the system that allows a user to share a certain file with others during the collaboration by aperiodic unicast or 1-to-N data delivery mechanisms [23]. We believe that this function accelerates the collaboration process because no necessary material should be searched on the Internet or shared folders of the group members – a user who has it will provide it in time, so that collaboration can be started immediately or be continued without being interrupted because of lack of the necessary information. Actually, this is what push technology is about – to provide necessary and timely information to save time; no boring and cumbersome search is needed.

Each member of the NetIsle network has a folder of files to push. We provide such a folder to make it possible to prepare necessary information and put in the folder before the collaboration is started. Therefore, all the files that may be pushed are always at hand. A user can easily select and copy information from any folder in his/her own computer to the specialized folder. Moreover,

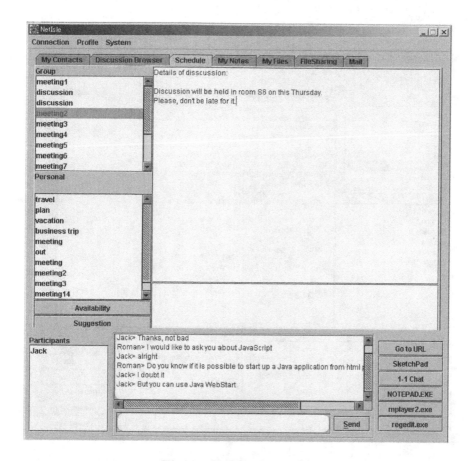

Fig. 2. NetIsle Scheduler

the folder can display all files, except music format files, video format files or images, that makes search of a necessary genre of files easier when a number of files becomes huge.

Files can be pushed in two ways:

- to all the nodes of the system when all the users need a certain file, and
- to specified users who can be selected from the list of online users.

This makes pushing quite flexible, so that the system can be used for pushing information whenever it is needed, not just in the process of group collaboration.

When one user is trying to send a file, a user who is going to receive it gets a notification about the incoming file. In this moment, he/she can reject or accept the incoming file. Only on the receiver's approval, the file is pushed through the NetIsle peer-to-peer network.

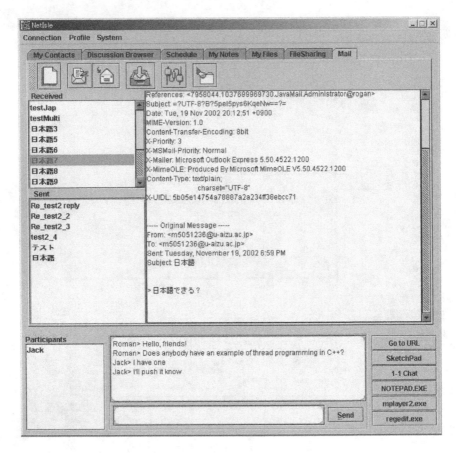

Fig. 3. NetIsle Mailer

Once a file is successfully downloaded, it can be viewed/listened by the NetIsle default player or any other player a user makes default for his/her NetIsle tools.

To implement and perform pushing, a simple FTP-like protocol has been implemented in this study.

4.2   Scheduler

Every group work needs scheduling to put the work into some certain order which every member will follow. That's why scheduler is a nondispensable tool for every group collaboration.

NetIsle provides two kinds of mutually dependent schedulers, as shown in Fig.2.:

– group scheduler which is for group purposes, and
– individual scheduler where a user writes his/her own plans.

By providing two schedulers in the system, we optimize scheduling mechanism to some extend. When one user plans a group meeting, he/she makes a suggestion to the entire group about date and time of the online meeting. Other members need to do nothing – a suggestion will travel from one scheduler to another checking personal schedulers of the members. If all the members do not have any personal plans for the suggested date and time, the suggestion will be automatically added to the group schedule of every member. Otherwise, a person who made a suggestion has to change date and time of the online meeting.

Before posting a suggestion, one can also check if all members are available in the suggested date and time by using "Availability" function.

It would be good to implement a function that could run at the background and notify a user about upcoming scheduled events, but such a function has not been implemented yet.

4.3   NetIsle Mailer

NetIsle Mailer shown in Fig.3. is a multilingual mail client program that has all main functions of any application of this kind, plus a direct message pusher. Here we will not describe common mail functions; instead we will pay attention to system-specific functions.

All collaboration group members may be interested in a received or a newly composed mail message, which can be pushed through the NetIsle network to be shared and discussed by all. It is a kind of serverless newsgroup where all messages have their unique ID, composed from a sender's name and a randomly generated number, and get into members' mailboxes. Such messages are grouped separately from ordinary mail messages and distinguished by color.

If some of the group members are offline, messages are not lost for them and will be delivered as soon as they come online. For this purpose, there is a simple mail agent which periodically checks if a certain message is delivered to all the online members. If some user was previously offline (he/she has not received the message) and becomes online, the agent finds it out and sends the message to that user. The message state for the user becomes "SENT." The agent is working in the background of the system, therefore, it does not hinder the main work being done by a user.

4.4   Other Functional Units

Besides the functional units we described above, there are two other utilities that make use of push technology in the system. They are Personal Contacts List and NetIsle Notepad.

Personal Contacts List is a list of one's friends and associates who do not necessarily use the NetIsle system. By choosing a certain item in the list, one can easily get a friend's profile, go to his/her home page or send an email. A profile can be viewed, added, modified and deleted.

Furthermore, every new user who wants to use a NetIsle application has to create his/her own profile and if that user wants to share it with all group members or one certain member, he/she can push the profile through the NetIsle network and get it added to the contact list of another user on that user's permission. So that no manual adding should be done.

NetIsle Notepad is just another simple editing program that allows users to write their ideas, save them and share now or later.

Again, since NetIsle utilizes push technology to its full, a text that is being edited in the notepad can be pushed to other peers and opened in the main window or another window not to overwrite other user's writings (it is done on the receiver's selection). Sometimes we can't write a long text in the chat window because it is very time-consuming and sometimes we want to share our ideas soon. In this case, NetIsle Notepad can be used.

5   Conclusions

This paper describes push technology and its usage in group collaboration through NetIsle groupware system which is based on its strengths. Push technology enables users to be not only passive information receivers, but also be active information providers. Information is not searched by all collaborative group members – it is provided by a member who possesses the piece of information when it is necessary. That is why we consider the use of push technology that is important in groupware implementation, though it has some disadvantages, such as unnecessary and irrelevant information can be supplied. But in the case of NetIsle such information can be rejected and the group itself is supposed to be small and task-oriented, so that unnecessary information is not likely to be pushed.

The present pilot system is implemented as a general-purpose groupware. The next phase of development is to apply it for educational purpose using MOO (Multi user dimension Object-Oriented) [24] environments and additing other education-specific tools. The system is constantly being developed and enhanced. Although it has been tested and a preliminary evaluation has been done, it should be evaluated in a real time situation of group collaboration.

Acknowledgment

This work has been partly supported by 2000-2002 JSPS (Japan Society for the Promotion of Science) Grant-in-Aid for Scientific Research Contract No. 12558012, 2002 University of Aizu Research Grants Nos. R-9-1 and G-25, and 2003 Waseda University Grant for Special Research Project No. 2003A-917. The authors wish to express their gratitude.

References

[1] IBM Lotus Software, http://www.lotus.com/   177
[2] Microsoft Exchange Server, http://www.microsoft.com/exchange/   177
[3] Novell GroupWize 6, http://www.novell.com/products/groupwise/   177
[4] GroupPORT, http://www.groupport.com/   177
[5] The Source for Java (TM) Technology, http://java.sun.com   178
[6] McGrath, J., and Hollingshead, A., *Groups Interacting with Technology* Thousand Oaks, Califf.. Sage, 1994.   178
[7] Shtykh, R., and Jin, Q., "A Push-Type Groupware System to Facilitate Small Group Collaboration," *Proceedings of First International Symposium on Cyber Worlds*, November 2002, pp.354–363.   179, 181
[8] Johansen, R., *Groupware: Computer Support for Business Teams*, New York: Free Press, 1988.   179
[9] Turchin, V., and Joslyn, C., "The Metasystem Transition," http://pespmc1.vub.ac.be/MST.html   179
[10] Campbell, D. T., and Heilighen, F., "Human society," http://pespmc1.vub.ac.be/SOCIETY.html   179
[11] Kendall, Julie E., and Kendall, Kenneth E., "Information delivery systems: an exploration of Web pull and push technologies," *Communications of the AIS*, April 1999.   180
[12] LEARN THE NET: Glossary, http://www.learnthenet.com/english/glossary/push.htm   180
[13] Keryxsoft, http://keryxsoft.hpl.hp.com/   180
[14] Liao, Tie, "Webcanal: Multicast Based Push," http://webcanal.inria.fr/arch/w3c_push_ws /w3c_push_liao.html   180
[15] InfoGate Inc., http://www.pointcast.com/   180
[16] Kamba, T., Sakagami, H., and Koseki, Y., "Automatic Personalization on Push News Service," http://www.w3.org/Architecture/9709_Workshop/paper02/paper02.ppt   180
[17] Bonifati Angela, Ceri Stefano, and Paraboschi Stefano, "Pushing reactive services to XML repositories using active rules," *Proceedings of the Tenth International Conference on World Wide Web*. April 2001, pp.633–641.   180
[18] Celik Aslihan, and Datta Anindya, "A scalable approach for broadcasting data in a wireless network," *Proceedings of the 4th ACM International Workshop on Modeling, Analysis and Simulation of Wireless and Mobile Systems*, July 2001, pp.131–138.   180
[19] Olsson Daniel, and Nilsson Andreas, "MEP: a media event platform," *Mobile Networks and Applications*, June 2002, Volume 7, Issue 3, pp.235–244.   180
[20] Netpresenter, http://www.netpresenter.com   180
[21] BackWeb, http://www.backweb.com   180
[22] Borghoff, U., and Schlichter, J., "Computer-Supported Cooperative Work: Introduction to Distributed Applications," Springer-Verlag, 2000.   181
[23] Franklin Michael, and Zdonik Stan, "Data in your face": push technology in perspective," *ACM SIGMOD Record, Proceedings of the 1998 ACM SIGMOD International Conference on Management of Data*, June 1998, Volume 27, Issue 2, pp.516–519.   182
[24] MOO home page, http://www.moo.mud.org/   186

An Improved Optimistic
and Fault-Tolerant Replication Protocol*

Luis Irún-Briz, Francesc D. Muñoz-Escoí, and Josep M. Bernabéu-Aubán

Instituto Tecnologico de Informatica, Universidad Politécnica de Valencia
46071 Valencia, Spain
{lirun,fmunyoz,josep}@iti.upv.es
iti@iti.upv.es

Abstract. In this paper, a protocol is proposed that provides the advantages of lazy approaches, forestalling their traditionally found disadvantages. Thus, our approach reduces the abortion rates, and improves the performance of the system. It can also use a dynamic computation of the protocol threshold, approximating its results to the optimal ones. In addition, fault tolerance has been included in the algorithm, using a pseudo-optimistic approach, and avoiding to block any local activity, and minimizing the interference over any node in the system.
A complete description of these algorithms is presented here. Finally, and empirical validation is also discused.

1 Introduction

Consistency requirements introduce a new parameter in the problem of replication in order to achieve fault tolerance and performance enhancement in distributed systems. In some areas – as distributed databases – this conforms a main problem to solve.

The concurrency control can be solved[1, 2, 3] using different techniques. Pessimistic techniques use "locks" to avoid conflicting transactions to break the consistency, and optimistic techniques are based on timestamps. The main disadvantage of pessimistic techniques is the degradation of the performance, due to the temporal block of the concurrent transactions. Its main advantage is the low abortion rate that the pessimistic techniques introduce.

Moreover, the optimism principle is also applied in the propagation of the updates in models where a particular transaction is not executed in every node in the system. In such systems, a notification of the updates performed by a transaction must be propagated to the rest of nodes.

The pessimistic propagation is commonly known as *Eager*, and performs the entire diffusion of the updates during the commit phase, making the commit phase more expensive, but ensuring that every replica in the system holds an

---

* This work has been partially supported by the EU grant IST-1999-20997 and the Spanish grant TIC99-0280-C02-01.

N. Bianchi-Berthouze (Ed.): DNIS 2003, LNCS 2822, pp. 188–200, 2003.

updated value for its objects. In the other hand, optimistic propagation[4] – described in the literature as *Lazy update protocols*[5, 6] –, delays the update propagation over the commit phase. This makes the commit phase faster, but complicates the consistency control, and increases the abortion rate, due to the accesses to outdated objects.

The inconvenience of lazy and optimistic approaches can be attenuated if the probability of an object to be outdated is included in a more careful design of the concurrency protocol.

Moreover, fault tolerance can also be benefitted from this approach, including it in a modification of the basic algorithm. Many recovery protocols use eager pessimistic approaches, making it necessary to temporally block transactions alive during the recovery process. In the other hand, lazy optimistic approaches for recovery protocols increase the abortion rate in the node being recovered. In the middle point, our proposal avoids to block transactions, and minimizes the abortion rate, using the principle of role migration.

We provide in this paper an statistical exploit of the expression for the abortion rate caused by the use of lazy replication, describing a new algorithm to solve the concurrency control in a distributed transactional system (e.g. distributed databases). Moreover, this algorithm makes use of the lazy paradigm, and maintains the optimistic approach in a certain degree. In addition, we provide fault-tolerance to the protocol, making use of the same principle, avoiding to block any transaction in the system during the recovery phase.

To this end, the following section describes a basic optimistic lazy protocol for the concurrency control. Section 3 presents a modification of the basic algorithm, introducing a prediction of the probability of outdate in order to improve the behavior of the abortion rate, and an experimental validation of the expression is then shown. In section 4, the modification to provide self-recovery ability to the protocol is detailed. Section 5 compares this protocol with other systems. Finally, section 6 gives some conclusions.

2   An Optimistic Lazy Protocol

The basic consistency protocol presented in this section is a variation of one of the consistency protocols currently implemented in the GlobData Project[7] (described in [8]).

In the GlobData project, a software platform is used to support database replication. This platform, is called COPLA, and provides an object-oriented view of a network of relational DBMSs. The COPLA architecture is structured in three different layers, which interact using CORBA interfaces, enabling the placement of each layer in a different machine. Thus, multiple applications (running in different nodes) may access the same database replica using its local "*COPLA Manager*". The COPLA Manager of each node propagates all updates locally applied to other database replicas using its replication management components.

One of the problems solved by COPLA is to ensure the consistency among transactions being executed in different database replicas. The solution to this problem depends mainly on the update propagation model: eager or lazy. COPLA is flexible enough to allow multiple update approaches, each one being managed by a dedicated consistency protocol. A particular COPLA component implements the consistency protocol. Multiple implementations of its interfaces are possible, thus allowing that a GlobData system could change its consistency protocol at will. So, the COPLA architecture can be used to experiment with different consistency protocols.

The basic optimistic Lazy Protocol implemented in GlobData is named "*Lazy Object Multicast Protocol*" (LOMP). It will be described in 2.2; further clarifications are presented in the subsections thereafter.

2.1   Node Roles

Considering a given session that tries to commit, the nodes involved in its execution may have four different roles:

- *Active node.* The node where the COPLA Manager that has served the session's execution is placed.
- *Owner node.* For a concrete object, the node where this object was created. During the consensus process performed at commit time of a session, the owner of an object will be asked to allow this session to complete the commit. Thus, it is the manager for the *access confirmation requests* sent by the active nodes at commit time. The management of these access confirmation requests is similar to lock management, but at commit time. These requests are detailed in section 2.2.
  We will denote that a node N_k owns an object o_i with the expression $N_k = own(o_i)$.
- *Synchronous nodes.* If one of our goals is fault tolerance, it becomes necessary a set of nodes that provides guarantees about the last version written for a certain object. So, for each session that is committing, the owner of each written object must multicast this update to a set of synchronous nodes, within the commit phase.
  We will denote that a node N_k is a synchronous replica of an object o_i with the expression $N_k \in S(o_i)$.
- *Asynchronous nodes.* For an object, all the other nodes that have a COPLA Manager replicating the database. In these nodes, the session updates will be eventually received.
  We will denote that a node N_k is an asynchronous replica of an object o_i with the expression $N_k \in A(o_i)$.
  Note that: $own(o_i) \in S(o_i)$, and $A(o_i) \cap S(o_i) = \emptyset$

2.2   Protocol

As described above, the GlobData-LOMP consistency protocol multicasts object updates to all synchronous nodes when a session is allowed to commit. Consistency conflicts among sessions are resolved with an optimistic approach, using object versions. To this end, the protocol uses some meta-data tables in the database where the current object versions can be stored.

In summary, it processes the following steps:

1. There is no consistency control when a session performs an access to an object.
2. At commit time, the consistency control performs a voting round for every owner node of the accessed objects of the session.
3. If all the owner nodes conform this commit, the session can continue, and completes the commit. Then, an update message is multicasted to every synchronous replica for each updated object.
4. If any of the owner nodes reply with a denial vote, then the conflicting objects are updated (the adequate value is included in the denial message), and the session is aborted.
5. An asynchronous process is run in the system in order to multicast to every asynchronous replica the updated objects in each node.

The full description of the protocol process can be found in [9].

3 COLUP: The Cautious Optimistic Lazy Update Protocol

An expression for the probability for an object o_i to cause the abortion of a session has been presented in [9]. This expression can be used to predict the convenience for a session to ensure that an object that is asynchronously updated has a recent version in the local database.

The complete expression can be written as follows:

$$PA_{outd}(o_i) = 1 - \left(1 - \frac{\sum_k nw_k}{K \times N}\right)^{\delta(o_i) \times \sum_k wtps_k} \tag{1}$$

Where:

- K is the number of nodes in the system.
- N is the amount of objects maintained by the system (i.e. the distributed database).
- nw_k is the number, in mean, of objects written per write-transaction in the node k of the system.
- $wtps_k$ is the number of write-transactions committed per second in the node k of the system.
- $\delta(o_i)$ the elapsed time the object o_i has not been updated in the node where the session accessing the object is executed.

The expression can be calculated with a few parameters. Only nw_k and $wtps_k$ must be collected in the nodes of the system in order to obtain the expression. Thus, it becomes possible for a node to estimate the convenience for an object to be locally updated before being accessed by a session. This estimation will be performed with a certain degree of accuracy, depending on the "freshness" of the values of nw_k and $wtps_k$ the node has.

In order to apply these results, it becomes necessary to establish a threshold of $PA(o_i)$ to consider the object "convenient to be updated". An adequate value for this threshold should minimize the number of abortions caused by accesses to outdated objects, and keeping low the number of updates for the system.

The higher the threshold is, the less number of abortions will occur in the system, but the higher updates will be done, and a higher overhead will be introduced in the system. This threshold can be approximated at run time, dealing with a behavior near to the optimum.

To implement this principle a new request message is required. Now, the active node for a session sends "update requests" to the owners of the accesses objects, in order to get the updated versions for such objects. This update request message can be sent along the session execution, in order to update (in a certain degree) the objects accessed by the session.

This technique reduces the probability of abortion caused by the accesses to outdated objects within the sessions.

3.1   Modification of the LOM Protocol

The way the COPLA manager decides to send or not an update request for an object that is about to be accessed is quite simple:

1. During the life of a session, an access to an object o_i is requested by the application. This access is intercepted by the COPLA manager of the active node, and then the probability of being outdated is calculated for the object o_i. If the active node is a synchronous (or owner) node for o_i, this probability is 0. This is because the protocol ensures that incoming updates of the object will abort every transaction conflicting with the updated object.
   If the active node is an asynchronous node for o_i, then the COPLA manager will use the expression of $PA(o_i)$. To perform this calculation, it is needed $\delta(o_i)$: the time elapsed from the last local update of o_i.
2. If this probability exceeds a certain threshold T_c, then the COPLA manager sends the update request to the owner of o_i. If the threshold is not reached, the protocol continues as described in section 2.2. This value can be adjusted at run time, in order to obtain results near to the optimum.
3. In other case, after the COPLA manager allows the session to continue, it waits for the update response. This response indicates whether the local version of o_i is updated, or outdated (then, the response contains the newest version for the object). If the local version must be updated, then the update is applied in the local database, and the update time is also written down.
4. Once the COPLA manager has ensured that o_i is updated, the required access to the object can continue.

By forcing to update an object before the session accesses it, the COPLA manager decreases the value of δ_i, to the length of the session. Thus, the chance for a session to success the commit phase is higher.

This technique implies that every update performed in the asynchronous nodes of an object must include a timestamp of the instant the update is performed at. Note that it is not necessary to use global time, but it is only necessary the local time for each node.

3.2   Validation and Accuracy of the Improvement

We have validated the expression used in the protocol, by implementing a simulation of the algorithm. In this simulation, we have implemented nodes that concurrently serve sessions, accessing to different objects of a distributed database. A complete description of this simulation and its results can be found in [9].

The improvement provided by our approach has been empirically observed, both using a simulation, and a real implementation. The results of these experiments have shown that the COLU protocol provides an increase in the performance of the system, keeping the abortion rate below reasonable levels.

The main effect of the overhead of the COLU protocol can be found in the "LocalUpdate" messages. The more *accurate* these messages are, the more efficient the improvement is.

When the expression exceeds the established threshold for an object, and an update request is sent, it is possible for the response of this request to contain the same version for the requested object (e.g. when the object was, in fact, up to date). We name this situation "Inaccurate prediction".

This *accuracy* depends on the expression used to evaluate the convenience of the LocalUpdate, and on the established threshold in the algorithm. Higher values for the threshold should provide more accurate predictions. In the other hand, higher values of the threshold makes it possible to let outdated values for objects. This is determined by the completeness of the prediction function: the correlation between the prediction and the real world will avoid accesses to outdated objects.

In the figure 1 we show the correlation between the prediction and the real abortion rate. The proximity of the predicted abortion rate to the experimental observations validates the expression.

The figure 2 shows the evolution of the inaccuracy of the prediction and the abortion rates. For higher values of the threshold, the number of vain updates is reduced, because the probability for an object to be outdated is also low. In contrast, the abortion rate trends to be increased for higher values of the threshold, providing the rates reached with lazy replication.

For the simulated scenario, it can be observed that for thresholds around 0,1 the lower number of abortions can be achieved. For this threshold, the 50% of the update requests obtain the same version, and the abortion rate is near to the minimum provided by eager replication.

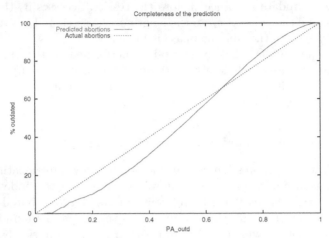

Fig. 1. Completeness

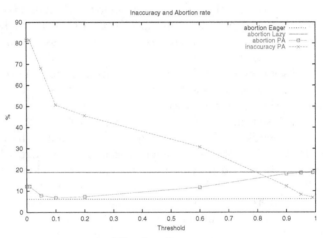

Fig. 2. Accuracy

4   Providing Self-Recovery Ability to COLUP

In section 3 we have presented a lazy update protocol, with a good behavior in respect to the abortion rate and an empirical mechanism to obtain the optimum value for the threshold of $P(o_i)$ has been also shown. However, the calculus of $PA(o_i)$ can be used for other techniques than the evaluation of the convenience for an update. This is the case of the *Fault Tolerance*. In this section, we will show a modification of the COLU Protocol, in order to provide fault tolerance to the protocol. This modification is based on two principles: role migration, and the calculation of $PA(o_i)$.

4.1 Modification of the COLU Protocol

Each node in the system runs a copy of a *membership monitor*. This monitor is a piece of software that observes a preconfigured set of nodes, and notifies its local node about any change in this set (either additions or eliminations). Each node is labeled with a number, identifying it, and providing an order between every node in the system. The membership monitor used for the LOM Protocol is described in [10], and can be also used to provide the membership service to our COLU Protocol. The rest of this section shows the differences between the LOM and the COLU protocols.

1. When the membership monitor notices a node failure (let N_f be the failed node), a notification is provided to every surviving node in the system. This notification causes for each receiving node to update a list of *alive nodes*. The effect of these notifications will be a logical migration of the ownerships of the failed node. Further steps will explain the term *logical*.

2. During the execution of a session, a number of messages can be sent to the different owners of the objects accessed by this session. If a message must to be sent to a failed owner N_f, then it will be redirected to the new owner for the involved object. This new owner can be assigned in a deterministic way from the set of synchronous replicas of the object (e.g. electing as new owner the node with an identifier immediately higher to the failed one). Let N_n be the new owner for the accessed object.
   The determinism of the election is important to guarantee that every surviving node redirects its messages to the same node (N_n).
   Note that the messages sent to a node can involve more than one object. This will generate a unique message to the new owner, because every object in the original message had the same owner, and so, will have the same substitute.

3. When the synchronous replica N_n receives a message considering the node as an owner, then the message is processed as if N_n was the original owner. To this end, if the received message was an *access confirmation request*, then the lock management must be performed by N_n, replying the request as shown in section 2.2. Moreover, if the received message was an *update request*, then the new owner should reply to the message sending the local version of the object. The update message will be detailed in further steps.
   This behavior maintains the consistence because the new owner of an object will be always elected from the set of synchronous replicas of the object. This guarantees that the value for the object maintained in the new owner is exactly the same value the failed owner had.

4. Whenever the original owner node N_f is recovered from the failure, every alive node will be notified by its local membership monitor. Then, further messages sent from the nodes to the owner N_f must not be redirected to N_n, because the node N_f has been recovered now.
   The alive nodes recognizes the recently recovered node by sending a *greeting message*. A *greeting message* sent from a node N_a to the recently recovered

node N_f contains a list of locks granted to the node N_a by the temporally owner N_n. Using the contents of these lists, the node N_f can generate the structures needed to manage the locks again. Thus, there becomes unnecessary for the N_n to continue managing these locks.

Step 8 includes a more detailed description of the contents of the *greeting messages*.

5. Nevertheless, a recently recovered node N_f will receive request messages concerning owned objects that can have been updated during the failure period. In order to manage this situation, a recovered node must consider every object held in its local database as an "asynchronous replica". This consideration will be done for an object o_i until either an *update reply* or *access confirmation reply* is received from a synchronous replica of the object. These replies will be received in the situations described in steps 6 and 7.

6. If an *access confirmation request* is received by a recently recovered node N_f, and the involved object has not been already *synchronized* in the node (i.e. the concerning object has not been already updated from a synchronous replica), then N_f must force the synchronization. This synchronization is performed with an *update message* sent to a synchronous replica of the object. The reply to this *update message* will ensure the local database to hold an updated version of the requested object.

   Once the object is updated in the local database, the *access confirmation request* can be processed as described for a standard owner node.

7. The recovered node can also process sessions during the synchronization period. These sessions will access to a set of objects. As we see in step 5, every accessed object must be temporally considered as an *asynchronously maintained* node until the object is synchronized.

   The treatment for the objects accessed by a local session will depend on the next classification:

   – Objects with a synchronous maintenance (i.e. either objects owned by the active node, or objects for which the active node is a synchronous replica.
   – Objects for which the active node is an asynchronous replica.

   The treatment for the objects with a synchronous maintenance in the active node will be similar to the recovery of the synchrony described in step 6. When the session ask its local COPLA manager about an object *originally* owned by the node, then an *update request* is sent to a synchronous replica of the object. The reply to this *update message* will ensure the database of the active node to hold an updated version of the requested object, and the response to the session can be completed.

   For the objects maintained asynchronously, the standard treatment can be used, taking into account that the period of outdatedness should include the time the active node was down.

8. Another way for a node N_f to recover the ownership of an object can be found in the *greeting messages* received by N_f from each alive node. This messages were introduced in step 4. When a node N_a sends a *greeting message* to N_f,

the message not only contains a list of locks obtained by N_a, but it also contains the last version for each locked object o_i. This information is enough for N_f to consider synchronized each object o_i.

9. In order to ensure that a recently-recovered node N_f achieves a correct state for its originally synchronized objects (i.e. the node receives an update message for each object o_j that satisfy $N_f \in S(o_i)$), an asynchronous process becomes necessary to be run.

   This process, will be executed as a low-priority process, and will send an *update request* for each object not already synchronized in N_f.

   Note that the interference of such process in the performance of N_f should be low, because it will only be scheduled during idle periods.

10. The asynchronous process should also include the update, in the local database of the recovered node N_f, of any new object created during the time the node was failed. To perform this update, a simple algorithm may be followed by N_f just at the beginning of its recovery:

    – When N_f recovers from a failure, a query is performed to the local database in order to retrieve the identifier for the more recently inserted object owned by every node in the system. This can be done due to the construction of the object identifiers. As a consequence of these requests, N_f knows, for each node, the last inserted object.

    – Until N_f has received the information from its local database, it will be locked any update in its local database. This ensures that the response of the requests does not includes any update performed after the recovery of N_f.

    – In addition, and concurrently with these requests, every node in the system sends the *greeting message* to the recovered node. In this message, explained in 8, additional information can be included. Moreover, a *greeting message* sent from a node N_i to N_f will include the identifier of the more recently object created by the node N_i.

    – The comparison of the information contained in the *greeting messages*, with the values collected from the local database, makes N_f know, for each node N_i, the *lost insertions* for each node (i.e. the range of objects inserted during the failure).

    – In addition to these object identifiers, the asynchronous process performs further requests to its local database in order to retrieve a complete list of object identifiers owned by each node in the system, and managed in a synchronous way in N_f.

    – Objects contained in this list of *synchronous identifiers* will be considered as asynchronously maintained objects, until an update message will be sent to its owner node, and an up-to-date value is guaranteed in the local database of N_f. Then, the identifier can be removed from the list of *synchronous identifier*.

In order to update every object in the local database, the asynchronous process will use the collected information about *lost insertions* to perform *update requests* to each owner node about these objects.

The behavior described in this section can be summarized by the rewriting of the expression for P presented in (1), and considering $d(N_f)$ as the set of objects with synchronous management in N_f, but not already synchronized (note that $\forall o_i \in d(N_f) : N_f \in S(o_i)$):

$$P(o_i) = \begin{cases} 1 & , o_i \in d(N_f) \\ 0 & , o_i \notin d(N_f) \wedge N_f \in S(o_i) \\ PA_{outd}(o_i) & , N_f \in A(o_i) \end{cases} \tag{2}$$

The expression includes either the access to already synchronized objects, or the access to synchronous objects that have not already been synchronized.

5   Related Work

Current work in consistency protocols for replicated databases can be found using either eager [11, 1] or lazy protocols [5, 6].

Each one has its pros and cons, as described in [12]. Eager protocols usually hamper the update performance and increase transaction response times but, on the positive side, they can yield serializable execution of multiple transactions without requiring too much effort. On the other hand, lazy protocols may allow a transaction to read outdated versions of objects, hamper the abortion rate, but they can improve transaction response times. Lazy replication is used in the presented approach, and have been implemented in a real environment (COPLA [8]).

A good classification of consistency control protocols was presented in [1], according to three parameters: server architecture, server interaction and transaction termination. Among the alternatives resulting from combining these three parameters, only two of them seem to lead to a good balance of scalability and efficiency: those based on "update everywhere" and "constant interaction", that increase the load distribution, and require low communication costs.

The use of "locks" in pessimistic consistency control[13] minimizes the number of aborted transactions, but degrades the performance of the system, because the complexity introduced by the management of the locks.

On the other hand, the traditional use of "versions" (or "timestamps" [14]) for optimistic consistency control[2] provides as an advantage the reduction of the blocking time of the transactions, but increases the abortion rate.

Lazy update protocols, introduced in [5, 6], presented a new approach for the propagation of the updates, in contrast to the traditionally used "eager replication". Lazy update protocols take advantage of the fact that an object can be written several times for different transactions before another transaction reads it.

In respect to recovery protocols, since the first attempts based on dynamic reassignment of the voting roles in pessimistic consistency control, many work has been made in order to provide fault tolerance minimizing the time the system is unaccessible. To this end, approaches like *active replication*[15] improves the simplicity, at the cost of load distribution, and *passive replication*[16] increases the load distribution, at the cost of recovery time.

6 Conclusion

Lazy update protocols have not been widely exploited due to its excessive abortion rate on scenarios with high probability of access conflicts. Nevertheless, such protocols can provide important improvements in the performance of a distributed system, when the abortion rate can be kept low, and the locality of the accesses is appreciable.

We have presented an algorithm based on statistical techniques, that makes use of the prediction of the probability for an accessed object to be out of date $(PA_{outd}(o_i))$, and cause a further abortion of the accessing transaction.

This protocol, remains a lazy update behavior, and uses this prediction to reduce its abortion rate, improving thus the performance of the system. In addition, the design of this protocol allows its variation from a pure lazy protocol, to a "paranoid" behavior (in the last case, it is comparable to an eager protocol).

In addition, a modification of this protocol is also described, providing self-recovery ability, in order to include fault tolerance in the algorithm. This modification, introduced as a lazy recovery mechanism, allows the re-incorporation of a fault node without interfere in the rest of nodes in the system, and avoiding to block any transaction in the system -even in the recovered node- during the recovery phase.

As a result, the complete protocol provides the advantages of lazy approaches, forestalling their traditionally found disadvantages, and including fault tolerance at a very low costs. Thus, our approach reduces the abortion rates, improving the performance of the system, and allowing the recovery phase to avoid blocking of the sessions during the recovery process.

References

[1] Wiesmann, M., Schiper, A., Pedone, F., Kemme, B., Alonso, G.: Database replication techniques: A three parameter classification. In: Proc. of the 19th IEEE Symposium on Reliable Distributed Systems (SRDS'00). (2000) 206–217   188, 198

[2] Kung, H.T., Robinson, J.T.: On optimistic methods for concurrency control. ACM Transactions on Database Systems **6** (1981) 213–226   188, 198

[3] Eswaran, K.P., Gray, J., Lorie, R.A., Traiger, I.L.: The notions of consistency and predicate locks in a database syste m. Communications of the ACM **19** (1976) 624–633   188

[4] Thomas, R.H.: A majority consensus approach to concurrency control for multiple copy databases. ACM Transactions on Database Systems **4** (1979) 180–209   189

[5] Breitbart, Y., Korth, H.F.: Replication and consistency: being lazy helps sometimes. In: Proceedings of the sixteenth ACM SIGACT-SIGMOD-SIGART symposium on Principles of Database Systems, ACM Press (1997) 173–184   189, 198

[6] Holliday, J., Agrawal, D., Abbadi, A.E.: Database replication: If you must be lazy, be consistent. In: Proceedings of 18th Symposium on Reliable Distributed Systems SRDS'99, IEEE Computer Society Press (1999) 304–305   189, 198

[7] Instituto Tecnológico de Informática: GlobData Web Site (2002) Accessible in URL: *http://globdata.iti.es.* 189

[8] Muñoz, F., Irún, L., Galdámez, P., Bernabéu, J., Bataller, J., Bañul, M.C.: Globdata: A platform for supporting multiple consistency modes. Information Systems and Databases (2002) 137–143 189, 198

[9] Irún, L., Muñoz, F., Decker, H., Bernabéu-Aubán, J.M.: Colup: The cautious optimistic lazy update protocol. In: XI Jornadas de Concurrencia. (2003) 191, 193

[10] Muñoz Escoí, F.D., Gomis Hilario, O., Galdámez, P., Bernabéu-Aubán, J.M.: HMM: A membership protocol for a multi-computer cluster. In: Anexo de las actas de las VIII Jornadas de Concurrencia, Cuenca, España (2000) 195

[11] Agrawal, D., Alonso, G., El Abbadi, A., Stanoi, I.: Exploiting atomic broadcast in replicated databases. Lecture Notes in Computer Science **1300** (1997) 496–503 198

[12] Gray, J., Helland, P., O'Neil, P., Shasha, D.: The dangers of replication and a solution. In: Proc. of the 1996 ACM SIGMOD International Conference on Management of Data, Canada (1996) 173–182 198

[13] Bernstein, P.A., Shipman, D.W., Rothnie, J.B.: Concurrency control in a system for distributed databases (SDD-1). ACM Transactions on Database Systems **5** (1980) 18–51 198

[14] Bernstein, P.A., Hadzilacos, V., Goodman, N.: Concurrency Control and Recovery in Database Systems. Addison Wesley, Reading, MA, EE.UU. (1987) 198

[15] Schneider, F.B.: Replication management using the state-machine approach. In Mullender, S.J., ed.: Distributed Systems. 2^a edn. ACM Press, Addison-Wesley, Wokingham, Reino Unido (1993) 166–197 ISBN 0-201-62427-3. 198

[16] Budhiraja, N., Marzullo, K., Schneider, F.B., Toueg, S.: The primary-backup approach. In Mullender, S.J., ed.: Distributed Systems. 2^a edn. ACM Press, Addison-Wesley, Wokingham, Reino Unido (1993) 199–216 ISBN 0-201-62427-3. 198

Visual Data Mining of Large Spatial Data Sets

Daniel A. Keim, Christian Panse, and Mike Sips

University of Konstanz, Germany
{keim,panse,sips}@informatik.uni-konstanz.de

Abstract. Extraction of interesting knowledge from large spatial databases is an important task in the development of spatial database systems. Spatial data mining is the branch of data mining that deals with spatial (location) data. Analyzing the huge amount (usually tera-bytes) of spatial data obtained from large databases such as credit card payments, telephone calls, environmental records, census demographics etc. is, however, a very difficult task. *Visual data mining* applies human visual perception to the exploration of large data sets. Presenting data in an interactive, graphical form often fosters new insights, encouraging the formation and validation of new hypotheses to the end of better problem-solving and gaining deeper domain knowledge. In this paper we give a short overview of visual data mining techniques, especially the area of analyzing spatial data. We provide some examples for effective visualizations of spatial data in important application areas such as consumer analysis, e-mail traffic analysis, and census demographics.

Keywords: Information Visualization, Visual Data Mining, Visualization of Spatial Data, Visualization and Cartography, Spatial Data Mining

1   Visual Data Mining

Progress in technology allows today's computer systems to store and exchange amounts of data that until very recently were considered extraordinarily vast. Almost all transactions of everyday life, such as purchases made with a credit card, web pages visited or telephone calls made are recorded by computers. This data is collected because it is a potential source of valuable information, providing a competitive advantage to its holders. The data is often automatically recorded via sensors and monitoring systems. Government agencies also provide a wealth of statistical information that can be applied to important problems in public health and safety, combined with proprietary data. Even simple transactions of every day life, such as paying by credit card or using the telephone, are typically recorded by computers. Usually many parameters are recorded, resulting in data with a high dimensionality. With today's data management systems, it is only possible to view quite small portions of this data. If the data is presented textually, the amount of data that can be displayed is in the range of some hundred data items, but this is like a drop in the ocean when dealing with data sets containing millions of data items. Having no possibility to adequately explore the large amounts of data that have been collected because of

N. Bianchi-Berthouze (Ed.): DNIS 2003, LNCS 2822, pp. 201–215, 2003.

their potential usefulness, the data becomes useless and the databases become 'Data Dumps'. Finding valuable details that reveal the structure hidden in the data, however, is difficult.

1.1 Visual Exploration Paradigm

Visual Data Exploration usually follows a three step process: *Overview first, zoom and filter, and then details-on-demand* (which has been called the Information Seeking Mantra [35]). First, the user needs to get an overview of the data. In the overview, the user identifies interesting patterns or groups in the data and focuses on one or more of them. For analyzing these patterns, the user needs to drill-down and access details of the data. Visualization technology may be used for all three steps of the data exploration process. Visualization techniques are useful for showing an overview of the data, allowing the user to identify interesting subsets. In this step, it is important to keep the overview visualization while focusing on the subset using another visualization. An alternative is to distort the overview visualization in order to focus on the interesting subsets. This can be performed by dedicating a larger percentage of the display to the interesting subsets while decreasing screen space for uninteresting data. To further explore the interesting subsets, the user needs a drill-down capability in order to observe the details about the data. Note that visualization technology does not only provide visualization techniques for all three steps but also bridges the gaps between them.

1.2 Classification of Visual Data Mining Techniques

There are a number of well known techniques for visualizing large data sets, such as x-y plots, line plots, and histograms. These techniques are useful for data exploration but are limited to relatively small and low dimensional data sets. Over the last years, a large number of novel information visualization techniques have been developed, allowing visualizations of multidimensional data sets without inherent two- or three-dimensional semantics. Nice overviews of the approaches can be found in a number of recent books [5] [32] [37] [42]. The techniques can be classified based on three criteria [17] (see also figure 1):

- the data to be visualized
- the visualization technique
- and the interaction technique used

The **data type to be visualized** [35] may be *one-dimensional data*, such as temporal (time-series) data, *two-dimensional data*, such as geographical maps, *multidimensional data*, such as relational tables, *text and hypertext*, such as news articles and web documents, *hierarchies and graphs*, such as telephone calls, and *algorithms and software*.
The **visualization technique** used may be classified as: *Standard 2D/3D displays*, such as bar charts and x-y plots, *Geometrically transformed displays*, such

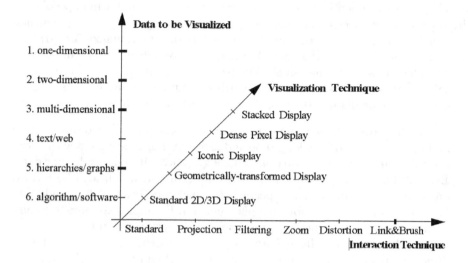

Fig. 1. Classification of visual data exploration techniques

as hyperbolic plane [40] and parallel coordinates [15], *Icon-based displays*, such as chernoff faces [6] and stick figures [29] [30], *Dense pixel displays*, such as the recursive pattern [2] and circle segments [3], and *Stacked displays*, such as treemaps [16] [34] and dimensional stacking [41]. The third dimension of the classification is the *interaction technique* used. Interaction techniques allow users to directly navigate and modify the visualizations, as well as select subsets of the data for further operations. Examples include: Dynamic Projection, Interactive Filtering, Interactive Zooming, Interactive Distortion, Interactive Linking and Brushing. Note that the three dimensions of our classification - data type to be visualized, visualization technique, and interaction technique - can be assumed to be orthogonal. Orthogonality means that any of the visualization techniques may be used in conjunction with any of the interaction techniques for any data type. Note also that a specific system may be designed to support different data types and that it may use a combination of visualization and interaction techniques. More details can be found in [20].

2   Visualizing Spatial Data

Spatial data is different from other kinds of data in that spatial data describes objects or phenomena with a specific location in the real world. Large spatial data sets can be seen as a result of accumulating samples or readings of phenomena in the real world while moving along two dimensions in space. In general, spatial data sets are discrete samples of a continuous phenomenon. Nowadays, there exist a large number of applications, in which it is important to analyze relationships that involve geographic location. Examples include global climate modeling (measurements such as temperature, rainfall, and wind-speed), environmental records, customer analysis, telephone calls, credit card payments, and crime data. Because of this special characteristic, the visualization strategy for spatial data is straightforward. We map the spatial attributes directly to the two physical screen dimensions. The resulting visualization depends on the spatial **dimension** or **extent** of the described phenomena and objects. Spatial phenomena may be distinguished to according their spatial dimension or extent:

- **Point Phenomena** - have no spatial extent, can be termed zero-dimensional and can be specified by a longitude and latitude coordinate pairs with a statistical value z. Examples are census demographics, oil wells, and crime data.
- **Line Phenomena** - have length, but essentially no width, can be termed one-dimensional and can be specified by unclosed series of longitude and latitude coordinate pairs for each phenomenon. Examples are large telecommunication networks, internet, and boundaries between countries.
- **Area Phenomena** - have both length and width, can be termed two-dimensional and can be specified by series of longitude and latitude coordinate pairs that completely enclose a region and a statistical value z for each phenomenon. Examples are lakes, and political units such as states or counties.

For each of the phenomena, several visualization approaches have been developed over the last years. In the following, we provide an overview of interesting novel visualization techniques in some of the most important application areas. More details about spatial visualization and cartography can be found in [26] [27] [31] [36].

2.1   Point Phenomena

The basic idea of visualizing spatial data which describes point phenomena is to place a pixel where that phenomenon occurs. Point phenomena with statistical values can be displayed as colored pixels. This simple visualization is called **Dot Map** (see figure 2). Dot Maps can be an elegant medium for communicating a wealth of information about the spatial relationships of spatial point phenomena, in a compact, convenient and familiar format. However, when large spatial data sets are drawn on a map, the problem of overlapping or overplotting of data points arises in highly populated areas, while low-population areas are virtually empty since spatial data are highly non-uniformly distributed in real world data sets. Figure 2 shows the overlapping problem for the New York / New England Area. Examples for such spatial data sets are credit card payments, telephone calls, health statistics, environmental records, crime data and census demographics. Note that the analysis may involve multiple parameters that may be shown on multiple maps. If all maps show the data in the same way, it may be possible to relate the parameters and detect local correlations, dependencies, and other interesting patterns. There are several approaches to coping with dense spatial data already in common use [11]. One widely used method is a 2.5D

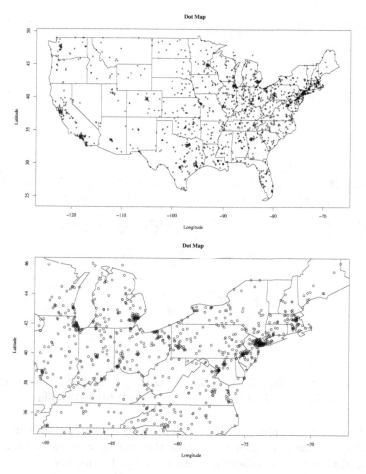

Fig. 2. Dot Map of the 1999 USA Population - every pixel represents the spatial location of people in the USA. Note that we have a overlapping of about 80 %

visualization showing data points aggregated up to map regions. This technique is commercially available in systems such as VisualInsight's In3D [1] and ESRI's ArcView [10]. An alternative that shows more detail is a visualization of individual data points as bars according to their statistical value on a map. This technique is embodied in systems such as SGI's MineSet [14] and AT&T's Swift 3D [18]. A problem here is that a large number of data points are plotted at the same position, and therefore, only a small portion of the data is actually visible. Moreover, due to occlusion in 3D, a significant fraction of the data may not be visible unless the viewpoint is changed.

VisualPoints One approach that does not aggregate the data, but avoids overlap in the two-dimensional display, is the *VisualPoints* approach [21]. The idea

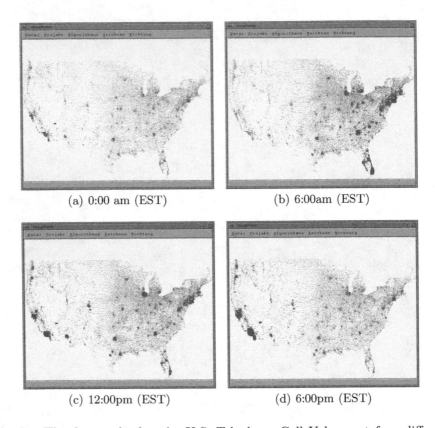

(a) 0:00 am (EST)   (b) 6:00am (EST)

(c) 12:00pm (EST)   (d) 6:00pm (EST)

Fig. 3. The figures display the U.S. Telephone Call Volume at four different times during one day. The idea is to place the first data items at their correct position, and then move overlapping data points to the nearby free position

is to reposition pixels that would otherwise overlap. The basic idea of the repositioning algorithm is to recursively partition the data set into four subsets containing the data points in equally-sized subregions. Since the data points may not fit into the four equally size subregions, we have to determine new extents of the four subregions (without changing the four subsets of data points) such that the data points in each subset can be visualized in their corresponding subregion. For an efficient implementation, a quadtree-like data structure manages the required information and supports the recursive partitioning process. The partitioning process works as follows. Starting with the root of the quadtree, in each step the data space is partitioned into four subregions. The partitioning is made such that the area occupied by each of the subregions (in pixels) is larger than the number of pixels belonging to the corresponding subregion. A problem of *VisualPoints* is that in areas with high overlap, the repositioning depends on the ordering of the points in the database. That is, the first data item found in the database is placed at its correct position, and subsequent overlapping data points are moved to nearby free positions, and so locally appear quasi-random in their placement. Figure 3 presents four time steps of such visualizations, showing the U.S. Telephone Call Volume within a 10 minute interval at the given time. The time sequence clearly shows the development of the call volume over time. The visualizations allow an intuitive understanding of the development of the call volume, showing the wake-up from east to west, the drop down in call volume at commuting and lunch time, etc. The visualizations show expected patterns but also reveal unexpected patterns such as the locations of nation wide call centers in the middle of the US (see figure 3(a)).

2.2   Line Phenomena

The basic idea to visualize spatial data describing linear phenomena is to represent linear phenomena as line segments between two end points. Today, **Network Maps** are widely used. Some approaches only display the structure of networks (usually modeled as graphs) to interpret and understand the general behavior and structure of networks. The goal is to find a good geometric representation of the network on a map. There are several approaches to visualize networks and data on these networks. Eick and Wills [9] use functions such as aggregation, hierarchical information, node position and linked displays for investigating large networks with hierarchies but without a natural layout. They used color and shape for coding node information and color and line width for coding link information. Researchers at NCSA [28] added 3D graphics to their network maps to display animations of Internet traffic packets within the network backbone. Becker, Eick and Wilks [4] describe a system called SeeNet, which is motivated by statistical research in dynamic graphics. The basic idea is to involve the human and let him/her interactively control the display to focus on interesting patterns. They use two static network displays to visualize the geographic relationships and a link matrix, which gives equal emphasis to all network links. Another interesting system for visualizing large network data is the AT&T's SWIFT-3D System [19]. The SWIFT-3D system integrates a collection of relevant visualization techniques ranging from familiar statistical displays, to pixel-oriented overviews with interactive 3D-maps and drag+drop query tools. The visualization component maps the data to a set of linked 2D and 3D views created by different visualization techniques: Statistical 2D Visualizations, Pixel-oriented 2D Visualizations, and Dynamic 3D Visualizations. In all mentioned approaches, however, the visualization of large networks on maps leads to the overlapping or overplotting problem of line segments in dense areas.

E-mail Traffic Analysis One of the first uses of the internet is the electronic mailing (e-mail). Messages are sent between users of computer systems to different places all over the world and the computer systems are used to hold and transport the messages. There are several advantages of electronic mailing, as it is a fast, cheap, and comfortable communication method. The number of internet users increases exponentially and therefore more and more people are able to

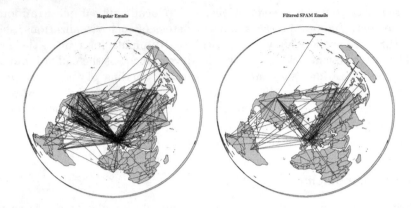

Fig. 4. The figures display the world wide e-mail routes of one of our *IMAP* users. The *IMAP* server is located in Konstanz, Germany (*37 41.0N / 09 08.3E*). In our department, SPAM hits one fourth of our e-mail traffic

send and receive e-mails. Today, corporate and university networks are becoming increasingly clogged by e-mail pitches for pornography, money-making schemes and health, products, and there's little relief on the horizon. In our department, about one fourth of our e-mail traffic are SPAM's. In 2002, we had one SPAM for every 20 legitimate e-mail messages; today the ratio is closer to one in four. Using Anti-SPAM software on specialized servers can discern SPAM from legitimate e-mail. The software can also upload potentially new forms of SPAM for analysis, and develop recognition algorithms to identify and filter new types of SPAM e-mail. An other interesting approach is to visualize the path of SPAM e-mail to see interesting patterns and behavior. The path information can be derived from the e-mail headers. Figure 4 shows the regular and SPAM e-mails path of one of the authors. The e-mail paths displayed in the plot have been stored since 2000. Each spatial location corresponds to a computer system from which the e-mails were sent. Each line segment describes the path of an e-mail message between two computer systems. The picture on the right displays only SPAM e-mails. Visualizing e-mail paths may help to find important patterns of the e-mail traffic. The picture on the left shows that a major amount of e-mails arrives from the USA. On the right hand side one can see that there is a strong accumulation of hosts in the eastern countries, where SPAM e-mails originate from.

2.3   Area Phenomena

The basic idea to visualize area phenomena is to represent the area phenomenon as a closed contour, a set of coordinates where the first and the last points are the same. Closed contours may be for example states, counties, cities, etc. Today, two types of maps, called **Thematic Map** and **Choropleth Map**, are used in

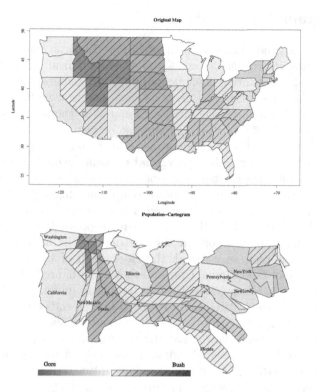

Fig. 5. The Figure displays the U.S. state population cartogram with the presidential election result of 2000. The area of the states in the cartograms corresponds to the population and the color (shaded and not shaded areas) corresponds to the percentage of the vote. A bipolar colormap depicts which candidate has won each state

Cartography and GIS-Systems. Thematic Maps are used to emphasize the spatial distribution of one or more geographic attributes. Popular thematic maps are the Choropleth Map (Greek: choro = area, pleth = value), in which enumeration units or data collection units are shaded to represent different magnitudes of a variable. Often the statistical values are encoded as colored regions on the map. On both types of maps, high values are often concentrated in densely populated areas, and low statistical values are spread out over sparsely populated areas. These maps, therefore, tend to highlight patterns in large areas, which may, however, be of low importance. In US Census Demographics Data Sets, for example, such maps tend to highlight patterns in areas where few people live, e.g. the large territorial states in the USA with less than 7 inhabitants per square mile. Advanced map distortion techniques such as density equalized maps or cartograms are a powerful way of visualizing area phenomena.

3   Cartograms

A cartogram is a generalization of an ordinary thematic map, which is distorted by resizing its regions according to a geographically-related input parameter. Example applications include population demographics [38], election results [25], and epidemiology [13]. Because cartograms are difficult to make by hand, the study of computer generated automated methods is of special interest [7] [8] [12] [33] [38] [39]. Cartograms can also be seen as a general information visualization technique. They provide a mean for trading shape against area to improve a visualization by scaling polygonal elements according to an external parameter. In population cartograms, more space is allocated to densely populated areas. Patterns that involve many people are highlighted, while those involving fewer people are less emphasized. Figure 5 shows a conventional map of the 2000 US presidential elections along with a population-based cartogram presenting the same information. In the cartogram, the area of the states is scaled to their population, so it reveals the close result of a presidential election more effectively than the Original Choropleth Map in figure 5. For a cartogram to be effective, a human being must be able to quickly understand the displayed data and relate it to the original map. Recognition depends on preserving basic properties, such as shape, orientation, and contiguity. This, however, is difficult to achieve and it has been shown that the cartogram problem is unsolvable in the general case [22]. Even when allowing errors in the shape and area representations, we are left with a difficult simultaneous optimization problem for which currently available algorithms are very time-consuming.

3.1   The Cartogram Problem

The cartogram problem can be defined as a map deformation problem. The input is a planar polygon mesh (map) $\mathcal{P}$ and a set of values $\mathcal{X}$, one for each region. The goal is to deform the map into $\overline{\mathcal{P}}$ so that the area of each region matches the value assigned to it, doing this in such a way that the overall shape of the regions is so preserved that they all remain recognizable.

Problem (The Cartogram Problem):

Input: A planar polygon mesh $\mathcal{P}$ consisting of polygons $p_1, \ldots, p_k$, values $\mathcal{X} = x_1, \ldots x_k$ with $x_i > 0, \sum x_i = 1$. Let $A(p_i)$ denote the normalized area of polygon p_i with $A(p_i) > 0, \sum A(p_i) = 1$.

Output: A *topology-preserving* polygon mesh $\overline{\mathcal{P}}$ consisting of polygons $\overline{p}_1, \ldots, \overline{p_k}$ such that the function $f(\overline{S}, \overline{A}) = \omega \cdot \sum_{i=1}^{k} s_i + (1 - \omega) \cdot \sum_{i=1}^{k} a_i$ is minimized with

$$\overline{S} = \{s_1, \ldots, s_k\} \text{ where } s_i = d_S(p_i, \overline{p}_i) \qquad \textbf{(Shape Error)}$$

$$\overline{A} = \{a_1, \ldots a_k\} \text{ where } a_i = d_A(x_i, A(\overline{p}_i)) \qquad \textbf{(Area Error)}$$

$\forall j = 1, \ldots, k$ and the weighting factor ω with $0 \leq \omega < 1$.

Intuitively, topology preservation means that the faces of the input mesh must stay the same, i.e. the cyclic order of adjacent edges in $\mathcal{P}$ must be the same as in $\overline{\mathcal{P}}$. This can be expressed formally by saying that the pseudo-duals[1] of the planar graphs represented by $\mathcal{P}$ and $\overline{\mathcal{P}}$ should be isomorphic. Even a simple variant of the cartogram problem, which even ignores issues of shape preservation ($\omega = 0$), is likely to be NP-complete. Since it may be impossible to simultaneously fulfill the area and shape constraints, the functions $f(\cdot\cdot), d_S(\cdot, \cdot)$ and $d_A(\cdot, \cdot)$ model the error of the output cartogram.

3.2   The *CartoDraw* Algorithm

The basic idea of *CartoDraw* is to incrementally reposition the vertices of the map's polygons by means of scanlines. Local changes are applied if they reduce the total area error without introducing an excessive shape error [22]. The main loop iterates over a set of scanlines. For each scanline, it computes a candidate transformation of the polygons, and checks it for topology and shape preservation. If the candidate transformation passes the tests, it is made persistent, otherwise it is discarded. The order of scanline processing depends on their potential for reducing area error. The algorithm iterates over the scanlines until the area error improvement over all scanlines falls below a threshold. The input scanlines are arbitrary lines and may be automatically computed or interactively entered. The idea for distorting the polygon mesh is to use line segments (called *cutting lines*) perpendicular to scanlines at regular intervals. Consider the two edges on the boundary of the polygon intersected by a cutting line on either side of the scanline. These edges divide the polygon boundary into two connected chains. Now, if the area constraints require that the polygon expands, the algorithm applies a translation *parallel* to the scanline to each vertex of the two connected pieces of the boundary (in opposite directions) to *stretch* the polygon at that point. Similarly, if a contraction is called for, the direction of translation is reversed.

3.3   *VisualPoints*-Approach

The basic idea of using the visual point approach for Cartogram generation is to insert points into each polygon, where the number of these points corresponds to the statistical parameter. After the quadtree is constructed, it is applied to distort the vertices of the polygon mesh. Each vertex is repositioned separately: First the cell of the quadtree containing the vertex is determined. Then the new position of the vertex is calculated by scaling the cells of the quadtree on each level according to the desired size of the cells (corresponding to the number of pixels). By repositioning each vertex, we iteratively construct the distorted polygon mesh. Figure 6 shows a *VisualPoints* (see also section 2.1) population cartogram representing the accomplished bachelor degrees in the USA in comparison with a CartoDraw cartogram. A comparison of both approaches can be found in [23] [24].

---

[1] The *pseudo-dual* of a planar graph is a graph that has one vertex for each face and an edge connecting two vertices if the corresponding faces are adjacent.

Fig. 6. The Figure displays (1) the U.S. state population cartogram computed with *VisualPoints*, and (2) the U.S. state population cartogram computed with *CartoDraw* showing the accomplished bachelor degrees or higher in the USA in 2000. The area of the states in the cartograms corresponds to the population and the grey level of the areas correspond to the percentage of the accomplished bachelor degrees or higher

4   Conclusion

Visual Data Mining is an important research area. Many data sources provide data with spatial attributes. In this article, we describe an overview of methods for visualizing large spatial data sets containing point, line and area phenomena. The results show that the visualization of spatial data can be extremely helpful for visually exploring large spatial data sets.

Acknowledgements

We would like to thank Florian Mansmann for helping us with the e-mail traffic analysis and Carmen Sanz Merino for her useful comments.

References

[1] I. Advizor Solutions. Visual insight in3d. http://www.advizorsolutions.com/, Feb. 2003.

[2] M. Ankerst, D. A. Keim, and H.-P. Kriegel. Recursive pattern: A technique for visualizing very large amounts of data. In *Proc. Visualization '95, Atlanta, GA*, pages 279–286, 1995.

[3] M. Ankerst, D. A. Keim, and H.-P. Kriegel. Circle segments: A technique for visually exploring large multidimensional data sets. In *Visualization '96, Hot Topic Session, San Francisco, CA*, 1996.

[4] R. A. Becker, S. G. Eick, and A. R. Wilks. Visualizing network data. *IEEE Transactions on Visualization and Computer Graphics*, 1(1):16–28, 1995.

[5] S. Card, J. Mackinlay, and B. Shneiderman. *Readings in Information Visualization*. Morgan Kaufmann, 1999.

[6] H. Chernoff. The use of faces to represent points in k-dimensional space graphically. *Journal Amer. Statistical Association*, 68:361–368, 1973.

[7] B. D. Dent. *Cartography: Thematic Map Design, 4th Ed., Chapter 10*. William C. Brown, Dubuque, IA, 1996.

[8] J. A. Dougenik, N. Chrisman, and D. R. Niemeyer. An algorithm to construct continuous area cartograms. *The Professional Geographer*, 37(1):75–81, 1985.

[9] S. G. Eick and G. J. Wills. Navigating large networks with hierarchies. In *Proc. IEEE Conf. Visualization*, pages 204–210, 25–29 1993.

[10] ESRI. Arc view. http://www.esri.com/software/arcgis/arcview/index.html, Feb. 2003.

[11] G. Geisler. Making information more accessible: A survey of information, visualization applications and techniques.
http://www.ils.unc.edu/~geisg/info/infovis/paper.html, Feb. 2003.

[12] S. Gusein-Zade and V. Tikunov. A new technique for constructing continuous cartograms. *Cartography and Geographic Information Systems*, 20(3):66–85, 1993.

[13] S. Gusein-Zade and V. Tikunov. Map transformations. *Geography Review*, 9(1):19–23, 1995.

[14] S. M. Homepage. Sgi mineset. http://www.sgi.com/software/mineset.html, Feb. 2002.

[15] A. Inselberg and B. Dimsdale. Parallel coordinates: A tool for visualizing multidimensional geometry. In *Proc. Visualization 90, San Francisco, CA*, pages 361–370, 1990.

[16] B. Johnson and B. Shneiderman. Treemaps: A space-filling approach to the visualization of hierarchical information. In *Proc. Visualization '91 Conf*, pages 284–291, 1991.

[17] D. Keim. Visual exploration of large databases. *Communications of the ACM*, 44(8):38–44, 2001.

[18] D. Keim, E. Koutsofios, and S. C. North. Visual exploration of large telecommunication data sets. In *Proc. Workshop on User Interfaces In Data Intensive Systems (Invited Talk), Edinburgh, UK*, pages 12–20, 1999.

[19] D. Keim, E. Koutsofios, and S. C. North. Visual exploration of large telecommunication data sets. In *Proc. Workshop on User Interfaces In Data Intensive Systems (Invited Talk), Edinburgh, UK*, pages 12–20, 1999.

[20] D. Keim and M. Ward. *Visual Data Mining Techniques, Book Chapter in: Intelligent Data Analysis, an Introduction by D. Hand and M. Berthold*. Springer Verlag, 2 edition, 2002.

[21] D. A. Keim and A. Herrmann. The gridfit algorithm: An efficient and effective approach to visualizing large amounts of spatial data. *IEEE Visualization, Research Triangle Park, NC*, pages 181–188, 1998.

[22] D. A. Keim, S. C. North, and C. Panse. Cartodraw: A fast algorithm for generating contiguous cartograms. *Trans. on Visualization and Computer Graphics*, March 2003. Information Visualization Research Group, AT&T Laboratories, Florham Park.

[23] D. A. Keim, S. C. North, C. Panse, and J. Schneidewind. Efficient cartogram generation: A comparison. In *InfoVis 2002, IEEE Symposium on Information Visualization, Boston, Massachusetts*, pages 33–36, October 2002.

[24] D. A. Keim, S. C. North, C. Panse, and J. Schneidewind. Visualpoints contra cartodraw. *Palgrave Macmillan – Information Visualization*, March 2003.

[25] C. J. Kocmoud and D. H. House. Continuous cartogram construction. *Proceedings IEEE Visualization*, pages 197–204, 1998.

[26] M.-J. Kraak, F. Ormeling, and M.-J. Kroak. *Cartography: Visualization of Spatial Data*. Addison-Wesley Pub Co, 1996.

[27] A. M. MacEachren. *How Maps Work: Presentation, Visualization, and Design*. The Guilford Press, New York, 1995.

[28] NCSA. Visualization study of the nsfnet, Feb. 2003. http://archive.ncsa.uiuc.edu/SCMS/DigLib/text/technology/Visualization-Study-NSFNET-Cox.html.

[29] R. M. Pickett. *Visual Analyses of Texture in the Detection and Recognition of Objects*. Academic Press, New York, 1970.

[30] R. M. Pickett and G. G. Grinstein. Iconographic displays for visualizing multidimensional data. In *Proc. IEEE Conf. on Systems, Man and Cybernetics, IEEE Press, Piscataway, NJ*, pages 514–519, 1988.

[31] E. Raisz. *Principles of Cartography*. McGraw-Hill, New York, 1962.

[32] H. Schumann and W. Müller. *Visualisierung: Grundlagen und allgemeine Methoden*. Springer, 2000.

[33] S. Selvin, D. Merrill, J. Schulman, S. Sacks, L. Bedell, and L. Wong. Transformations of maps to investigate clusters of disease. *Social Science and Medicine*, 26(2):215–221, 1988.

[34] B. Shneiderman. Tree visualization with treemaps: A 2D space-filling approach. *ACM Transactions on Graphics*, 11(1):92–99, 1992.

[35] B. Shneiderman. The eye have it: A task by data type taxonomy for information visualizations. In *Visual Languages*, 1996.

[36] T. A. Slocum. *Thematic cartography and visualization*. Prentice Hall, Upper Saddle River, NJ, 1999.

[37] B. Spence. *Information Visualization*. Pearson Education Higher Education publishers, UK, 2000.

[38] W. Tobler. Cartograms and cartosplines. *Proceedings of the 1976 Workshop on Automated Cartography and Epidemiology*, pages 53–58, 1976.

[39] W. Tobler. Pseudo-cartograms. *The American Cartographer*, 13(1):43–40, 1986.

[40] J. Walter and H. Ritter. On interactive visualization of high-dimensional data using the hyperbolic plane. In *Proc. ACM SIGKDD International Conference on Knowledge Discovery and Data Mining*, pages 123–131, 2002.

[41] M. O. Ward. Xmdvtool: Integrating multiple methods for visualizing multivariate data. In *Proc. Visualization 94, Washington, DC*, pages 326–336, 1994.

[42] C. Ware. *Information Visualization: Perception for Design*. Morgen Kaufman, 2000.

An Analysis and Case Study
of Digital Annotation

Paolo Bottoni, Stefano Levialdi, and Paola Rizzo

Department of Computer Science, University of Rome "La Sapienza"
Via Salaria 113, 00198, Rome. Italy
{bottoni,levialdi}@dsi.uniroma1.it
rizzo.paola@virgilio.it

Abstract. Digital annotation of multimedia objects is an activity central to many important tasks, such as studying, commenting on, indexing and retrieving. Although annotation is becoming widespread, a formal account of it is lacking. We argue that an algebraic definition of the functions and of the data types involved in digital annotation is essential in the design of tools. Moreover, it allows designers to establish syntactic, semantic and pragmatic aspects of the annotation activity. This paper starts this enterprise by providing a formal analysis of digital annotations, seen as special types of documents dependent on the existence of other documents. This analysis allows a distinction to be made between annotations and other types of digital entities. Moreover, we identify operations and procedures that should be enabled by annotation systems. As a case study, the UCAT annotation system is described.

1 Introduction

Annotation is an important modality of interaction with digital objects (web pages, text files, programs, etc.) besides browsing and editing. It supports crucial cognitive and collaborative functions [1] such as: *remembering* – by highlighting the most significant parts of the annotated document; thinking – by adding one's own new ideas, critical remarks, questions; *clarifying* – by reshaping the information contained in the document into one's own verbal representations; and *sharing* – by supporting discussion about the document.

Several tools are starting to offer the possibility of constructing personalised annotations. Among them we quote Annotea and Banco, which will be more thoroughly discussed in Section 9. Such tools make it possible to create personal data bases of annotated digital documents. On the other hand, the possibility of publishing such personal annotations poses the problem of defining some common semantics, or at least convention, which make different personal annotations usable within a community or across communities. To this end, some formal definition of what a digital annotation is appears to be a prerequisite to this enterprise. Strangely enough, there is not an agreement yet on the definition of digital annotation, or on how to distinguish it from other digital entities (e.g. hyperlinks, metadata, newsgroup messages). Furthermore, an analysis of

N. Bianchi-Berthouze (Ed.): DNIS 2003, LNCS 2822, pp. 216–231, 2003.

the basic operations, to be enabled by a digital annotation system, seems to be lacking. This paper addresses such issues and describes a case study.

In our view, a digital annotation can be considered a digital object (or simply an object) attached to (portions of) other objects. A user is any person who can access, process, annotate and retrieve an object. In the next two sections, we formally define digital objects as tuples of attribute-value pairs, and annotations as objects with additional specific attributes.

The relationship between an object and an annotation is defined in Section 4 by specialising the notion of visual sentence (**vs**) [2] to multimedia objects. Visual sentences were originally introduced in relation to images; here, a **vs** is specialised to be a tuple formed by: (a) the annotated object; (b) the related annotations, (c) a *comment* function from structures in the object to the annotations, and (d) a *localisation* function from annotations to structures in the object.

The distinction between annotations and other objects, addressed in Section 5, is based on a special attribute of annotations named **location**. Section 6 describes a set of basic operations on objects and annotations that should be supported by annotation systems. In Section 7, the UCAT system (User Centered Annotation Tool) [3] is described as a case study. Section 8 describes related work, while the last section concludes the paper and mentions future work.

2   Digital Objects

A digital object o is a typed tuple of attribute-value pairs: $o = typeName((attr_1; val_1), (attr_2; val_2), \ldots, (attr_n; val_n))$. The *type name* denotes the category an object belongs to: it is a string such as *program, file, image, annotation*, and the like. Types are defined in an object hierarchy; here we only define annotations as a specialisation of objects. The attributes can be used for indexing and retrieving the object, and may for instance be **author**, **title**, **creationDate**, **modificationDate**, **size**. Two mandatory attributes are the following:

id. A unique identifier; its value is an element from an infinite set of identifiers. In this paper, identifiers are represented by alphanumeric strings. There can be several copies of an object, i.e. objects having the same values for the same attributes except **id**. Multiple copies of an object can have different annotations related to them.

contents. The actual content of a digital object; its value is specified by a function $f : S \rightarrow V$, that may be empty. The *support S* of the object is a subset of a Cartesian product formed with initial segments of the integer numbers; the vocabulary V, on which the value of **contents** is formed, is a finite set of symbols. The content can in general be considered as some sentence from a language, and it can be formed according to some syntax or semantics. The vocabulary can consist of different types of symbols according to the object type: characters for text, colors for images, image sequences for movie clips, and so on. A vocabulary may mix symbols of different kinds (as in multimedia objects), or may include symbols which are interpreted as references to other objects (e.g. a web page may contain links to image, sound, or movie objects). For example, in a textual object, the support is simply the set $\{1, \ldots, n\}$, where n is the number of characters in the object, and V is formed by alphanumeric and punctuation symbols. In a similar way, if the object is an image, the support is given by the cartesian product of two sets, usually rows and columns, and the vocabulary is formed by the possible grey values or RGB triples, etc., according to how the pixel is coded. In some cases, the content can also include symbols whose meaning conveys information for rendering (portions of) the document, as is the case of HTML tags. It is often the case that the value of **contents** for an object is not rendered completely, or even in coherence with any ordering imposed on the set S. For example a video projection can be stopped, rewound, replicated, etc. We can then speak of *views* of digital objects to indicate the portion of **contents** that is rendered at any given instant or interval of time.

3   Digital Annotations

A *digital annotation* (or simply annotation) is an object a of type *annotation*, related to (portions of) of the content of one or more objects. Analogously to any other object, an annotation can be defined by functions on different supports and vocabularies, i.e. it can be an image, or text, etc. An annotation can be annotated in its turn. An object of type *annotation* has at least the following additional attributes.

location. A reference to the annotated portion(s) of the object(s). In our approach, the value of this attribute is computed by a *localisation* function that will be defined in the next section.

placeHolder. This allows the rendering of indications of the presence of annotations. It takes values in an alphabet of symbols, to each of which a possible representation in the different sensory modalities is associated. So, for instance, if a text document is presented visually and a visual representation is provided for the symbol ph denoting the value of the **placeHolder**, ph will be represented by a visual mark (such as an icon, or an oval surrounding a portion of the object contents). If the same text is presented aurally, ph will be rendered via some auditory mark in the sound stream (if such a mark is defined for it). In general, it is the task of the rendering system to present the place holders in the chosen modality. In some situations the rendering of the **placeHolder** can be exploited to access the **contents** of the annotation, whereas in others it only signals the presence of an annotation. Typically, in visual systems, the **placeHolder** is a hot-spot. When clicking on it, the relative annotation is shown. In auditory modalities some special sound indicates the presence of some annotation relative to the contents at that location, but some other tool must be used to access the annotation. The representations of the **placeHolder** may have a shared semantics, i.e. a meaning common to a set of users (e.g., underlining a sentence might be used for signalling that the sentence is important), or it might have a private semantics, i.e. a meaning understandable only to the annotation creator (e.g., a symbol near a sentence may imply that the sentence is not understood, badly written, or meaningful). In general, the presentation of ph must be studied so as to provide saliency, drawing attention to relevant portions of the material, without hindering its global understanding [4].

role. This attribute describes the communicative relation between the contents of an annotation and the annotated object. The domain of the attribute is a set of names, called $\mathcal{ROL}$. If the role of an annotation is unspecified, then the annotation is called *untyped*, otherwise it is called *typed*. In the latter case, as a shortcut, we say that the annotation "is of type" x, with $x \in \mathcal{ROL}$. As an example, let us consider the case of a maths lesson and an annotation that explains a formula. In this case, we can say that the annotation is of type "explanation". There can be many different communicative roles played by annotations with regard to annotated objects. A set of communicative roles inspired by the Rethorical Structure Theory [5] and specifically tailored to the case of annotations has been used in [3]. Similarly to **placeHolder**, the **role** attribute may have a shared or private semantics, and it can be perceptually signalled in a given modality.

accessibility. It describes capabilities of users over an annotation, in analogy to user rights over files in operating systems. Its value is a pair $(usrs, op)$, where $usrs$ is a predicate defining a set of users, and op is a variable specifying the types of operation (*read, write, activate*) available to users in that set.

4 Relations between Objects and Annotations

The relation between an annotation and the annotated object is analogous to the relation between nucleus and satellite described in the Rhetorical Structure Theory [5], where nuclei and satellites are non-overlapping portions of text. The nucleus is independent of the satellite (if the satellite is removed from the text, the nucleus is still understandable, while the opposite is not true). Similarly, it can be said that an annotation depends on an annotated object. Here we propose to formalise the relations between objects and annotations by generalizing the notion of visual language introduced in (Bottoni et al, 1997).

4.1 Visual Languages

In visual HCI, the messages exchanged between human and computer are images visible on the computer screen. An *image* produced during an interaction is a function $i : \{1, \ldots, rw_i\} \times \{1, \ldots, cl_i\} \rightarrow V \cup \{\tau\}$, where rw_i and cl_i are two integers indicating the size of the image, V is a generic alphabet, and τ is a special symbol deemed *transparent*. A *pixel* in i is a triple (rw, cl, v), where $rw \in \{1, \ldots, rw_i\}$ is called the pixel *row*, $cl \in \{1, \ldots, cl_i\}$ the pixel *column*, and $v \in V \cup \{\tau\}$ the value of the pixel. A pixel whose value is in V is said *visible*, a pixel with value τ is said *transparent*. The set $\{1, \ldots, rw_i\} \times \{1, \ldots, cl_i\}$ is called the *support* of i.

Humans interpret images by recognising *characteristic structures* (**css** or *structures* for short), i.e. sets of image pixels forming functional or perceptual

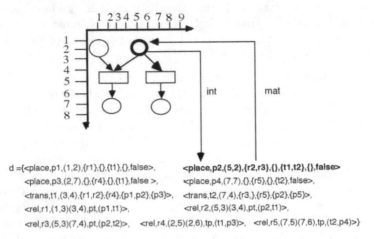

d ={<place,p1,(1,2),{r1},{},{t1},{},false>,   <place,p2,(5,2),{r2,r3},{},{t1,t2},{},false>
   <place,p3,(2,7),{},{r4},{},{t1},false >,   <place,p4,(7,7),{},{r5},{},{t2},false>,
   <trans,t1,(3,4),{r1,r2},{r4}.{p1,p2},{p3}>,   <trans,t2,(7,4),{r3,},{r5},{p2},{p5}>,
   <rel,r1,(1,3)(3,4),pt,(p1,t1)>,   <rel,r2,(5,3)(3,4),pt,(p2,t1)>,
   <rel,r3,(5,3)(7,4),pt,(p2,t2)>,   <rel,r4,(2,5)(2,6),tp,(t1,p3)>,   <rel,r5,(7,5)(7,6),tp,(t2,p4)>}

Fig. 1. An example of visual sentence

units. The **cs** recognition results in the association of that structure with a meaning. From an abstract point of view, a **cs** is a copy of an image in which selected pixels maintain the original values and the others are mapped to the transparent symbol. Formally, given an image i and a selection function $sel_{cs} : \{1, \ldots, rw_i\} \times \{1, \ldots, cl_i\} \to \{0, 1\}$, the function induces a restriction of the i function to a set E, made up of elements (r, c) such that $sel_{cs}(r, c) = 1$. The set E is called the *support* of the structure.

The computer, on its side, captures every gesture of the user and interprets it with respect to the image using a description of the latter. The description is a set of attributed symbols: each of them consists of a type name – the *symbol* – and a tuple of properties which uniquely describes the **cs**. A **cs**, its associated attributed symbol, and the relation between them identify a characteristic pattern (**cp**). The relation between the **css** in the image and the attributed symbols in the description is specified by two functions. An interpretation function (*int*) associates **css** in an image with attributed symbols in a description. A materialisation function (*mat*) associates attributed symbols in a description with **css** in an image. A visual sentence (**vs**) is defined as a triple (*image, description, (int, mat)*). A visual language (**VL**) is a set of **vss**.

Figure 1 shows an example of **vs**. The image (top) is a diagram representing a Petri net, where circles stand for places, rectangles stand for transitions, and arrows stand for the relations between them (the two axes are used only as reference and are not part of the image component). The description (bottom) is a set d of attributed symbols, each of them corresponding to a **cs** (a circle, rectangle, or arrow) in the image and describing its functional meaning in the Petri net. In the synthetic syntax used in Figure 1, the type name (*place, trans, rel*) is the first value of each tuple and the second value is the **identifier**; the other values are for attributes concerning the location of each component of the net and its relations with respect to other components. The two arrows

> The operation of almost all modern digital computers is based
> on two-valued or binary systems. Binary systems were known
> in the ancient Chinese civilisation and by the classical Greek
> philosophers who created a well structured binary system,
> called propositional logic, in which propositions may be TRUE
> or FALSE, and are stated as functions of other propositions
> which are connected by the three basic logical connectives:
> AND, OR, and NOT.

Fig. 2. Three **css** (in gray) selected from the contents of a textual object

from the image to the set d and vice versa show two ordered pairs belonging
to *int* and *mat* respectively: *int* maps a **cs** in the image (a circle, i.e. a place)
onto the corresponding symbol in the description, while *mat* maps that symbol
onto the corresponding **cs** (the circle). The selected **cs**, its associated attributed
symbol, and the relation between them, specified by the two functions, form
a characteristic pattern (**cp**). The mappings between each **cs** and each symbol
in the description form a **vs**; the set of **vss** formed on all possible Petri nets
constitutes the **VL** of Petri nets.

4.2   From Visual Languages to Digital Objects

The concepts described above are here reconsidered to be applied not only to
images and descriptions, but also to any digital object and to annotations.

Characteristic Structures of Objects. Given a digital object, a **cs** is a subset
of its content that forms a functional or perceptual unit for the human. Formally,
a **cs** is defined on the contents c of an object o, as a restriction f' of the f
function: $f' = f \mid E$, where E is a set of elements $\{s_i, \ldots, s_j\} \subseteq S(c)$, and $S(c)$ is
the support for c. It may be possible that $E = S(c)$, i.e., that a **cs** corresponds
to the whole content of o rather than a proper subset of it. For example, in
a textual object, a **cs** could be any significant unit for the user, such as a letter,
word, sentence, paragraph, or the whole contents of the object (see Figure 2).

Multistructures of Objects. In the case of images and descriptions, **css** are
considered independent from one another, and there is a one-to-one correspondence between **css** in a single image and symbols in the description of that
image. By contrast, in the case of digital objects and annotations, one or more
css belonging to one or more objects can be mapped onto several annotations.
The possibility of defining annotations on several objects is related to a view of
a multimedia object as a collection of digital objects connected by some syn-
chronisation constraint on their rendering, so that annotation is performed on
simultaneous views of the related objects. We can now introduce the notion of
multistructure (**MS**) defined on a *multiobject* (**MO**). A multiobject *mo* is an
indexed set of objects $\{o1, \ldots, on\}$, possibly of different types, where the index
set $I = \{1, \ldots, n\}$, $n \geq 1$, is totally ordered. A **MS** is an ordered sequence of

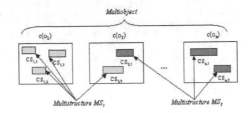

Fig. 3. Two multistructures on a multiobject

css belonging to one or more objects, i.e. an indexed family of function restrictions $\{f'_{1,1}, \ldots, f'_{m,n}\}$, where $f'_{j,i}$ is the j-th restriction of the content function of the i-th object. The mapping between the set of objects and the family of corresponding function restrictions is left implicit. An example of **MO** with two **MS**s defined on it is given in Figure 3.

The Commenting Function. Moving from images and descriptions to digital objects and annotations, the *int* function has been specialised to be a commenting function $com : MS(o) \rightarrow \mathcal{P}(A(o))$, where $MS(o)$ is the family of all **MS**s defined on a **MO** o, and $A(o)$ is the set of all annotations related to o. In other words, given a multistructure *ms*, the *com* function returns the set of annotations that are related to it.

The Localisation Function. The *mat* function, that maps symbols in a description onto css in images, is specialised to be a *localisation* function $loc : A(o) \rightarrow MS(o)$, with $A(o)$ and $MS(o)$ as above. Given an annotation, *loc* returns the **MS** that corresponds to it. As mentioned in Section 3.2, the *loc* function allows the valuation of the **location** attribute for any given annotation. The *com* and *loc* functions are visually exemplified in Figure 4.

Annotation Sentence and Language. Once the *com* and *loc* functions have been defined, a characteristic pattern (**cp**) on digital objects and annotations can be defined as a **MS**, its associated annotations, and the relations between them. We can also define an *annotation sentence* as a triple (*multiobject, set of annotations, (com, loc)*); an *annotation language* is a set of annotation sentences. We have here a difference with **cp**s in the visual language setting, in that the attributed symbols in the description of a **cs** did not contain an indication of the location of the structure, which could be recovered via the *int* function. In this case, on the contrary, this indication is needed, as the annotation cannot be independent of the structure it annotates.

4.3   Representing Annotations

It is common for an object to be annotated in the same modality in which it is presented. For instance, an object displayed in a visual modality usually has

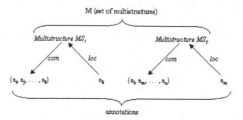

Fig. 4. The com and loc functions applied to multistructures and annotations

visual annotations attached to it. However, it might be possible to display objects and annotations in different modalities. For example, a visually displayed object might have an annotation presented in auditory modality, and vice versa.

Place holders need to be rendered in some way which is coherent with the current rendering of the document. Typically, in the visual modality one has icons superimposed on the display of the document. Such a solution allows a simple management of the relation between the **location** of the annotation and its **placeHolder**. However, this is not an absolute requirement. Indeed, one could think of exploiting eye-fixation to materialise non visual representations of place holders, for example by emitting some sound when the readers' gaze meets some annotated structure. Conversely, consider a scenario in which an audio file is being played, to which somebody has added some textual annotation, and suppose that a visual representation of the audio document is available, such as to enforce a sequential reading, for example the score of music played. Then, an icon visually representing the place holder may be shown, only when the annotated portion of sound is about to be played, in correspondence of the onset of the annotated portion in the score.

5   Annotations vs. Other Objects

The definition of annotation given above should help distinguish between annotations and other types of digital objects that could "look like" annotations. In fact, a digital object o_1 (*origin*) can be related to another object o_2 (*target*) in many ways: for instance, a web page might have a hyperlink to a sound, movie, or another web page; a reply to an email, bulletin board, or newsgroup message usually contains a reference to that message. However, in such cases o_2 has no **location** attribute containing a reference to the contents of o_1: in fact, it is not possible to specify (multi)structures on the contents of o_1 to be annotated. Think for instance of email or newsgroup messages: replies to those messages can only have a reference to the subject or thread, but cannot be related to (portions of) their contents. When this is necessary, portions of the original message have to be incorporated in the new one. Hence, a crucial difference between annotations and other digital objects concerns the location attribute, through which an annotation explicitly relates to the (sub)contents of another digital object.

Another important distinction is between annotations and metadata. The latter are usually attributes that can be added to an object for automatic processing, indexing, and retrieval. They usually refer to the contents of the object, and can be based on ontologies, i.e. formal descriptions of a set of concepts and of their relationships. Metadata can be represented separately from the object contents, or they can be represented within the contents, by means of a markup language such as XML. An object contents that has been marked up is often said to be "annotated", and the marks within the contents are considered annotations. According to our definition, annotations properly named differ from metadata for two reasons: (a) annotations consist in sets of attribute-value pairs, one of which is the contents. By contrast, metadata are additional attributes of an object, and need not have their own attributes, nor some contents; (b) metadata, when represented as marks, alter the contents of the object, while annotations do not modify the contents of the annotated object, but exploit the *com* and *loc* functions to specify the relations between object and annotations.

6   Operations and Procedures

In a user-computer interaction, objects may be accessed, processed, and annotated. We identify a set of operations and procedures that an annotation system should offer to its users. Such utilities operate on (multi-) objects and structures, annotations, and the *com* and *loc* functions. In addition, a set of procedures should receive objects and annotations as input, and produce different views in a given modality. We specify here operations and procedures, using a synthetic version of the style for abstract data type specifications, i.e. by presenting the signatures of the operations and the equations describing their behaviour. We assume the existence of the following domains: $\mathcal{O}$ of digital objects, $\mathcal{MO}$ of multiobjects, $\mathcal{S}$ of structures, $\mathcal{MS}$ of multistructures, $\mathcal{A}$ of annotations, $\mathcal{AS}$ of annotation sentences, $\mathcal{PH}$ of place holders, $\mathcal{ROL}$ of roles and $\mathcal{PRED}$ of predicates, with values in the boolean domain $\mathcal{BOOL}$. The set of all attribute names is denoted by $\mathcal{ATT}$ and the domain for an attribute *attr* is denoted by $Dom(attr)$.

6.1   Editing Operations

We present the algebraic specifications for operations made available to users, distinguishing them according to the types of elements which are manipulated.

Objects and Multiobjects $mkMO : \mathcal{O} \rightarrow \mathcal{MO}$ allows the construction of a **MO** formed by a single object. $addObj : \mathcal{MO} \times \mathcal{O} \times \mathcal{BOOL} \rightarrow \mathcal{MO}$ and $rmvObj : \mathcal{MO} \times \mathcal{O} \rightarrow \mathcal{MO}$ manage **MO**s. The equations $rmvObj(addObj(mo, o, true), o) = addObj(rmvObj(mo, o), o, true) = (mo \setminus \{o\}) \cup makeCopy(o)$ and $rmvObj(addObj(mo, o, false), o) = addObj(rmvObj(mo, o), o, false)) = mo$ hold, where *makeCopy* produces a fresh copy of its argument (with a new identifier). The operational interpretation of *addObj* is that an object *o* is inserted into a multiobject *mo*. If the value of the boolean variable *b* is *true*, a copy of *o* is inserted into mo rather than o itself. The operational interpretation of $rmvObj$ is the removal of o from mo.

Structures and Multistructures $mkMS : S \to \mathcal{MS}$ allows the construction of a **MS** formed by a single structure. $addStruct : \mathcal{MS} \times S \times \mathcal{BOOL} \to \mathcal{MS}$ and $rmvStruct : \mathcal{MS} \times S \to \mathcal{MS}$ allow the management of **MS**s and are connected by equations analogous to those for the pair $addObj$ and $rmvObj$ seen above. $getMO : \mathcal{MS} \to \mathcal{MO}$ relates a **MS** to the **MO** from which the restrictions are taken. $getMS : \mathcal{MO} \to \mathcal{P}(\mathcal{MS})$ extracts all the **MS**s defined on a **MO**.

Annotations $mkAn : \mathcal{MS} \times \mathcal{PH} \times \mathcal{ROL} \to \mathcal{A}$ allows the construction of annotations from **MS**s on **MO**s. Let $getLoc : \mathcal{A} \to \mathcal{MS}$, $getPhl : \mathcal{A} \to \mathcal{PH}$, and $getRol : \mathcal{A} \to \mathcal{ROL}$ be three operations extracting information from an annotation. Then the annotation constructed via $mkAn$ is specified by three equations: $getLoc(mkAn(ms, h, r)) = ms$, $getPh(mkAn(ms, h, r)) = h$, $getRol(mkAn(ms, h, r)) = r$. Moreover, $mkAn(ms, h, r) \in com(ms)$.

$addAn : \mathcal{AS} \times \mathcal{A} \to \mathcal{AS}$ and $rmvAn : \mathcal{AS} \times \mathcal{A} \to \mathcal{AS}$ allow the management of annotation sentences, updating their loc and com functions. They are defined by the obvious equations $rmvAn(addAn(anSent, a), a) = addAn(rmvAn(anSent, a), a) = anSent$. Note the difference between $getLoc$, obtaining the value of the **location** attribute for a specific annotation and the loc function of an annotation sentence. $modifyAn : \mathcal{A} \times \mathcal{ATT} \times \bigcup_{att \in \mathcal{ATT}}(Dom(attr)) \to \mathcal{A}$. If we assume the existence of a function $getattr : \mathcal{A} \to Dom(attr)$ for each attribute $attr \in \mathcal{ATT}$, then we characterise the behaviour of $modifyAn$ by the equation $getattr(modifyAn(a, attr, v)) = v$ if and only if $v \in Dom(attr)$.

$getAn : \mathcal{MS} \to \mathcal{P}(\mathcal{A})$ retrieves annotations related to a **MS**. These can be filtered out by using some predicate p and a function $eval : \mathcal{PRED} \times \mathcal{A} \to \mathcal{BOOL}$, so as to construct a function $filterAn : \mathcal{MS} \times \mathcal{PRED} \to \mathcal{P}(\mathcal{A})$ defined by: $a \in filterAn(ms, p)$ if and only if $a \in getAn(ms) \wedge eval(p, a) = true$. The evaluation of the empty predicate produces the value true for all annotations.

6.2   Procedures

These procedures allow the presentation of annotations in some well-defined views. We assume the existence of some rendering mechanism which is implicitly invoked to present the output of the procedure in the specified view. Actually, these operations are used for their side effects.

$showAn : \mathcal{O} \times \mathcal{A} \to \mathcal{PH}$. Given an annotation a and an object o, such that $getMO(loc(a)) = mkMO(o)$, it holds $showAn(o, a) = getPh(a)$, and the placeholder for a is shown in the same view as o.

$hideAnn : \mathcal{O} \times \mathcal{A} \to \mathcal{PH}$. Given an annotation a and an object o, such that $getMO(loc(a)) = mkMO(o)$, it holds $hideAnn(o, a) = getPh(a)$, and the rendering of the placeholder for a is removed from the current view of o.

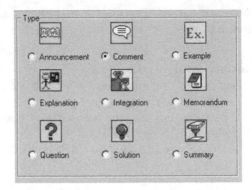

Fig. 5. Icons for denoting roles

$listAnn : \mathcal{P}(\mathcal{A}) \to \mathcal{P}(\mathcal{A})$. The behaviour of this procedure is to act as an identity on its arguments, but to produce a representation of the placeholders for all the annotations in its argument. Such a representation is displayed in an *ad hoc* view, separate from any other view.

7   A Case Study: UCAT

UCAT (User-Centered Annotation Tool) [3] is an annotation system based on Amaya [6], a web browser/editor that complies with the World Wide Web Consortium (W3C) standards, and that has annotation functionalities based on the W3C Annotea project [7].

The Role Attribute. The **role** of an annotation takes its value from a list exploiting some roles defined in the Rhetorical Structure Theory [5]. Each attribute value is represented by an icon, as shown in Figure 5. The available values have a semantics common to the set of users. Usability studies have been performed in order to assess the non-ambiguity of icons representing the different annotations (some slight modifications were introduced to guarantee a unique meaning to each icon). A group of nearly ten university students (typical population of candidate users of an annotation tool) was chosen. They were asked to perform the full annotation process (select a textual component, an annotation class, fill the annotation window and, retrieve the annotated text on the basis of author, date and annotation class). It was observed that icons facilitate the memory process by means of which the different classes can be remembered. Moreover the use of filters to avoid viewing all the annotations performed on the text has also proved useful from the user's viewpoint.

The placeHolder Attribute. When the **role** attribute has a specified value, the **placeHolder** for the annotation is visually rendered by the icon representing

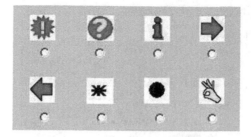

Fig. 6. Icons for place holders

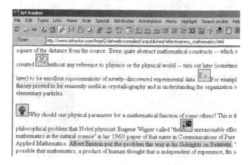

Fig. 7. An annotated page

it. Conversely, if the role attribute is unspecified, the **placeHolder** may be visually rendered with an icon from a different set. For example, if the user wants to create an annotation for signaling a point to be remembered, he/she can choose from the set of icons shown in Figure 6, without specifying the **role** attribute. Figure 7 shows a view of an annotated web page where several place holders are displayed. Other types of rendering, other than visual, are not currently implemented in UCAT, but are under study.

Annotation Search. Any annotated object can be sought in order to find annotations related to it. Figure 8 shows the window available for setting the search parameters, while Figure 9 displays the result of a search: an annotation (on the left window in the forefront) and its **placeHolder** (on the bottom in the background).

8   Related Work

A formal definition of annotation seems to be missing in the literature. Usually the notion of annotation is defined pragmatically, by specifying what it is for (role) and how it is supported by a software system (architecture and interface).

[1] analyses the cognitive roles of annotations, and [8, 9] illustrate field studies on them. [1] also presents a wide overview of implemented annotation systems

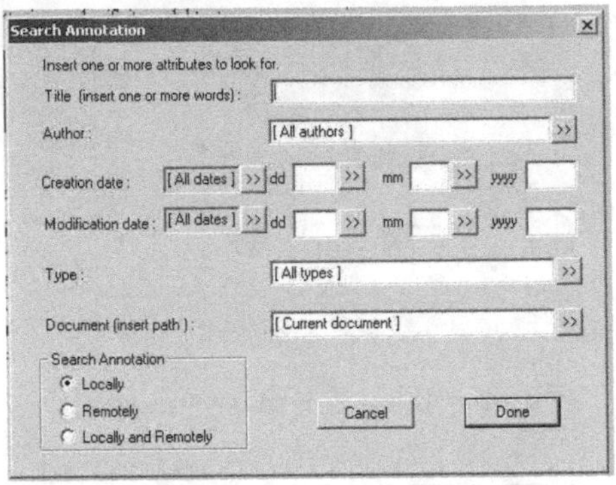

Fig. 8. The Search window

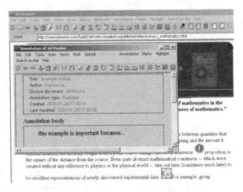

Fig. 9. An annotation and its placeHolder as returned from a search

and analyses architectural issues. The systems are compared along several dimensions, such as sharing of annotations, position of annotations (in our terms **placeHolders**), range of contents (text *vs* other media), availability of search engines. As no formal definition of annotations and of related operations is given there, the systems are not compared along such features.

Several other annotation systems are currently in use. MyLifeBits enables annotations on multimedia data. It is a database of resources (media) and links, where a link indicates that one resource annotates another [10]. Annotations consist in collections, with a recursive semantics (a collection contains all its descendants). In contrast, an annotation may not apply recursively to items annotated by the resource(s) it is linked to. Another example is the Annotation Toolbar, a plug-in for Internet Explorer inspired to the Amaya interface and architecture [11]. Finally, Yawas is an annotation sytem based on the Document Object Model (DOM) level 2 [12]. Thanks to the DOM, the application can easily manipulate the contents of a document, and in particular the "range objects". These are subparts of a document that may be selected by the user for being annotated, and that correspond to the **location** of annotations.

Annotations are also useful in digital libraries, enabling the use of shared comments on the indexed material (e.g. [8, 13]), and in e-learning environments (e.g. [14, 15, 16]). In the latter, students browse and annotate web-based teaching material in order to understand and summarise the most important concepts, and may want to share their own annotations with others (both students and lecturers) so as to collaboratively solve problems and exercises, ask for help, or clarify some information. On the other hand, lecturers provide the web-based lessons, and may incrementally annotate them for signaling related information, posting announcements, or addressing some questions raised by a student.

An important effort concerning annotation is the Annotea project at the W3C [7]. It starts from a similar definition of annotation as a statement made by an author about a Web document. Annotations are external to the documents and can be stored in one or more annotation servers, from which they can be retrieved. Some client implementations of Annotea are now available, such as Amaya or Annozilla. Annotea also provides an ontology of annotations. We complement that approach by establishing our ontology in the framework of the Rhetorical Structure Theory, which maintains some similarity with the Annotea one. As typical of Amaya, we use XPointers to implement the **location** attribute, which mitigates the negative effects of orphan ones (occurring whenever part of the original text is modified/deleted), by moving the pointer to the enclosing context for the original text.

The integration of tools for annotation of images and of text is an important line of research. The BANCO system [17] allows the production of annotations on images by producing other images with marked structures. The images constituting annotations can be retrieved and examined independently or with reference to the original images. Its flexible architecture, which allows the dynamic enrichment of the Document Object Model managed by the BANCO browser, seems to be a promising platform for such an integration.

9   Conclusions and Future Work

Objects and annotations are specific types of digital objects, with operations and procedures that should be available on them. This helps define Web-based annotation systems. A further development would be to have annotation systems providing helpful functionalities in a multiuser environment, such as:

Notification/Polling. The system informs the user about new annotations that are added to the *com* function. This may occur in real time or at given times.

Information Retrieval. Given a set of annotations and a set of terms (keywords), the system searches the annotations in order to retrieve information relevant to the terms.

Users could also perform several operations supporting some kind of collaborative work based on annotations, such as the following:

Mailing. An annotation is mailed to another user.

Replying. A user replies to an annotation by creating a related annotation.

Voting. The user communicates to other users his/her vote about an annotation (e.g., an evaluation of the annotation, or the decision on whether publishing on the web the annotation or not).

References

[1] Ovsiannikov, I., Arbib, M., McNeill, T.: Annotation technology. International Journal of Human-Computer Studies **50** (1999) 329–362 216, 227

[2] Bottoni, P., Costabile, M.F., Levialdi, S., Mussio, P.: Defining visual languages for interactive computing. IEEE Transactions on Systems, Man, and Cybernetics **A-27** (1997) 773–782 217

[3] Bonifazi, F., Levialdi, S., Rizzo, P., Trinchese, R.: A Web-based annotation tool supporting e-learning. In: Proceedings of the Working Conference on Advanced Visual Interfaces: AVI 2002. (2002) 123–128 217, 219, 226

[4] Itti, L.: Models of Bottom-Up und Top-Down Visual Attention. Ph.D. Thesis, California Institute of Technology (2000) http://ilab.usc.edu/bu/. 219

[5] Mann, W.C., Thompson, S.A.: Rhetorical structure theory: A theory of text organization. Technical report, ISI/RS-87-90, Information Sciences Institute, University of Southern California (1987) 219, 226

[6] Vatton, I., Kahan, J., Carcone, L., Quint, V.: Amaya. Technical report, http://www.w3.org/Amaya (1996) 226

[7] Kahan, J., Koivunen, M.R., Prud'Hommeaux, E., Swick, R.R.: Annotea: An open RDF infrastructure for shared Web annotations. In: Proc. of the WWW10 International Conference. (2001) 226, 229

[8] Marshall, C.C.: Annotation: from paper books to the digital library. In: Proceedings of the ACM Digital Libraries '97 Conference. (1997) 131–140 227, 229

[9] Marshall, C.C.: Toward an ecology of hypertext annotation. In: Proc Hypertext '98. (1998) 40–49 227

[10] Gemmell, J., Bell, G., Lueder, R., Drucker, S., Wong, C.: Mylifebits: fulfilling the memex vision. ACM Multimedia (2002) 235–238 228

[11] Raman, R., Venkatasubramani, S.: Annotation tool for semantic web. In: Proceedings of WWW2002. (2002) 228

[12] Denoue, L., Vignollet, L.: An annotation tool for web browsers and its applications to information retrieval. In: Proceedings of RIAO2000. (2000) 228

[13] Nichols, D.M., Pemberton, D., Dalhoumi, S., Larouk, O., Belisle, C., Twidale, M.B.: DEBORA: Developing an interface to support collaboration in a digital library. In: Research and Advanced Technology for Digital Libraries. Springer, Lecture Notes in Computer Science, 1923 (2000) 239–248 229

[14] Bargeron, D., Grudin, J., Gupta, A., Sanocki, E., Li, F., LeeTiernan, S.: Asynchronous collaboration around multimedia applied to on-demand education. Journal of MIS **18** (2002) 117–145 229

[15] Smith, B., Blankinship, E., Lackner, T.: Annotation and education. IEEE Multimedia **7** (2000) 84–89 229

[16] LeeTiernan, S., Grudin, J.: Fostering engagement in asynchronous learning through collaborative multimedia annotation. In: Proc. INTERACT 2001. (2001) 229

[17] Carrara, P., Fresta, G., Mussio, P.: SVG: more than a markup language for vector graphics. In: Proceedings of EuroWeb 2001 International conference on "The Web in Public Administration. (2001)   229

Vectorization of Graphical Components
in Sketch-Based Interfaces

Fernando Ferri and Patrizia Grifoni

Istituto di Ricerche sulla Popolazione e Politiche Sociali, CNR
Via Nizza 128, 00198 Roma
{f.ferri,p.grifoni}@irp.rm.cnr.it

Abstract. Sketching rapidly communicates ideas through approximate visual pictures with low overhead (pencil and paper), it is easy to correct and revise and does not require specialized knowledge or precision. A picture can contain characters, symbols and graphical components. Usually, the recognition of graphical components and their vectorization follows the text and symbols detection phase in pattern recognition algorithms. This paper presents an algorithm which analyses a hand-drawn sketch and recognizes and vectorizes the graphical components of the sketch. The proposed algorithm is based on the assumption that the sketched picture is given by an array of pixel and the graphical components are represented by black pixels on a white background. The algorithm uses a representation based on coding horizontal sequences of black pixels identified in the image. The algorithm consists of two steps: the first one identifies the horizontal sequences of black pixels and stores them in a list L, the second step reads the list L, recognizes and stores the graphical components in different lists classified by types.

1   Introduction

Drawing is a simple, common, and expressive way to represent concepts, relationships and information. The most natural and convenient way to input graphic objects is to draw sketches on a tablet using a pen, just like drawing on a real sheet of paper. When drawing a visual image, the user tends to divide the graphic objects into several primitive shapes. Then the system analyzes the sketch and presents the user with the most similar but regular shape that is intended by the user. Users can also adjust the recognition and regularization results suggested by the system by interacting during the phase of recognition. This process is specified as graphic recognition. For example, in recognition of formal sketches (those created with a specific diagram notation), systems have been designed for UML, Math, Engineering diagrams, and others [1] [2] [3] [4] [5] [6]. Finite state machines, flowcharts, networks, program class structures, and file systems are only a few examples of applications that are easier to understand using this method.

The transformation from a raster representation to a vectorial one is a question that has to be frequently dealt with in the management and processing of visual images. Vectorial representation describes sketches in terms of graphical components (with their geometry). The transformation must preserve topological features and

N. Bianchi-Berthouze (Ed.): DNIS 2003, LNCS 2822, pp. 231-244, 2003.

relationships between initial graphical components, i.e. preservation of inclusion, touching, and other relationships. Indeed, components resulting from the acquired image need to be represented in a form suitable for further computer processing. These documents contain characters, symbols and graphical parts. Usually the detection phase of the text and symbols in pattern recognition algorithms and in vectorization algorithms for visual images is followed by the recognition of different graphical components and their vectorization.

Rosenfeld described a number of algorithms for raster to vector conversion [7] [8]. Other works [9] [10] [11] [12] focus on the best approximation of a raster image by means of a vector representation using different approximation approaches. In the present work, the goal of the algorithm is not only to convert raster to vector conversion (representing the result by means of a set of polylines), but also to recognize a set of graphical components of the sketch, each one represented by means of a sequence of coordinates. In fact, the algorithm considers two different kinds of graphical components: polylines and closed regions (points are considered a kind of polyline with only one couple of coordinates). The algorithm has been studied for a sketch-based geographical query language, but it is applicable to other fields in which the user draws sketches using a pen or other input devices. The proposed algorithm assumes that the input image is given by an array of black and white pixels.

The following section shows the data structure adopted for memorizing graphical components. Section three presents possible ambiguities related to sketches. Section four presents the algorithm. Finally, section five concludes the paper.

2   Input Characteristics and Data Structures

Depending on different application domains, sketches can have different characteristics and needs in representing concepts, objects and relationships. Figure 1 shows three sketches concerning the related different domains: geographical (Figure 1A), diagram representation (Figure 1B) and hypertext representation (Figure 1C). All the examples of sketches considered can be treated using the algorithm presented in this paper.

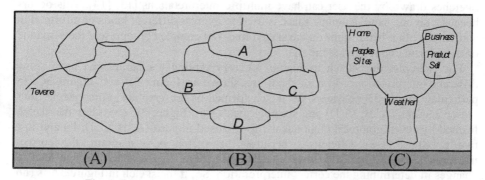

Fig. 1. Some examples of sketch in different application domains

The algorithm uses a representation based on coding horizontal sequences of black pixels identified in the sketch. Horizontal sequences of black pixels are stored in a record that contains the following fields:

- vv contains the row index,
- valInf contains the index of the column of the pixel which starts the horizontal sequence,
- valSup contains the index of the column of the pixel that ends the horizontal sequence.

Using this kind of representation, the part of a sketch formed by three horizontal sequences of black pixels, in Figure 2, could be stored using the following three records:

sequence1. vv:=14;	sequence2. vv:=15;	sequence3. vv:=15;
sequence1. valInf:=11;	sequence2. valInf:=9;	sequence3. valInf:=15;
sequence1. valSup:=14;	sequence2. valSup:=10;	sequence3. valSup:=16;

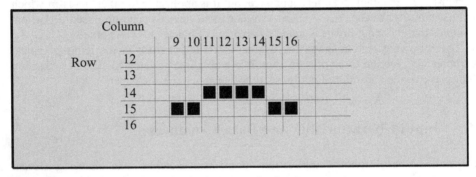

Fig. 2. A part of a sketch

3   Possible Ambiguities Contained in the Sketch

Sketches drawn by the user can have multiple interpretations [13] [14]. This occurs because, on one hand, a unique space is used to express different kinds of information and, on the other hand, signs on the sketch may not completely represent the semantic of the information related to the sign.

For example, the sketch in Figure 3A representing a diagram can have some different interpretations. Two of them are shown in Figure 3B and Figure 3C. In particular, Figure 3B considers the sketch formed by ten graphical components: four closed regions (A, B, C, D) and six polylines (1-6). Figure 3C considers the sketch formed by seven graphical components: five closed regions (A, B, C, D, E) and just two polylines (1-2). Obviously, because the sketch is a diagram, the correct interpretation is Figure 3B. However, changing the application domain can lead to changes in determining the correct interpretation. So, if the sketch in Figure 3A is (no longer a diagram but) a map, Figure 3B is probably the correct interpretation.

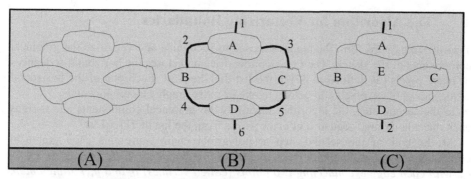

Fig. 3. A sketch and some of the possible interpretations

In figure 4A another example of ambiguity is presented. The sketch can have at least two interpretations, as shown in Figure 4B and Figure 4C. Obviously if the goal of the user is to sketch a river passing-through a region, the correct interpretation is represented in figure 4C.

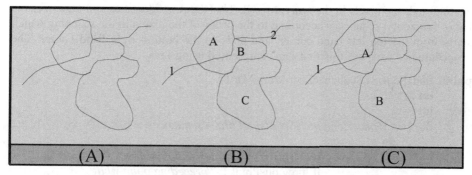

Fig. 4. Another sketch and some of the possible interpretations

It is possible to resolve ambiguities contained in the sketch by using different approaches (which may be integrated):

- the user's specification of the correct interpretation;
- considering the application domains and a significant set of sketch models for each domain;
- considering both the sketch and the actions performed in drawing the sketch in order to have the correct interpretation.

The algorithm does not dealt with ambiguities and their solution. Currently, the implemented version of the algorithm allows the user to specify the correct interpretation after a rough interpretation has been given by the system. However, the goal is to integrate, in the algorithm, the interpretation of the sketch and of the actions performed in drawing the sketch.

4 The Algorithm for Vectorizing Boundaries

Two different steps form the algorithm used to recognize and vectorize the graphical components of the sketch. The first step identifies and stores the horizontal sequences of black pixels (as defined in §2) in the list theHSeqList. Each one of the horizontal sequences of black pixels can belong to one or more graphical components.

In the second step, the algorithm identifies the graphical components and assigns each one a horizontal sequence of black pixels from the list theHSeqList.

At the end of the second step, a polygonal chain represents each graphical component. *A polygonal chain is a sequence of line segments (called edges) e_1, e_2, ... e_n, with each edge e_i connecting two points (called vertices) p_i and p_{i+1} of the chain.* Closed regions are represented by means of closed polygonal chains (in which $p_1 = p_{n+1}$). The graphical components are then stored in a second list, each one as the sequence of points $p_1,...,p_{n+1}$ which identifies the *polygonal chain*.

A. The First Step of the Algorithm: Storage of the Horizontal Sequences

The first step identifies all the horizontal sequences of black pixels in the sketch and examines all the pixels in the array M(i, j). TheHSeqList identifies and organizes the list of horizontal sequences according to the order of the pixels in the scanning which starts from the top left hand corner, and ends to the bottom right hand corner. The procedure that executes this first step is presented using Java:

```java
public theHSeqList SequenceList(Array M); {
        int i=1;
        int j=1;
        do  { // Memorize in theHSeqList all black sequences
                do {
                                if (M[j,i] == 1 ) { //current point black
                                if !previousPoint { //preceding point white
                                        lastChange=j;
                                }
                                previousPoint=true;
                        }

                        else { //current point white
                                if (previousPoint) {  //preceding point black
                                        aSequence.vv=i;
                                        aSequence.valInf=lastChange;
                                        aSequence.valSup=j-1;
                                        theHSecList.InsertLast(aSequence);
                                        lastChange=j;
                                }
                                previousPoint=false;
                        }
                        j=j+1;
                while (j>=m);
                i=i+1; j=1;
        while (i>=n);
}
```

The complexity of this first step is O(n X m) where n is the number of rows and m is the number of columns of the array associated with the sketch.

B. The Second Step of the Algorithm: The Vectorization of the Boundaries

This step identifies the different components of the sketch. The algorithm distinguishes two different kinds of horizontal sequences:

- sequences associated to an edge identified as typeA sequence,
- sequences which present a convergence among two or more than two different edges, identified as typeB sequence. The convergence point is the point in which two or more than two different edges of graphical components meet.

In Figure 5 typeB sequences are highlighted.

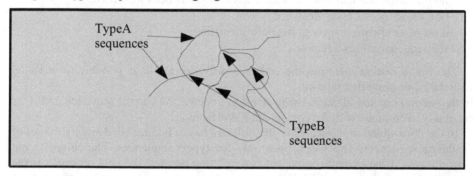

Fig. 5. Different kinds of sequences

The algorithm has to distinguish between two types of components: regions and polylines. The algorithm recognizes closed regions, by default, and any other horizontal sequence belongs to polyline components of the sketch. The algorithm starts from the horizontal sequence that it first meets, during the scanning of the sketch (from the top-left hand corner to the bottom-right hand corner).

After the first horizontal sequence the algorithm continues the scanning activity and performs two different actions:

- it identifies the horizontal sequence, belonging to the same component, which follows in a clockwise direction by making a local search in the TheHSeqList. This action stops when the algorithm meets the first convergence point or no further sequences have been detected,
- it identifies the horizontal sequence, belonging to the same component, that follows in a counterclockwise direction by making a local search in the TheHSeqList. This action continues until the algorithm meets the same convergence point met in the clockwise direction or no further sequences have been detected.

Local search only involves two rows adjacent to the row of the current sequence. Indeed, the sequence which follows may only involve these two rows. For this reason if the sequence is associated to the row value i, then the local search involves the i-1 and the i+1 rows. These sequences are adjacent to the current sequence in the

TheHSeqList according to the construction method of the TheHSeqList. These sequences are nearer to the sequence associated to the row value i than sequences associated to the i-2 and i+2 row indexes.

For this reason the local search for the nearest sequence stops when the first sequence with i-2 row index (for sequences which precedes the current sequence) and the sequence with i+2 row (for sequences which follows the current sequence) are met. The only sequences belonging to the i-1 and i+1 rows and having the index of the column contained in the range delimitated by jmin-1 e jmax+1 may be the sequence which follows the current sequence.

When the search for the candidate sequences (following the current one) is completed it is possible to distinguish four different situations:

– no one sequence which follows the current one has been identified;
– one sequence has been identified;
– a set of candidate sequences has been identified;
– the sequence closes a region

The first situation identifies the end of a polyline, and it is possible to continue with the component that follows.
In the second one the identified sequence has become the current sequence and it is necessary to continue with the component identification.

In the third situation the sequence that follows has to be identified among the set of candidate sequences. This can happen only for typeB sequences. The choice is not very relevant if the current component is a polyline because the new sequence is the first of a new component (polyline or region). On the contrary, when the current component is a region the new sequence to choose belongs to the same region. In this case, in order to continue with the same region, it is necessary to choose correctly the sequence that follows the current one from among the candidate sequences, using the criteria defined in theorem 1, which follows.

Finally, in the last situation a new component has been completely detected. This can happen both in typeA and typeB sequences.

For example, in the sketch in Figure 5, the algorithm recognizes regions and polylines as shown in Figure 6A.

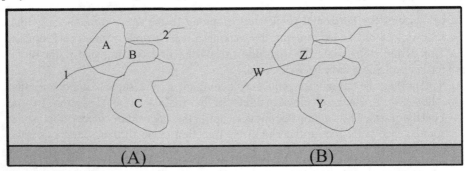

Fig. 6. Regions and polylines recognized by the algorithm

Theorem 1: In the convergence points, the horizontal sequence has to be chosen with the aim of minimizing the internal area of the region. The horizontal sequence that minimizes the internal area of the region is the sequence that minimizes internal pixels on the vertical co-ordinate of the considered sequence.

Demonstration: The demonstration begins with the hypothesis that pixels are examined in a counterclockwise direction (obviously, similar considerations can be made for a clockwise direction).

Moreover, it is possible to distinguish between two different situations: 1) the vertical coordinate is increased, 2) the vertical coordinate is decreased. In the first situation pixels belonging to the region which has the same vertical coordinate are potentially all pixels on the right in respect to the upper-bound of the sequence of black pixels (on the left considering the direction).

In the second situation (the vertical coordinate decreases) pixels belonging to the region which has the same vertical coordinate are potentially all pixels on the left in respect to the lower-bound of the sequence of black pixels (on the left considering the direction).

In order to simplify the presentation, it is possible to consider two regions only, and to generalize the algorithm in the case of more than two regions being involved. Let A and B be the two considered regions. Suppose that the algorithm is following the boundary of the A region and it meets the sequence in which A and B converge. Choosing the sequence that follows corresponds to choosing the A region or the *AUB* region. Each pixel belonging to the A region obviously belongs to the *AUB* region. For this reason the boundary of the A region is identified if the algorithm chooses the configuration which minimizes the number of pixels on the vertical coordinate. Choosing the sequence that follows in the convergence point between the A and the B regions requires the identification of the A or the A U complement (A U B).

Taking into account that each one of the pixels belonging to the A belongs to A U complement (A U B) too, but not all pixels belonging to the A U complement (A U B) belong to A too, you can consider a couple of sequences which minimize the number of pixels with the same vertical coordinates. A more general situation involving n (n>2) different regions A, B,...N can be treated considering the couple of regions A and (B U ... U N).

Now, it is necessary to consider the different possible configurations between a couple of sequences in order to establish rules for minimizing the internal area of the region.

Definition 1: Let us define the six different configurations between couples of consecutive horizontal sequences (shown in Fig. 7). Considering a couple of consecutive sequences, P is the preceding sequence, and S is the second element of the couple (successor).

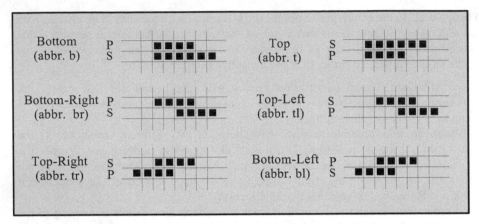

Fig. 7. Six different configurations between couples of consecutive horizontal sequences

If the current sequence is a TypeB sequence, more than one sequence is the candidate for the second one of the couple (successor). If that is the case, given the current sequence, the sequence that precedes has to be considered in identifying the successor sequence, by applying theorem 1. Indeed, it is possible to establish the order of sequences that minimizes the internal region according to the chosen direction (clockwise or counterclockwise) and the configuration given by the couple of current sequence and preceding sequence.

Theorem 2:   Table 1 gives the minimization rules (for the counter-clockwise direction) of the internal areas according to the configuration of the current and the preceding sequence, and the chosen order of the current and the successor sequence in order to minimize the internal region.

Table 1. Minimization rules of the internal areas

Preceding and current sequence configuration	Choosing configuration order of current sequence and successor sequence.	No valid configuration
bl	br, b, bl, tl, t	tr
tl	bl, tl, t, tr, b	br
t	bl, tl, t, tr, br, b	
tr	tl, t, tr, br, b	bl
br	t, tr, br, b, bl	tl
b	t, tr, br, b, bl, tl	

Demonstration: This is applying theorem 1 to the six different configurations, and choosing configuration which minimizes the internal region.

Example: The hypothesis is to vectorize the boundary of a closed region of sketches covering it by following a counter-clockwise direction. The preceding and current sequence configuration is represented by bl. That is, choosing the configuration order of current sequences and successor sequences the configuration (if more than one sequence is the candidate successor sequence) has to have the following order: br, b, bl, tl, t. Therefore tl configuration (and its sequence) may only be chosen if there are no horizontal sequences for br, b and bl configurations. A closed boundary (the current sequence coincides with the firstone) identifies the valid boundary of a region. If the horizontal sequence path does not identify a closed boundary, then a polyline is identified. This operation has to be repeated for all boundaries until all horizontal sequences of the TheHSeqList will be considered as a polyline or one or more closed regions.

The Algorithm

Also the procedure implementing the second step of the algorithm is presented in Java. For temporary memorization of horizontal sequences during the component detection the following data structures are used:

- a list of Record type Sequences (currentPath) in order to memorize the path performed in a counterclockwise direction do detect a new component. The currentPath is a compound of several edges delimited by convergence points. The sequences of the new component are a subset of the sequences of the path. All edges explored;
- lists of Record type Sequences (newComponent) in order to memorize the last detected component;
- three sequences of black pixels in order to choose the correct sequence following the convergence points during the component detection.

The algorithm distinguishes two cases:
- the path followed in a counterclockwise direction closes. In this case a region has been detected and both the first and the last edge can be deleted from the theHSeqList. These edges only belong to the detected region;
- the path followed in a counterclockwise direction does not close. In this case one or more polylines have been detected. If the path does not include convergence points a polyline (coincident to the path) has been detected. If the path in a counterclockwise direction includes convergence points and the path in clockwise direction does not include regions, two polylines have been identified which corresponds to the first and the last edges. In this case, the first and the last edges can be eliminated from the edgesList. On the contrary if the path in a counterclockwise direction includes convergence points and the path in a clockwise direction includes a region one polyline has been identified which corresponds to the last edge. In this case, the last edge can be eliminated from edgesList.

At the end, all detected boundaries are stored in two lists (regionsList and polylinesList).

```
public ComponentList boundaryDetection (BlackList theHSeqList); {
        Initialize the regionsList; Initialize the polylinesList;
        Initialize the edgesList; Initialize the newComponent;
        Initialize the currentPath; Initialize the currentEdge;
        Find the first horizontal sequence of black pixels;
        do {  //Loop to check the theHSeqList
                Find the candidates as following horizontal sequences in theHSeqList or in edgesList
                if (numberOfCandidates == 0) {
```

```
        if (current sequence closes the boundary ) {   // a boundary has been detected
                Assign the edges of the path to newComponent;
                Insert the newComponent in the regionsList;
                Delete the first and the last edges from the currentPath;
                Insert the remaining edges of currentPath to edgesList if not yet
                inserted;
                Initialize a newComponent;
                Find the first horizontal sequence of black pixels from edgesList or
                theHSeqList;
        }
        else { // one or two polylines has been detected
                if (path in clockwise direction closes a region or edges of
                currentPath ==1 )
                { //one polyline
                        Assign the last edge of the path to newComponent;
                        Insert the newComponent in the polylinesList;
                        Delete the last edge from the currentPath;
                        Insert the remaining edges of currentPath to edgesList
                        if not yet inserted;
                        Initialize a newComponent;
                        Find the first horizontal sequence of black pixels from
                        edgesList or  theHSeqList;
                }
                else {// two polylines
                        Assign the first edge of the path to newComponent;
                        Insert the newComponent in the polylinesList;
                        Initialize a newComponent;
                        Assign the last edge of the path to newComponent;
                        Insert the newComponent in the polylinesList;
                        Delete the first and the last edges from the currentPath;
                        Insert the remaining edges of currentPath to edgesList if not yet
                        inserted;
                        Initialize a newComponent;
                        Find the first horizontal sequence of black pixels from edgesList or
                        theHSeqList;
                }
        }
        Initialize the currentPath;
        Initialize the currentEdge;
        }
        else {
                if (numberOfCandidates == 1) { // sequence typeA detected
                        Update the currentEdge with the new sequence;
                        Delete the sequence from the theHSeqList;
                }
                else { //sequence of typeB detected
                        Choose the following sequence;
                        Insert the currentEdge in the edgesList;
                        Initialize the currentEdge;
                        Delete the sequence from the theHSeqList;
                }
        }
        } while (theHSecList is void);
}
```

Application of the Algorithm to a Sketch

The algorithm works by following paths on the sketch. When the path followed is
closed, a region has been found, when the path followed is not closed, one or more

polylines have been found. Fig. 8 shows the application of the algorithm to the sketch in Figure 1A. A row of Figure 8 refers to a different path and the last figure of a row shows the labels of the new components found by the algorithm at the end of the path. In particular, the first row considers the three edges constituting component A (Figure 8.1-A, Figure 8.1-B, Figure 8.1-C).

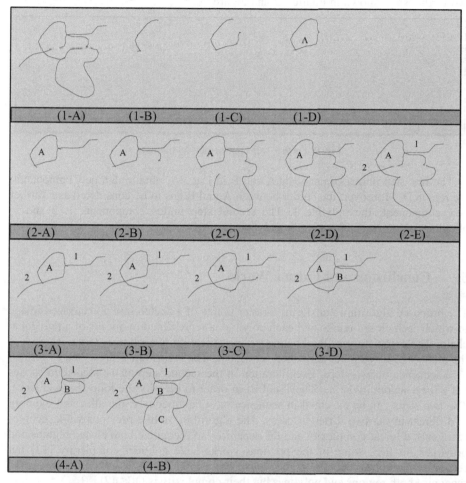

Fig. 8. Paths and graphical components detected from the algorithm

The second row shows a path compound of five edges from Fig. 8.2-A to Figure 8.2-E. Because the path does not close, two polylines are detected: components 1 and 2 of Figure 8.2-E.

The third row shows a path compound of four edges from Figure 8.3-A to Figure 8.3-D. The first edge is the border between component A and component B. This closed path allows the detection of component B.

Finally, in the fourth row, the path constitutes two edges. The first edge is the border between component B and component C, the second edge is considered in Figure 8.4-B.

The Further Steps Related to Multiple Interpretations

After using the algorithm the user can perform some simple operations on the detected components. Then, for example, if the correct interpretation of the sketch in Figure 1A is Figure 4C, it is possible to specify the correct interpretation by means of two further steps shown in Figure 9B and Figure 9C.

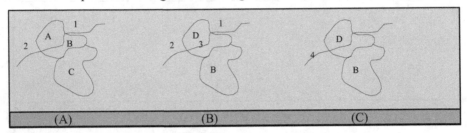

Fig. 9. Further steps performed by the user

The first step unites components A and B in Fig. 9A, obtaining a new component: the region D. Moreover, the border between A and B has to be considered as a further new component: the polyline 3. The second step unites components 1, 2 and 3, obtaining only one component: the polyline 4.

5   Conclusion and Future Works

The proposed algorithm transforms a raster image of a sketch into a vectorized image in which each closed region and each polyline is represented by means of a polygonal chain. The complexity of the boundary's identification algorithm is $O(k)$, where k is the number of black pixel horizontal sequences. The algorithm is presented as formed by a sequence of two steps. Each iteration in the second step of the algorithm carries out a local search in the list TheHSeqList in order to identify the following sequence. The two steps can be executed in sequence or simultaneously; the allocated memory is different in the two different cases. The algorithm, unlike previous work, achives two goals: a linear complexity and the capability to recognize both closed regions and polylines. In fact, some of the previous works have a linear complexity [12] but recognize polylines only (and the worst case complexity is $O(k^2)$), other works recognize both regions and polylines but their complexity is $O(k^2)$[7] [8].

Currently, the algorithm presented does not resolve the problems related to multiple interpretations of the sketch and its graphical components. The user obtains the correct interpretation of the sketch interactively after the application of the algorithm to the sketch by applying simple geometric operators (like union and difference) to the graphical components recognized by the algorithm. In order to improve automatic capabilities to recognize the correct interpretation of the sketch, it is necessary to consider the sketch drawing process, described in terms of the starting sketch and the subsequent modification of the graphical components (drawing of a new component, erasure and/or modification of an existing component). A correct interpretation of the different operations performed during the sketch drawing could allow automatic recognition reducing erroneous interpretation.

References

[1]   E. Lank, J. Thorley, S. Chen and D. Blostein, "An on-line system for recognizing hand drawn UML diagrams", Proceedings of the International Conference on Document Analysis and Recognition, ICDAR 2001, Seattle, September 2001, pp. 356-360.

[2]   R. Zanibbi, D. Blostein, J. Cordy, "Recognizing Mathematical Expressions Using Tree Transformation", *IEEE Transactions on Pattern Analysis and Machine Intelligence*, Vol. 24, No. 11, pp. 1455-1467, November 2002.

[3]   D. Blostein, E. Lank, R. Zanibbi, "Treatment of Diagrams in Document Image, in *Theory and Application of Diagrams*, Eds. M. Anderson, P. Cheng, V. Haarslev, Lecture Notes in Computer Science, Vol. 1889, Springer Verlag, 2000, pp. 330-344.

[4]   T. Kanungo, R. Haralick, D. Dori, "Understanding Engineering Drawings. A Survey." Proc. Int. Workshop on Graphic Recognition. University Park. Pennsylvania. Aug 1995. pp. 119-130.

[5]   A.D. Blaser, M. J. Egenhofer, "A Visual Tool for Querying Geographic Databases." Proc. ACM AVI 2000, Palermo 2000, pp. 211-216.

[6]   Lin, M. Thomsen, J.A. Landay, "A Visual Language for Sketching Large and Complex Interactive Designs" Proc. ACM CHI 2002, Minneapolis 2002, pp. 307-314.

[7]   Rosenfeld, "Algorithms for Image/Vector Conversion", Computer Graphics, n. 12, pp.135-139, 1978

[8]   Rosenfeld and A.C. Kak, Digital Image Processing, New York; Academic Press, Cap 11, 1987.

[9]   D. Dori, Orthogonal Zig-Zag: an Algorithm for Vectorizing Engineering Drawings Comared with Hough Transform, Advances in Engineering Software 1997, 28(1): 11-24.

[10]   U. Montanari, "A note on the minimal length polygonal approximation to a digitized contour." Communications of the ACM 1970; 13(1):41-47.

[11]   S.H.Y. Hung, T. Kasvald, "Critical points on a perfectly 8- or perfectly 6-connected thin binary line." Pattern Recognition 1983; 16:297-284.

[12]   D. Dori, W. Liu., "Sparse Pixel Vectorization: An Algorithm and its Performance Evaluation" *IEEE Transactions on Pattern Analysis and Machine Intelligence*, Vol. 21, No. 3, pp. 202-215, March 1999

[13]   F. Favetta, M.A. Aufaure-Portier, "About Ambiguities in Visual GIS Query Languages: A Taxonomy and Solutions". in *Advances in Visual Information Systems*, Ed. R. Laurini, Lecture Notes in Computer Science, Vol. 1929, Springer Verlag, 2000, pp. 154-165.

[14]   P. Bottoni, M.F. Costabile, S. Levialdi, P. Mussio, "Formalising visual languages. Proc. IEEE Symposium on Visual Languages '95, 1995, pp 45-52.

A Data Placement Method of HSM for Streaming Media Server in Network Environment[*]

Yaoqiang Xu[1], Chunxiao Xing[2], and Lizhu Zhou[2]

Department of Computer Science and Technology, Tsinghua University
Beijing, 100084, China
Fax: +86-10-62771138
[1] xuyq99@mails.tsinghua.edu.cn
[2] {xingcx,dcszlz}@mail.tsinghua.edu.cn

Abstract. Streaming media service, such as video-on-demand (VOD), is getting popular in network environment. To get high cost/performance ratio, Hierarchical Storage Management (HSM) is adopted by streaming media servers in such services. However, if HSM system places the media object, say a movie, exclusively in a tertiary storage device, the response time to an on demand service will be too long to be satisfactory. This paper presents a new data placement method based on prearrangement strategy in HSM for streaming media server. By prearranging the head part of media objects on disk, streaming data accesses can get immediate response, and in concurrent, tertiary storage device can be prepared for continuous access. The paper discusses a method to calculate the head data length of media objects and an algorithm to read data in HSM. Simulation result shows that with a low disk storage cost, the response time of the HSM system can be reduced to a large extent, and the performance of the whole system is enhanced significantly.

1 Introduction

With the development of network, streaming media services, e.g., video-on-demand (VOD), news-on-demand (NOD), etc., are becoming more and more popular. Large media server always has thousands of media objects, and need to deliver them to thousands of users over the network. To place all the objects, many of which are rarely accessed, in disk, the storage cost will be very high. As the result, distributed hierarchical storage is proposed to get high cost/performance ratio [1-3].

Figure 1 shows the typical structure of media servers based on distributed hierarchical storage. In this structure, media objects with high access probability are stored in Video File Server (VFS). VFS has local secondary storage device such as disk or RAID. It accepts on demand requests and delivers services. Other objects are stored in Archive Server (AS) on the network. The main storage device of AS is tertiary storage device, such as tape library and CD tower, whose storage cost is much

[*] Supported by the National Natural Science Foundation of China under Grant No.60221120146; the National Grand Fundamental Research 973 Program of China under Grant No.G1999032704.

N. Bianchi-Berthouze (Ed.): DNIS 2003, LNCS 2822, pp. 245-254, 2003.

lower than disks' while the access time can be tens of seconds and even several minutes because of its mechanical characteristic.

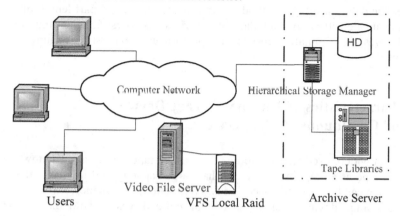

Fig. 1. Hierarchical Storage Based Media Service System

If the media object requested by user is not in VFS, it will be read from AS to VFS so that VFS can provide the on demand service. The straightforward method is to wait until the object is entirely in VFS. A pipeline mechanism in media server is presented in [8]. It starts delivering when some data has been copied to VFS, and avoids the long waiting time for object copy. In [2, 10], caching and data replacement algorithms between disks and AS were developed. In [4, 5], the authors presented algorithms to schedule the tape library to get higher throughput and lower response time. All of them are effective, but they still need to read data from tertiary storage device in AS, whose startup time is still too long for users.

The purpose of this paper is to introduce a better method to shorten the response time of AS, so that the users can get response quickly even the object is not in VFS.

Archive Server is often organized as a Hierarchical Storage System (or Hierarchical Storage Management, HSM) to enhance the performance by using additional secondary storage device. HSM researchers usually focus on how to minimize the media exchange times and how to reduce the total cost of data reading [6, 7]. As a result, they place most of the media objects entirely on tertiary storage device, and cache some object in the disks. However, the fact is that this kind of caching has little use in media server because the request probability of objects in HSM has little difference.

In this paper, we propose a data placement method for AS. While storing media objects in the HSM system, we place the head part of each media object with specified length on disk, and the other part on tertiary storage device such as a tape library. When serving on-demand request, continuous media data immediate response from disks and tertiary storage devices are concurrently initialized for continuous access. If the length of head part is appropriate, the initialization can be finished before the data on disk is consumed, so the data will switch to coming from the tertiary storage device smoothly. With this method, waiting time of reading continuous media data from HSM is close to the response time of the disk.

The remainder of this paper is organized as follows: section 2 discusses the characteristics of tertiary storage device and continuous media service, and section 3 introduces the data placement method. A way to calculate head part length of media object and an algorithm to read data in HSM is also described in this section. Section 4 gives the simulation results and performance analysis. Section 5 is the conclusion.

2   Characteristics of Tertiary Storage Device and Continuous Media Service

The two most widely used tertiary storage devices are tape library and CD tower. The former uses tape as storage media, which has large capacity and low cost; the latter uses CD which can be randomly accessed and has better performance.

Tertiary storage device usually has one or more drives to hold the removable media, many slots to place the media, and a robot arm to transfer media between the slots and the drives. The media is placed in the slot before and after being accessed. The response time for reading data from tertiary storage device can be calculated as

$$T\_response = T\_load + T\_mount + T\_seek \tag{1}$$

where T_load refers to the time needed for the robot arm to load the media from slot to drive, whose typical value is about 10 seconds; T_mount is the time between the media being put into the drive and ready to be operated; and T_seek refers to the time needed for the drive to seek to the desired position. T_seek is short for CD tower, while for tape libraries, it can be tens to hundreds of seconds, depending on the performance of the device and the target position.

When the media is ready, tertiary storage device can be read or written with high speed (see table 1).

Table 1. Performance Summary of Storage Device

Storage media	Response time(s)	Data read rate (Mega bytes/s)
Sony DTF tape library	143	12
Ampex DST tape library	25	14.2
IDE hard disk	0	8

Continuous media service requires short response time and specified data rate. Waiting is always boring when the user requests a media object, so the ideal response time should be zero. But the requirement for data rate is low. For instance, the playback rate of MPEG2 video stream is about 4.5Mbps, or 0.6Mbyte/s.

Table 1 shows the data read performance of two tape libraries and common IDE hard disk. The data of Sony DTF comes from [9] and that of Apex DST comes from [7]. We can see that the data reading rate of the storage device is much higher than the playback rate of media. However, when the response time is concerned, only secondary storage device can meet the need of media service.

Another feature of media service is: many requests only focus on a few media objects. This access rule approximately follows Zipf(0) distribution [1, 10]. That is, if the total count of media objects is M, then the nth most popular object's access probability is C/n, where C=1/(1+1/2+1/3+...+1/M).

3   A Data Placement Method of Continuous Media Object Based on Prearrangement

The method of this paper mainly considers most popular tape libraries that use helical scan drives, in which the tape will rewind to the Physical Begin Of Tape (PBOT) before being ejected. Unsurprisingly, this idea can be used in CD towers and other tape libraries as well.

3.1   The Method Description

Definition 1. Bit File: Continuous byte stream in HSM system, corresponding to the media object in the system.

Definition 2. Segment: Segment is the physical unit for storage of continuous bytes. A Bit File is made up of several Segments.

Definition 3. Segmentation Information of Bit File: Corresponding relationship between a Bit File and segments. It describes which Segments compose the Bit File.

Media objects are stored in HSM system in the form of Bit Files. Each Bit File is divided into two segments, as shown in Figure 2. The first Segment with length *L_head_seg* is stored in the disk, and the second segment containing the left data is stored in the tape. When the object is requested, the first segment will be read, and in the meantime the second segment is prepared for reading. To ensure that the tape will be ready before segment 1 is completely consumed, *L_head_seg* should satisfies the following constraint.

$$L\_head\_seg = V\_bit\_rate * (T\_response + T\_queue) \tag{2}$$

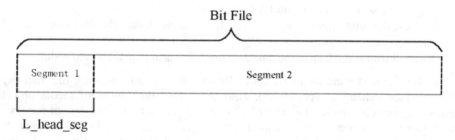

Fig. 2. Segmentation of Bit File

where *V_bit_rate* is the playback rate of the media object, *T_response* is the delay needed to read data from tape library, and *T_queue* is the queue time waiting for the tertiary storage device.

Ignoring the startup, the tape's seek time can be represented as:

$$T\_seek = \frac{S\_addr}{V\_seek}$$

(3)

where S_addr means the target position in the tape, and V_seek is the seek rate of the tape.

From expression (1), (2), and (3), we can get:

$$L\_head\_seg = V\_bit\_rate*(T\_load + T\_mount + \frac{S\_addr}{V\_seek} + T\_queue)$$

(4)

In this formula, T_queue is unknown before the request is actually executed. Now, the problem becomes finding an estimation method for computing T_queue.

3.2   Computation of T_queue

The appropriate computation of T_queue is got via simulation. To do this, we first build the queue model of the continuous media server. Secondly, we simulate the running of the system by giving different configuration (different system workload, different drive number etc.) and record the delay of every tape request. In this way, we get the distribution of T_queue. Finally, we determine an appropriate formula for T_queue to ensure that most HSM request will get response before Segment 1 is consumed.

The queue model of media server is shown in Figure 3, which is used to describe the response time. The procedure of reading data from HSM's disk is not described here because it can be ignored when compared with the response time.

If the media object referred by the On Demand request is in the local disk of VFS, it can be read and start playback immediately. Otherwise we need to get data from HSM system (the AS). With the data placement method above, this procedure should be divided into two parts: a) reading data from disk of HSM; b) reading data from tape of HSM. Procedure a) is ignored in Figure 3 for briefness because it's very simple. The processing steps of tape request are as follows:

- Stay in the schedule queue until a drive is free;
- Request the robot arm to load the tape to the drive, locate the data position and read the data;
- After all data is read, eject the tape and use robot arm to place it into a slot.

The On Demand requests usually obey Poisson distribution (because the intensity of the requests changes very slowly). And the access probability of media object follows Zipf(0) distribution. Let *Drive's Process Ability* μ be the number of requests that a drive can process in a time unit, and *Request Intensity* λ be the number of requests that arrive at the HSM system in a time unit. The number of drives is K. We define the workload of HSM system as

$$\rho(K) = \frac{\lambda}{K*\mu}$$

(5)

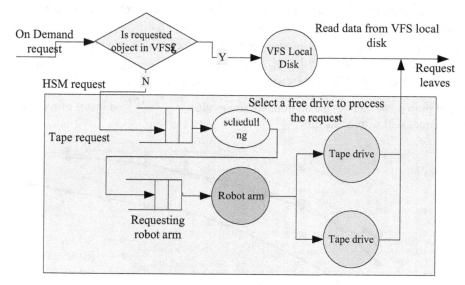

Fig. 3. Queue Model of Media Server

λ can be estimated from the intensity of users' On Demand request and the probability of the requested object residing in VFS.

We simulate the running of media server in different system workload level using Sim++ [11, 12]. Table 2 summarizes the parameters of our system.

Table 2. The parameters of our system

Symbol	Value	Note
TapeLoad_time	12.8s	Time for robot arm to take a tape from slot to drive
TapeUnload_time	17.2s	Time for robot arm to take a tape from drive to slot
TapeMount_time	51s	Time period between the time when the tape is placed into the drive and the time when the tape can be operated
TapeUnmount_time	18s	Time period between the time when the "unmount" command is issued and the time when the tape is extracted from the drive by the robot arm
Transfer_rate	12Mbyte/s	Persistent read/write rate of the tape
Seek_rate	300Mbyte/s	Quick seek rate of the tape
Tape_size	42G	Tape capacity
Object_size	2G	Size of each media object. Here we suppose all the sizes are equal.

Figure 4 shows the waiting time distribution of the HSM requests with different workload ρ. For a point (t, p) of a curve, p is the ratio of the requests whose waiting time is less than t to the total requests under the workload level represented by the curve. We use $p = F_{k,w}(t)$ to represent the curve of $\rho(k) = w$.

As we can see, waiting time of tape requests is concentrated in a small range. For example, in the case of $\rho(4) = 0.33$, for 70.5% of the tape requests, the waiting time is less than 200 seconds. Given the system configuration with known k and w, and the desired ratio p, we can get the appropriate time value $t = F_{k,w}^{-1}(p)$ so that p of requests can be processed within this time.

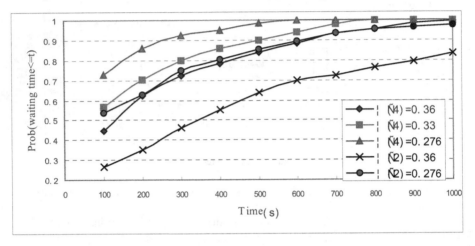

Fig. 4. Distribution of tape requests' waiting time in different workload

1.3   Data Reading Algorithm

For the discussed data placement method in previous section, we need to design a data-reading algorithm following this method. In addition, the algorithm needs to deal with the cases when the pre-placed segment 1 is too short to be consumed within the selected time that we just discussed.

To ensure the continuity of data stream, FIFO strategy is applied in the scheduling of tape library. The tape request's waiting time in this queue can be calculated according to the tasks in the queue. If this waiting time exceeds the range of Segment 1, HSM system will send a notice.

The algorithm description of HSM 's main thread is listed as below:

- Accept the HSM request to read an object from VFS.
- Query the Segmentation Information of corresponding Bit File.
- Append a task of reading Segment 2 to the task queue of tape library, and calculate its waiting time *T_wait*.
- If T_wait <= L_head_seg / V_bit_rate, jump to 5. Otherwise, notify the VFS, and wait for T_wait - L_head_seg / V_bit_rate.
- Read data from Segment 1 from the disk and send to VFS until the end of Segment 1.
- Request to access Segment 2. If the tape is not ready, raise exception.

–   Read data from Segment 2 in the tape and send to VFS until the end of
     Segment 2.

4   Simulation Result and Analysis

We simulate the running of the HSM system using the data placement method
described in section 3. In the simulation, the *T_queue* parameter is set as 200 seconds.
Other parameters are same as those in section 3.2. The distribution curve of the actual
waiting time of HSM requests is shown in Figure 5. Simulation shows that most of
the requests can get response immediately.

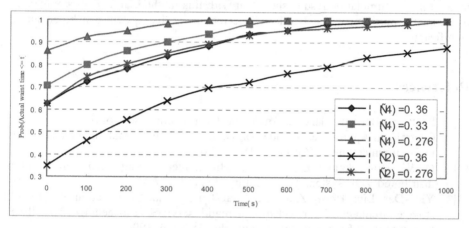

Fig. 5. Distribution of HSM requests' waiting time in different workload

Now we check the disk capacity needed to hold segment 1 of media objects.

Let T_object be the time length of a media object, then the storage cost for this
object can be calculated as Object_size = V_bit_rate * T_object . So the ratio of the size
of segment 1 to the total size is

$$r = \frac{L\_head\_seg}{Object\_size} = \frac{V\_bit\_rate * (T\_response + T\_queue)}{V\_bit\_rate * T\_object}$$

$$= \frac{T\_load + T\_mount + S\_addr/V\_seek + T\_queue}{T\_object} \tag{6}$$

For parameters shown in Table 2. T_object is about 4000 seconds, the mean of
S_addr is about 0.5*Tape_size, so the expectation of the ratio:

$$E(r) = \frac{E(T\_load + T\_mount) + E(S\_addr/V\_seek) + E(T\_queue)}{E(T\_object)}$$

$$= \frac{12.8 + 51 + 21000/300 + 200}{4000} = 0.083 \tag{7}$$

If the total capacity of the HSM system is R, the disk space for storing the first segments of objects is about R*0.083.

Another conclusion we can draw from Figure 4 is that under the same workload, the request's waiting time is shorter if there are more drives. As the result, we should try to use large tape libraries.

5   Conclusion

By analyzing the access characteristics of tertiary storage devices and the feature of media service system, this paper proposes a data placement method for continuous media service. Simulation results show that with this method, at a small storage cost the response performance of HSM and the media service system can be enhanced significantly.

References

[1]   Scott A. Barnett, Gary J. Anido. A Cost Comparison of Distributed and Centralized Approaches to Video-on-Demand. IEEE Journal on Selected Areas in Communications 14(6): 1173-1183, 1996

[2]   D. W. Brubeck and L. A. Rowe. Hierarchical storage management in a distributed VOD system. IEEE Multimedia, 3(3): 37-47, 1996

[3]   Ying-Dar Lin, Horng-Zhu Lai, Yuan-Cheng Lai. A hierarchical network storage architecture for video-on-demand services. Proceedings 21st IEEE Conference on Local Computer Networks, 355-364, 1996

[4]   S. W. Lau, J. C. S. Liu. Scheduling and data layout policies for a near-line multimedia storage architecture. Multimedia Systems, 5(5): 310-323, 1997

[5]   Jing Shi, Chungxiao Xing and Lizhu Zhou. Efficiently Scheduling Tape-resident Jobs. In the 19th IEEE Symposium on Mass Storage Systems, 305-309, 2002

[6]   S. Christodoulakis, P. Triantafillou, and F. Zioga. Principles of optimally placing data in tertiary storage libraries. Proc. of Intl. Conf. on Very Large Data Bases, Athens, Greece. 236-245, 1997

[7]   Jiangtao Li, Sunil Prabhakar. Data Placement for Tertiary Storage. In the 19th IEEE Symposium on Mass Storage Systems, 193-207, 2002

[8]   Shahram Ghandeharizadeh, Ali Dashti, and Cyrus Shahabi. A pipelining mechanism to minimize the latency time in hierarchical multimedia storage managers. Computer communications, 18(3): 170-184, 1995

[9]   T. Johnson and E. L. Miller. Performance measurements of tertiary storage devices. In Proc. of 24th Intl. Conf. on Very Large Data Bases, New York, 50-61, 1998

[10]   Yang Daoliang, Ren Xiaoxia and Chang Ming. Study on Data Replacement Algorithm in Continuous Media Server with Hierarchical Storage. 16th IFIP World Computer Congress, Beijing, 2: 1387-1394, 2000

[11] Paul A. Fishwick. Simpack: Getting Started with Simulation Programming in C and C++. In 1992 Winter Simulation Conference, Arlington, VA, 154-162, 1992

[12] SimPack Toolkit. http://www.cise.ufl.edu/~fishwick/simpack/simpack.html

[13] J. A. Buzacott and J.G. Shanthikumar. Stochastic Models of Manufacturing Systems, Prentice Hall, 1993

Application of Active Real-Time Objects and Rules in Semantic Web*

Sang Bong Yoo[1] and In Han Kim[2]

[1] School of Computer Science, Inha University
Incheon, Korea
Fax: 82-32-874-1435
syoo@inha.ac.kr
[2] Department of Architectural Engineering, Kyung-Hee University
Yong-In Si, Korea
ihkim@khu.ac.kr

Abstract. As more real-world data are included in the Web, requirements to capture more meaning of the data have rapidly increased. Semantic Web has been proposed by W3C to be the next generation of web by representing the metadata using RDF (Resource Description Framework). Even though the metadata encoded in RDF have rich semantics and high potential for providing lots of intelligent features, there have not been enough efforts to utilize them in practical Web application areas. In this paper, we model the Semantic Web as an active environment that consists of a set of real-time objects each consisting of a set of attributes, functions, and active rules. A real-time object can be changed spontaneously or triggered by demands (via messages) in real-time. The semantics of such a distributed, real-time object system can be described completely by a formal logical foundation that is the ordinary first order language (that is time-invariant) plus a set of time-varying constructs. The declarativeness and inference capability of formal logic are coupled with real-time distributed objects in order to enable the users to encode easily the domain knowledge into rules. The design and application of active real-time objects and rules are presented using working examples.

1   Introduction

As the Internet prevails all over the world, requirements to handle the data on the Web have been increased rapidly. The Semantic Web, which was initiated by W3C, is an effort to capture more meaning of the data on the Web [3, 9, 16, 20, 22]. RDF (Resource Description Framework) is the primary tool to serialize the metadata from the Web, which enables software agents or human can understand the contents [21, 23]. XML was introduced to enhance the syntax and semantics of Web data over HTML by using meaningful tags with structured schemata. For example, by using XML we

---

*   The work reported here has been supported by the Grant Number (R01-2001-000-00467-0) from the Korea Science & Engineering Foundation.

N. Bianchi-Berthouze (Ed.): DNIS 2003, LNCS 2822, pp. 255–269, 2003.

can represent the same person as an employee in one place or as a customer in another place. However, XML has a limited capability to capture the interrelationship among objects. Metadata and RDF have been introduced in order to complement XML with rich semantics of the relationship among objects. Even though many active research and development efforts are being conducted in order to apply the Semantic Web to practical uses, the current paradigm of the Semantic Web cannot handle effectively existing Web environments due to the followings:

-   **Active Objects:** Recently the Web accommodates a large number of autonomous "network devices" – (wired or wireless) PDA, workstations, databases, and other devices – that are all connected via an intranet or the Internet. These "network devices" are active: they not only receive information, but also deliver information (e.g., instructions, commands). In addition, many of such devices may possess states and need to be controlled dynamically (e.g., oxygen valves). To manage a dynamic environment as described, special control and communication mechanisms are required to be developed.
-   **Real-Time, Distributed Processes:** Because there are many indeterministic factors in real-time distributed environments (e.g., order and time of message deliveries), it usually needs trial and error to encode the overall distributed control processes in conventional programs. The domain knowledge is intermixed with program constructs in conventional programming methods, which makes the maintenance of the software labor-intensive especially in distributed environments. In this paper, we couple the declarativeness and inference capability of formal logic with real-time distributed objects in order to enable the users to encode easily the domain knowledge into rules.

An active environment has been modeled as a set of real-time objects each consisting of a set of attributes, states and methods that can be changed or executed spontaneously or triggered by demands (via messages) in real-time. The semantics of such a distributed, real-time object system can be described completely by a formal logical foundation called Active Real-Time Semantic Web (ARTSW) [24] that is the ordinary first order language (that is time-invariant) plus a set of time-varying constructs (see Fig. 1). The ARTSW can be used to describe the constraints on top of the real-time objects, or it can be used as a specification language that defines the semantics of a dynamic environment.

Not only the Web pages in HTML or XML but also all the resources connected through networks are identified and controlled in ARTSW. In the metadata defined by RDF and encoded in XML, summaries, classifications, relationship, contexts, or control logics as for network resources are specified. Each ARTSW agent runs on an embedded controller or on a stand-alone machine independently and communicates with the ARTSW server or other agents. Because each agent is portable and has built-in capability of real-time management and rule processing, the users only need to define the semantics and constraints into rules. With this approach, the knowledge encoded in rules is orthogonal to other built-in modules in ARTSW, therefore each rule is defined separately and can be easily updated with automatic validation. ARTSW can relieve the developers from real-time network programming details.

Because the number of agents is not limited, it is also scalable and can be effectively maintained.

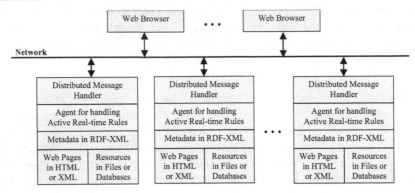

Fig. 1. Overall architecture of ARTSW environment

2   Related Work

The base element of the RDF model is the triple: a resource (the subject) is linked to another resource (the object) through an arc labeled with a third resource (the predicate). RDF triples are designed to easily represent the relationship among objects. Current research and developments of RDF can be considered in two groups. The first group focuses on the development of various applications such as library catalogs, worldwide directories, and syndication and aggregation of news, software, or personal collections [10]. In order to build applications, projects like Doublin Core[8] defines the terminology and hierarchy of metadata. Software tools such as a RDF parser and a browser are also actively developed.

The second group works on enhancing RDF by adding some knowledge processing features such as ontology or logic [12, 17]. Ontology mainly consists of a vocabulary of basic terms and a precise specification of what those terms mean. DAML+OIL is an example of Web ontology language, which defines a set of ontology in order to facilitate the exchange of knowledge that is defined with different terminology [22]. In order to utilize the power of declarativeness and inference, logical rules have been extensively studied for artificial intelligence, expert systems and deductive databases [7]. Even though many practical applications have been implemented, the need of high computing power and expensive knowledge acquisition prevent the rule-based systems from becoming general-purpose problem solving tools. Number of proposals have been made to incorporate the general logic into the Semantic Web [4, 11]. However the notorious computational complexity of general-purpose inference is also well acknowledged. A practical compromise would be to apply the logical rules only to the applications where we can control the computational complexity.

As an effort to provide the users with the knowledge management features that are orthogonal to programming, many research and development projects have also been conducted to extend the conventional programming environment into active systems by utilizing rules [6, 7, 15, 18]. Researches have been centered on three aspects of

active systems: optimizing the computation of the condition part, defining rule languages, and efficient event monitoring. Studies on rule languages have been published
in [1, 5, 19]. [5] describes a rule language with flexible execution modes for active
systems, which expresses not only simple triggering events but also composite triggering events and supports nested transaction model. [1] extends their previous rule
language, O++, to express integrity constraints and triggers. Triggers can be used to
monitor complex triggering events and to call appropriate procedures.

The semantics of the rules used in ARTSW is similar to that of production systems
and active database systems. ARTSW does not use rules for problem solving and is
not coupled with any database systems either. It is rather tightly coupled with real-time
distributed objects. Recent developments of real-time systems on top of such general-
purpose operating systems as Windows, Unix, and Linux enable rapid expansion of
real-time applications in distributed environments [14]. One of the major features of
ARTSW is describing the behavioral semantics and integrity constraints of networked
resources by logical rules. Because it is coupled with distributed real-time objects
rather than any off-the-shelf products (e.g., database or expert systems), it can efficiently run on various networked computing devices including embedded systems.
The declarativeness and inference capability of logic still enable the users to encode
effectively their domain knowledge into active rules, which can be effectively managed and validated using the unification procedures.

3   Describing Active Real-Time Objects
and Rules in Semantic Web

Active real-time rules will be defined on the framework of Semantic Web including
RDF, which specify the relationship and constraints among the resources connected
through the networks. In this section, the basic approaches of specification, execution,
and validation of active real-time rules are presented with examples.

3.1   RDF and Metadata

RDF (Resource Description Framework) is a recommendation of the World Wide
Web Consortium (W3C) to model metadata about the resources of the Web [2, 13].
Currently a wealth of information on every subject is available on the Internet. People
are able to use so many services wherever the network is connected. For example, we
can check the money exchange rate among international currencies, find out the real-
time score of a baseball game, or reserve an airline seat. The Internet has already
changed the lifestyle of many people and the possible uses of the network seem end-
less.

According to the characteristics of the Web, we must know the URI (Uniform Resource Identifiers) in order to access resources. Except a few well-known addresses,
most users or programs get the URI through some search engines such as Google or
Altavista. In many cases users are unsatisfied with the search results. Even though
there have been many efforts to improve the search results using many techniques such

as ranking or clustering results, current techniques cannot effectively handle the growth and change of the Web. This situation can be changed if all Web pages provide some description about the information stored. The description of information is metadata and RDF is a framework to specify it. For example, "author", "title", and "subject" are examples of metadata for books. Basic concept and terminologies used for RDF are described in [21, 23] and Fig. 2 depicts the classes and resources defined in RDF specifications in terms of sets and elements. A rounded rectangle and a bullet represent a class and a resource, respectively. An arc is directed from a resource to a class that the resource defines. As a convention, resources that define classes start with a capital letter and resources that represent properties start with a lower case letter. Predefined resources have namespaces such as *rdf* and *rdfs* in Fig. 2.

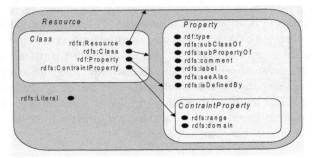

Fig. 2. Relationship among RDF classes and resources

3.2   Metadata Modeling Using RDF

In order to model metadata, an RDF schema needs to be modeled using the resources defined in RDF Model and Syntax Specification and RDF Schema Specification. Based on the RDF schema, metadata is modeled and encoded in XML. This process can be summarized in the following steps.

a)   Step 1: Model RDF schema
b)   Step 2: Model RDF data and encode them into XML

The process of modeling RDF schema is similar to that of modeling database schema using Entity Relationship. Fig. 3 is an example RDF schema for a Medical Information System. A simplified schema for this system consists of 3 classes: *Patient, Appointment,* and *Physician.* Class *Patient* has four literal properties (i.e., *patientID, name, address,* and *reference*) and a sequence of *Appointments.* Class *Appointment* has *appNumber, dateTime,* and *appWith* as properties. Class *Physician* has five properties (i.e., *physicianID, name, department, speciality,* and *officeNo*) and each of them has literal value. An DLG (Directed Labeled Graph) of this schema is shown in Fig. 3.

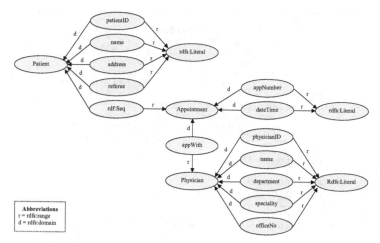

Fig. 3. An RDF Schema for a Medical Information System

The next step for modeling metadata is to instantiate the RDF schema defined in the previous step. The instantiation of metadata can also be represented by a DLG as in Fig. 4, where rectangular nodes represent literals and elliptical nodes represent other resources. Property names are labeled on arcs. In this example in Fig. 4, a patient named "John Doe" has two appointments with Dr. Jackson and Dr. Stevens.

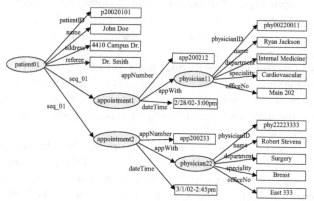

Fig. 4. An RDF model represented by a directed labeled graph

RDF metadata modeled as in Fig. 4 needs to be encoded in XML in order to be processed by software agents. There are two types of syntaxes for XML encoding, i.e., serialization syntax and abbreviation syntax. In serialization syntax, resources are specified by description elements and properties (the same property name can be repeated). In abbreviation syntax, the resource type is used as the element name instead of the description element. Because it is more simple and intuitive, the abbreviation syntax is employed in Fig. 5.

```
<Patient id="patient01">
        <patientID>p20020101</paticientID>
        <name>John Doe</name>
        <address>4410 Campus Dr.</address>
        <referee>Dr. Smith</balance>
        <seq_01 rdf:resource="#appointment1"/>
        <seq_02 rdf:resource="#appointment2"/>
</Patient>
<Appointment id="appointment1">
        <appNumber>app200212</appNumber>
        <appWith rdf:resource="#physician11"/>
        <dateTime>2/28/02-3:00pm</dateTime>
</Appointment>
<Appointment id="appointment2">
        ......
</Appointment>
<Physician id="physician11">
        ......
</Physician>
<Physician id="physician22">
        ......
</Physician>
```

Fig. 5. An RDF data encoded in XML

3.3   Active Real-Time Objects and Rules in RDF

In ARTSW, the semantics of a distributed, real-time object system can be described completely by a formal logical foundation. Rules (axioms) are defined in a subset of first-order logic and inferred by forward chaining. A rule is defined as $l_1 \wedge l_2 \wedge \ldots \wedge l_n \rightarrow r_1 \wedge r_2 \wedge \ldots \wedge r_m$, where each l_i, $1 \leq i \leq n$, and r_j, $1 \leq j \leq m$, is a literal that is a predicate or a negated predicate. Given this rule, all the literals on the right hand side $r_1, r_2, \ldots r_m$ should be true if all the literals on the left hand side $l_1, l_2, \ldots l_n$ are evaluated true at the same time. A predicate can represent a *condition* or an *action*. Condition predicates compare the variables of object instances with some values and action predicates trigger the methods defined in object classes. Each literal can have real-time arguments optionally.

A real-time argument is an instance of the class *time*, which has six literal properties: *year, month, day, hour, min*, and *sec*. An instance of the class *time* can have the values only for a subset of the six variables. In such case, the omitted variables act as wild cards and enable multiple matches. As an example, if an instance of the class *time* has the values *h*, *m*, and *s* for attributes *hour*, *min*, and *sec*, respectively, it matches at *h:m:s* every day.

Conditions that do not have real-time arguments are evaluated when the corresponding attribute is updated (i.e., *event-triggered*). The conditions that do not have real-time argument can be defined in ordinary manner. An example of the ordinary condition predicate is:

<lessthan about= "attr"> □ *</lessthan>* // true if the attribute *"attr"* is less than □

The conditions that have real-time arguments are evaluated on appropriate time (i.e., *time-triggered*). A condition that has real-time arguments can be defined as follows:

```
<equals about="attr" at="t"> α </attr>  // true if the attr has value α at time t
<greaterThan about="attr" at="t"> α </attr>  // true if the value of attr is greater than α at time t
<greaterThanOrEqualTo about="attr" at="t"> α </attr>
                                // true if the value of attr is greater than or equal to α at time t
< lessThan about="attr" at="t"> α </attr>  // true if the value of attr is less than α at time t
< lessThanOrEqualTo about="attr" at="t"> α </attr>
                                // true if the value of attr is greater than α at time t
<equals about="attr" from="ts" to="te"> α </attr>
                                // true if the attr has value α from time ts to time te
<greaterThan about="attr" from="ts" to="te"> α </attr>
                                // true if the value of attr is greater than α from time ts to time te
< greaterThanOrEqualTo about="attr" from="ts" to="te"> α </attr>
                                // true if the value of attr is greater than or equal to α from time ts to time te
<lessThan about="attr" from="ts" to="te"> α </attr>
                                // true if the value of attr is less than α from time ts to time te
< lessThanOrEqualTo about="attr" from="ts" to="te"> α </attr>
                                // true if the value of attr is less  than or equal to α from time ts to time te
```

Action predicates are defined using the procedural methods defined in object classes. Similarly to the condition predicates, an action predicate can have no real-time argument, one real-time argument or two real-time arguments. Examples of action predicates are as follows:

```
<function id = "name" var1 = "a1" var2= "a2" ... varn= "an"> function_body </function>
                                // trigger the function with input arguments a1, a2, ..., an
<function id= "name" var1 = "a1" var2= "a2" ... varn= "an" at= "t"> function_body </function>
                                // trigger the function with input arguments a1, a2, ..., an at time t
<function id = "name" var1 = "a1" var2= "a2" ... varn= "an" from="t1" to="t2"> function_body
</function>              // trigger the function with input arguments a1, a2, ..., an at time t1 to time t2
```

Example 1. The following function computes the number of days of hospitalization for each inpatient. Because variables are referenced by their URI, all variables are *call-by-reference*.

```
<function id = "daysOfStay" var1= "dateIn" var2= "dateOut" var3= "numDays">
      #numDays = #dateOut - #dateIn
</function>                                                                           Σ
```

The aggregate functions operate on a set of persistent objects and can have real-time arguments optionally. There are five aggregation functions: *count, sum, avg, max*, and *min*.

Example 2. The following function uses the aggregation function *count*.

```
<function id = "numberOfInpatients">
      <if> <forall about = "http://www.AmericaHospital.com">
            <greaterThan count about = "inpatients"> numberOfBeds  </greaterThan> </forall>
      <then>
            <rdf:description about = "http://www.AmericaHospital.com/inpatients/availBeds">
            0  </rdf:description>
      </then>
      </if>
</function>
```

This function works on a Web site (i.e., *http://www.AmericaHospital.com*) and count the number of current inpatients. If the count is greater than the number of beds, then set the value of *http://www.AmericaHospital.com/inpatients/availBeds* to 0.   Σ

The literals in the left hand side of a rule are condition predicates and the literals in the right hand are either condition predicates or action predicates. When condition predicates are on the right hand side of a rule, the rule specifies the integrity constraints of the distributed Semantic Web. On the other hand, action predicates on the right hand side of a rule specify the behavior of the given system. When all condition predicates on the left hand side of a rule are evaluated true at the same time, the literals on the right hand side of the rule are processed as follows.

–   Condition predicates on the right hand side should be evaluated true. Otherwise, the integrity constraints specified by the rule are violated.
–   Action predicates on the right hand side will be triggered.

The time to execute the methods corresponding the triggered predicates depends on the numbers of real-time arguments included in the predicates.

–   The method that does not have any real-time argument will be executed immediately
–   The method that has one real-time argument will be executed at time t
–   The method that has two real-time arguments will be executed from *ts* to *te*

In RDF files, rules can be defined in the following syntax:

```
<rule id = "name">
      <if>
            condition
      <then>
            action
      </then>
      </if>
</rule>
```

Example 3. Supposing that a ARTSW agent is running in an intensive care center of a hospital, we could have the following rule:

```
<rule id = "arrhythmiaAlertEmergency">
      <forall about = "http://www.AmericaHospital.com/patient">
            <if>
                  <and>
                        <equals about= "nameOfDisease">arrhythmia</>
                        <greaterThan about= "pulseRate" at= "::00">100 </>
                        <greaterThan about= "bloodPressure" at= "::00"> 140 </>
                  </and>
            <then>
                        <alertEmergency var1 = "name" />
            </then>
            </if>
      </forall>
</rule>
```

This rule specifies that all patient who suffer arrhythmia (i.e., irregular pulses) should be monitored every minute. If their pulse rate is greater than *100* beats per minute and their blood pressure is greater than *140* mm Hg, this emergency situation should be alerted to a staff in the hospital. Because the time *::00* specifies only *00* second but no hour and minute, the conditions are evaluated every minute. This rule specifies the behavior of a distributed Semantic Web. Σ

Example 4. The following rule specifies an integrity constraint:

```
<rule id = "roomShare">
        <forall id= "P" about = "http://www.AmericaHospital.com/patient">
                <if> <exists id= "Q" about= "http://www.AmericaHospital.com/patient">
                        <and>
                                        <equals about= "#P/nameOfDisease">dyspnea</>
                                        <equals about= "#Q/nameOfDisease">influenza </>
                        </and> </exists>
                <then>
                                <not> <equals about= "#P/roomNo"> #Q/roomNo</equals></not>
                </then>
                </if>
        </forall>
</rule>
```

Because this rule includes two patients, instance variables of class patient P and Q are defined. This rule states that a dyspnea patient should not share a room with an influenza patient. The condition predicate on the right hand side of a rule will be evaluated immediately. If it is evaluated to false, an appropriate action should be taken or an exception will be thrown. Σ

Rules in ARTSW can be either *local* or *global*. As described in details in the next section, the ARTSW server and agents run separately but communicate each other via networks. Rules that specify integrity constraints or behavior of the objects in a single agent are named local. Global rules specify the relationship among the objects from two or more agents in ARTSW environments. The syntax and semantics of global and local rules are the same but evaluation strategies are different. Because the objects included in a global rule can be defined in several agents, the ARTSW server should request each of those agents for the information that is required to evaluate the rule.

Example 5. Supposing that the persistent data of *patients* and *staffs* are defined and executed in different agents, we can define a global rule as follows:

```
<rule id = "staffOnDuty">
        <if><forall id= "P" about = "http://www.AmericaHospital.com/patient">
                <forall id= "Q" about = "http://www.AmericaHospital.com/staff">
                <and>
                                <greaterThen count about= "#P"
                                        where= "nameOfDisease == dyspnea"> 5 </>
                                <greaterThen conut about= "#P"
                                        where= "nameOfDisease == influenza> 5 </>
                                <lessThan count about= "Q"
                                        where= "(onDuty == true) and (major == pulmonary)"> 2 </>
                </and>
        <then>
                        <addStaffOnDuty var1= "pulmonary"/>
        </then> </forall> </forall>
        </if>
</rule>
```

This rule specifies that if the numbers of patients who suffer from dyspnea is grater than 5, the numbers of patients who suffer from influenza are also greater than 5 and the number of staff who is on duty and whose major is pulmonary is less than 2 then a staff whose major is pulmonary should be added to the duty list. In order to evaluate this rule, the ARTSW server should request the agents that manage the persistent objects for the numbers of patients and staffs who meet the given conditions.   Σ

4   Validation of Active Real-Time Rules

One of the main advantages of using logical rule is that we can analysis a set of rules based on mathematical unification and inference methods. In this work, we will extend the knowledge assimilation procedure to the rules with real time. We will explore the concepts of *contradiction*, *redundancy*, and *independency* of a set of logical rules with time and develop the procedures to verify these properties. Given a set of existing rules R and a rule k to be added, we can classify the knowledge assimilation problem into the following cases:

a) *Contradiction* between A New Rule and The Current Rule Base.
    k is said to be inconsistent with R if $(k \wedge R)$ can derive a contraction, which is represented by the empty clause, *nil*.

b) *Subsumption*.
    In general, one clause $C1$ subsumes another clause $C2$ if all the conditions and conclusions of some instance of $C1$ are contained among the conditions and conclusions of $C2$. The subsuming clauses are more general than the subsumed clause and possibly have fewer conditions or fewer conclusions. Although redundancy can be traced as a special case of subsumption such that k is said to be redundant with respect to R if k can be derived from R. In this work, redundant rules will be handled differently even if a redundant rule is a special case of subsumed rules. For example, consider the case in which we try to add a rule $p_1(a, Y) \wedge p_2(Y, Z) \rightarrow p_3(a, Z)$ into a rule base which has the rule $p_1(X, Y) \wedge p_2(Y, Z) \rightarrow p_3(X, Z)$ explicitly or implicitly. In this case, the new rule is redundant because it can be obtained by instantiating the variable X with a constant a.

c) *Independency*.
    A rule is said to be independent on the current rule base if the rule neither contradicts nor is provable from the current rule base. In this case, the rule can be assimilated into the rule base.

Several knowledge assimilation methods have been proposed for logic and deductive databases. Because the logic system used in this work includes the real-time arguments, the proposed methods should be modified. Because real-time arguments not only specify exact times but also define time intervals, the assimilation process needs special considerations.

Example 6. The following two clause do not match each other but contradict because it specify different values for the same object.

<rdf:description about= "temperature" from= ":9:00" to= ":11:00"> 70 </>
<rdf:description about= "temperature" from= ":10:00" to= ":12:00"> 80 </>

The first clause specifies the temperature to 70 between 9:00 and 11:00 and the second clause specifies it to 80 between 10:00 and 12:00. These two clauses do not match in conventional unification procedures. However they contradict each other between 10:00 and 11:00.   Σ

In order to handle real-time properly in the knowledge assimilation procedure, we need to build a meta-knowledge base. An example of meta-knowledge can be as follows.

$$X(A, T1, T2) \wedge X(B, T3, T4) \wedge (T1 < T4) \wedge (T2 > T3) \rightarrow (A == B)$$

With this meta-rule, we can derive a contradiction from the two clauses in Example 6. Because the active rules defined in first-order logic can be validated by the knowledge assimilation methods, the quality of specification and control can be improved without fatal failures.

5   Working Scenario

A scenario to apply ARTSW in networked environments is discussed in this section. A part of distributed system for a medical center is depicted in Fig. 6, where one server and three agents are included. Recently, as more medical instruments and information systems are connected to networks, the need to automate their operation has been rapidly increased. In this example, three different ARTSW agents are running for an intensive monitoring system, a duty desk, and an administrator, respectively. The intensive monitoring system keeps track of the results of automatic measuring for such basic test items as blood pressure, body temperature, pulse rate, and so on. The agent on a duty desk manages the data of staffs including doctors and nurses. The third agent handles the administrative job for patients. For example, it allocates an empty bed for a new patient and takes charge of bookkeeping.

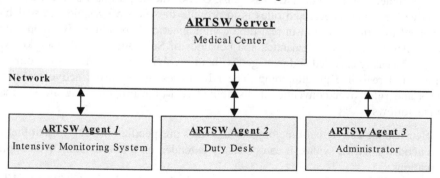

Fig. 6. An example of ARTSW environment

In agent *1*, local rules for the intensive monitoring system are stored and evaluated. The rule in Example 3 is stored in agent *1*, which collects the measurement values and deals with abnormal cases. The rule in Example 4 specifies the restrictions on sharing a room among patients and it is stored in agent 2. The global rule in Example 5 monitors the numbers of patients and staffs on duty. If the number of staffs on duty is less than certain regulation it automatically run a function to add more staffs. This global rule is stored in the Medical Center Server.

Having defined the above three rules in agent 1, agent 3, and the server, respectively, rule triggering modules continuously monitor the literals on left hand sides. In agent 3, in case any patient having dyspnea is allocated to the same room with a patient having influenza, the local rule defined in agent 3 is violated. Once a violation occurs, the allocating procedure is blocked and the situation is informed to an administrator. The conditions in the rule defined in agent 1 are evaluated every minute. If any patient having arrhythmia suffers from high pulse rate and blood pressure as defined on the left hand side of the rule, the patient's name will be informed to the staffs in agent 2.

Supposing that the persistent objects of staffs and patients are managed by agent 2 and agent 3, respectively, the aggregate function *count* in the global rule should be evaluated by agent 2 and agent 3. Because the given literals are event-triggered, they will be evaluated whenever the values of patients and staffs are updated. Suppose that the numbers of patients having dyspnea and influenza are 5 and 6, respectively, and the number of on-duty staff whose major is pulmonary is 1. Currently not all the conditions of the left hand side of the rule are true. Once a new patient having dyspnea is checked in, the rule will be fired and the function *addStaffOnDuty* will be executed in agent 2.

6   Conclusion

The design principles and operational model of the active real-time objects and rules is presented in this paper. As networks (i.e., the Internet and intranets) proliferate in recent computing environments, software development and maintenance become a major bottleneck in distributed Web systems. One of the major goals of the providing the active real-time objects and rules is to provide the users a portable and scalable distributed tool that has built-in real-time communication capabilities. By supporting formal rules to define the semantics and behavior of Semantic Web, domain knowledge can be easily encoded and managed without involving into the details of communication and real-time programming. The advantages of using the active real-time objects and rules over conventional distributed real-time programming are summarized as follows:

–   Because the active real-time objects and rules arespecified in RDF format that is encoded in XML syntax, it can be easily extended on top of existing Web applications.
–   Because all the resources connected through the network can be identified by URI, the active real-time objects and rules can be directly built on HTML, XML, or other file systems. With proper optimization modules, it will outperform existing information systems by eliminating data transformations.

–   Defining the business rules or control logics in terms of the first order logic, it relieves the users from complicated real-time and network programming and maintenance.
–   Because the active rules are defined in first-order logic can be validated by knowledge assimilation methods, the quality of specification and control can be improved without fatal failures.

Prospected application areas of the active real-time objects and rules are many soft real-time distributed Web systems such as Distributed Control and Management Systems, Electronic Commercial Systems, information appliances, VOD systems, and game software. In order to be more powerful, it needs to be extended with various development tools. Even current execution model allows cascade rule triggering; the users are responsible for the consequences. In order to be more reliable tool, more rule analysis and simulation tools should prevent possible malfunctions such as infinite triggering and indeterministic behaviors.

References

[1]   R. Agrawal and N. Gehani, "Ode(Object database and environment): The language and the data model," *Proceedings of the ACM SIGMOD International Conference on Management of Data,* pp36-45, Portland, Oregon, May 1989.
[2]   Kal Ahmed et al., *Professional XML Meta Data,* Wrox Press, Nov. 2001.
[3]   Tim Berners-Lee, J. Hendler, and Ora Lassila, "The Semantic Web – A new form of Web content that is meaningful to computers will unleash a revolution of new possibilities," *Scientific American,* May 2001.
[4]   H. Boley, S. Tabet, and G. Wagner, "Design Rationale for RuleML: A Markup Language for Semantic Web Rules," *Proc. of Semantic Web Symposium,* Stanford University, July 2001.
[5]   S. Chakravarthy, B. Blaustein, A.P. Buchmann, M.Carey, U.Dayal, D.Goldhirsch, M.Hsu, R.Jauhari, R.Ladin, M.Livny, D.McCarthy, R.McKee, and A.Rosenthal, "HiPAC: A research project in active, time-constrained database management," *Technical Report XAIT-89-02,* Xerox Advanced Information Technology, Cambridge, Massachusetts, July 1989.
[6]   S. Ceri, C. Gennaro, S. Paraboschi, and G. Serazzi, "Effective scheduling of detached rules in active databases," IEEE Trans. on Knowledge and Data Engineering, Vol. 15, Issue 1, Jan/Feb 2003, pp. 2-13.
[7]   Datta and S.H. Son, "A study of concurrency control in real-time, active database systems," IEEE Trans. on Knowledge and Data Engineering, Vol. 14, Issue 3, May/Jun 2002, pp. 465-484.
[8]   Doublin Core Metadata Initiative website http://dublincore.org/
[9]   Stefan Decker et al., "The Semantic Web: The Roles of XML and RDF," *IEEE Internet Computing,* Vol 4(5), pp. 63-74, Sept/Oct 2000.
[10]   Andreas Eberhart, *Survey of RDF data on the Web,* Dec 2001, available at http://www.i-u.de/schools/eberhart/rdf/

[11] James Farrugia, "Logics for the Semantic We," *Proc. of Semantic Web Symposium,* Stanford University, July 2001.

[12] R. Fikes and D. McGuinness, *An Axiomatic Semantics for RDF, RDF Schema, and DAML+OIL,* Technical Report KSL-01-01, Knowledge Systems Laboratory, Stanford University, 2001.

[13] Johan Hjelm, Creating the Semantic Web with RDF: Professional Developer's Guide, John Wiley & Sons, 2001.

[14] Kim, K. H., "Real-time Object-oriented Distributed Software Engineering and The TMO Scheme," *International Journal of Software Engineering and Knowledge Engineering,* Vol. 9, No. 2, 251-276, 1999.

[15] K. C. Kim, S. B. Yoo, K. W. Ko, and S. K. Cha, "Active System for Heterogeneous ODBMS Using Mobile Rule Codes," *Lecture Notes in Computer Science 1884 (2000 ADBIS-DASFAA),* Springer-Verlag, pp. 93-106, September 2000.

[16] McBride, "Jena: a semantic Web toolkit," IEEE Internet Computing, Vol. 6, Issue 6, Nov/Dec 2002, pp. 55-59.

[17] Drew McDemott and Dejing Dou, *Embedding Logic in DAML/RDF,* Nov. 2001, available at ftp://ftp.cs.yale.edu/pub/mcdermott/papers/wwwconf.pdf

[18] Paton, N. W. and Diaz, O., "Active Database Systems," *ACM Computing Surveys,* 31(1), pp. 63-103, 1999.

[19] Steve Ross-Talbot, "Java Rules in J2EE," *Java Developer's Journal,* Vol. 6, Issue 9, September 2001.

[20] Sheth, "Managing Semantic Content for the Web," IEEE Internet Computing, Vol. 6, Issue 4, July/Aug 2002, pp. 80-87.

[21] World Wide Web Consortium, Resource Description Framework (RDF) Schema Specification 1.0, W3C Candidate Recommendation 27 March 2000, available at http://www.w3.org/TR/2000/CR-rdf-schema-20000327/

[22] World Wide Web Consortium website http://www.w3.org/2001/sw/

[23] World Wide Web Consortium, Resource Description Framework (RDF) Model and Syntax Specification, W3C Recommendation 22 February 1999, available at http://www.w3.org/TR/1999/REC-rdf-syntax-19990222/

[24] S. Yoo and P.C-Y. Sheu, "Describing Distributed Real-time Objects with Logic," Sixth International Conference on Integrated Design and Process Technology, Pasadena, California, USA, June 2002, pp. 1-7.

Author Index

Lecture Notes in Computer Science

For information about Vols. 1–2730
please contact your bookseller or Springer-Verlag